1a 1b 1uno

¡En español!

LECTURAS PARA TODOS

with TEST PREPARATION

McDougal Littell
A DIVISION OF HOUGHTON MIFFLIN COMPANY
Evanston, Illinois • Boston • Dallas

Cover photo by Martha Granger/EDGE Productions

Acknowledgments

"Cumpleaños," from *Cuadros de familia* by Carmen Lomas Garza. Copyright © 1990 by Carmen Lomas Garza. All rights reserved. Reprinted by permission of Children's Press Books.

"La exclamación" by Octavio Paz, from *The Collected Poems of Octavio Paz: 1957–1987,* edited by Eliot Weinberger. Copyright © Octavio Paz. Reprinted by permission of Maria José Paz.

"En Uxmal" by Octavio Paz, from *The Collected Poems of Octavio Paz: 1957–1987,* edited by Eliot Weinberger. Copyright © Octavio Paz. Reprinted by permission of Maria José Paz.

"Palma sola," from *El libro de los sones* by Nicolás Guillén. Copyright © 1982 Nicolás Guillén. Editorial Letras Cubanas, Instituto Cubano Del Libro, La Habana, Cuba. Reprinted by permission.

Excerpt from *Como agua para chocolate* by Laura Esquivel. Copyright © 1989 by Laura Esquivel. Reprinted by Anchor Books, a division of Random House, Inc.

"Oda al tomate," by Pablo Neruda. Copyright © 1954 by Pablo Neruda and Fundación Pablo Neruda. Reprinted by permission of Agencia Literaria Carmen Balcells, S.A.

Illustration and **Photography Credits** appear on page 250.

ISBN: 0-618-33488-2

1 2 3 4 5 6 7 8 9 – PBO – 07 06 05 04 03

Table of Contents

En voces *continued*

Literatura adicional 129

Academic and Informational Reading

Test Preparation Strategies

Introducing *Lecturas para todos*

Lecturas para todos
is a new kind of reading text.
As you will see, this book helps
you become an active reader.
It is a book to mark up, to
write in, and to make your
own. You can use it in class
and take it home.

Reading Skills Improvement— in Spanish *and* English

You will read selections from your textbook, as well as
great literature. In addition, you will learn how to understand
the types of texts you read in classes, on tests, and in the
real world. You will also study and practice specific strategies
for taking standardized tests.

Help for Reading

Many readings in Spanish are challenging the first time
you encounter them. **Lecturas para todos** helps you
understand these readings. Here's how.

Para leer The page before each reading gives you
background information about the reading and a key to
understanding the selection.

  Reading Strategy Reading strategies help you decide
  how to approach the material.

  What You Need to Know A preview of every selection
  tells you what to expect before you begin reading.

Reading Tips Useful, specific reading tips appear at
points where language is difficult.

A pensar... Point-of-use, critical-thinking questions help
you analyze content as you read.

Márcalo This feature invites you to mark up the text by underlining and circling words and phrases right on the page.

Gramática As you read, this feature highlights key grammar concepts.

Vocabulario This feature helps you with the new vocabulary as you read the selection.

Análisis This feature appears in the *Literatura adicional* section and encourages you to focus on one aspect of literary analysis as you read.

Reader's Success Strategy These notes give useful and fun tips and strategies for comprehending the selection.

Challenge These activities keep you challenged, even after you have grasped the basic concepts of the reading.

Vocabulary Support

Palabras clave Important new words appear in bold. Their definitions appear in a *Palabras clave* section at the bottom of any page where they occur in the selection. You will practice these words after the selection.

Vocabulario de la lectura Vocabulary activities follow each selection and give you the opportunity to practice the *Palabras clave.* Active vocabulary words from the *etapa* appear in blue.

Comprehension and Connections

¿Comprendiste? Questions after each selection check your understanding of what you have just read.

Conexión personal These short writing activities ask you to relate the selection to your life and experiences to make what you have read more meaningful.

Links to ¡En español!

When using McDougal Littell's *¡En español!,* you will find *Lecturas para todos* to be a perfect companion. *Lecturas para todos* lets you mark up the *En voces* selections as you read, helping you understand and remember more.

Read on to learn more!

Academic and Informational Reading

Here is a special collection of real-world examples—in English—to help you read every kind of informational material, from textbooks to technical directions. Why are these sections in English? Because the strategies you learn will help you on tests, in other classes, and in the world outside of school. You will find strategies for the following:

Analyzing Text Features This section will help you read many different types of magazine articles and textbooks. You will learn how titles, subtitles, lists, graphics, many different kinds of visuals, and other special features work in magazines and textbooks. After studying this section you will be ready to read even the most complex material.

Understanding Visuals Tables, charts, graphs, maps, and diagrams all require special reading skills. As you learn the common elements of various visual texts, you will learn to read these materials with accuracy and skill.

Recognizing Text Structures Informational texts can be organized in many different ways. In this section you will study the following structures and learn about special key words that will help you identify the organizational patterns:
• Main Idea and Supporting Details
• Problem and Solution
• Sequence
• Cause and Effect
• Comparison and Contrast
• Persuasion

Reading in the Content Areas You will learn special strategies for reading social studies, science, and mathematics texts.

Reading Beyond the Classroom In this section you will encounter applications, schedules, technical directions, product information, Web pages, and other readings. Learning to analyze these texts will help you in your everyday life and on some standardized tests.

Test Preparation Strategies

In this section, you will find strategies and practice to help you succeed on many different kinds of standardized tests. After closely studying a variety of test formats through annotated examples, you will have an opportunity to practice each format on your own. Additional support will help you think through your answers. You will find strategies for the following:

Successful Test Taking This section provides many suggestions for preparing for and taking tests. The information ranges from analyzing test questions to tips for answering multiple-choice and open-ended test questions.

Reading Tests: Long Selections You will learn how to analyze the structure of a lengthy reading and prepare to answer the comprehension questions that follow it.

Reading Tests: Short Selections These selections may be a few paragraphs of text, a poem, a chart or graph, or some other item. You will practice the special range of comprehension skills required for these pieces.

Functional Reading Tests These real-world texts present special challenges. You will learn about the various test formats that use applications, product labels, technical directions, Web pages, and more.

Revising-and-Editing Tests These materials test your understanding of English grammar and usage. You may encounter capitalization and punctuation questions. Sometimes the focus is on usage questions such as verb tenses or pronoun agreement issues. You will become familiar with these formats through the guided practice in this section.

Writing Tests Writing prompts and sample student essays will help you understand how to analyze a prompt and what elements make a successful written response. Scoring rubrics and a prompt for practice will prepare you for the writing tests you will take.

En voces

Point-of-use comprehension support helps you read selections from *¡En español!* and develop critical-thinking skills.

Reading Strategy
This feature provides reading tips and strategies that help you effectively approach the material.

What You Need to Know
This section provides a key to help you unlock the selection so that you can understand and enjoy it.

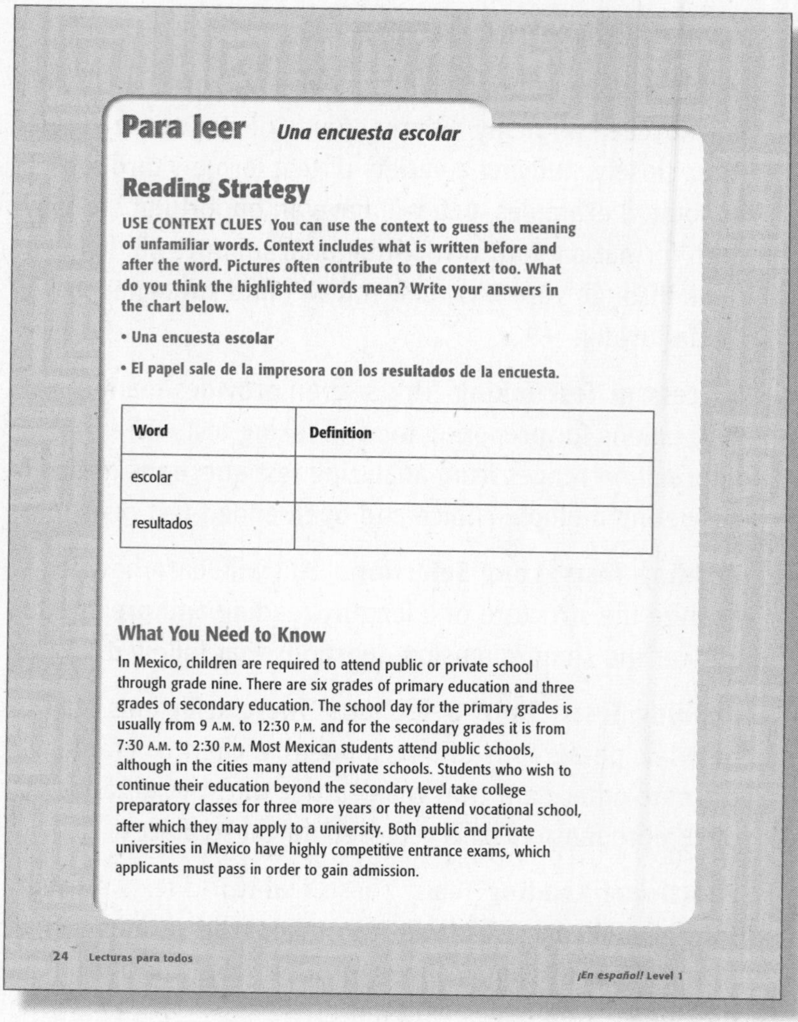

Para leer *Una encuesta escolar*

Reading Strategy

USE CONTEXT CLUES You can use the context to guess the meaning of unfamiliar words. Context includes what is written before and after the word. Pictures often contribute to the context too. What do you think the highlighted words mean? Write your answers in the chart below.

- **Una encuesta escolar**
- **El papel sale de la impresora con los resultados de la encuesta.**

Word	Definition
escolar	
resultados	

What You Need to Know

In Mexico, children are required to attend public or private school through grade nine. There are six grades of primary education and three grades of secondary education. The school day for the primary grades is usually from 9 A.M. to 12:30 P.M. and for the secondary grades it is from 7:30 A.M. to 2:30 P.M. Most Mexican students attend public schools, although in the cities many attend private schools. Students who wish to continue their education beyond the secondary level take college preparatory classes for three more years or they attend vocational school, after which they may apply to a university. Both public and private universities in Mexico have highly competitive entrance exams, which applicants must pass in order to gain admission.

24 Lecturas para todos

¡En español! Level 1

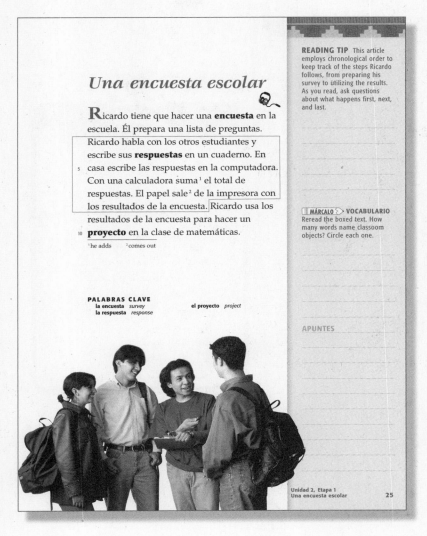

Una encuesta escolar

Ricardo tiene que hacer una **encuesta** en la escuela. Él prepara una lista de preguntas.

Ricardo habla con los otros estudiantes y escribe sus **respuestas** en un cuaderno. En 5 casa escribe las respuestas en la computadora. Con una calculadora suma[1] el total de respuestas. El papel sale[2] de la impresora con los resultados de la encuesta. Ricardo usa los resultados de la encuesta para hacer un 10 **proyecto** en la clase de matemáticas.

[1]he adds [2]comes out

PALABRAS CLAVE
la encuesta *survey*   el proyecto *project*
la respuesta *response*

||| MÁRCALO ⟩ VOCABULARIO
Reread the boxed text. How many words name classoom objects? Circle each one.

APUNTES

Unidad 2, Etapa 1
Una encuesta escolar   25

||| MÁRCALO ⟩
VOCABULARIO
This feature helps you with the new vocabulary as you read the selection. Underlining or circling the example makes it easy for you to find and remember.

PALABRAS CLAVE
Important vocabulary words appear in bold within the reading. Definitions are given at the bottom of the page.

En voces *continued*

A pensar...

Point-of-use questions check your understanding and ask you to think critically about the passage.

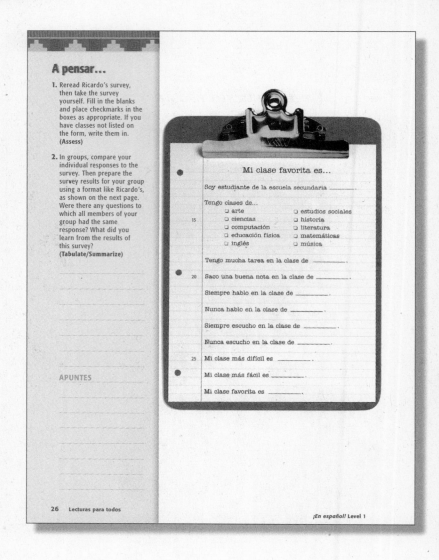

A pensar...

1. Reread Ricardo's survey, then take the survey yourself. Fill in the blanks and place checkmarks in the boxes as appropriate. If you have classes not listed on the form, write them in. **(Assess)**

2. In groups, compare your individual responses to the survey. Then prepare the survey results for your group using a format like Ricardo's, as shown on the next page. Were there any questions to which all members of your group had the same response? What did you learn from the results of this survey? **(Tabulate/Summarize)**

APUNTES

¡En español! Level 1

Mi clase favorita es...

Soy estudiante de la escuela secundaria _____

Tengo clases de...
15
- ❑ arte
- ❑ ciencias
- ❑ computación
- ❑ educación física
- ❑ inglés

- ❑ estudios sociales
- ❑ historia
- ❑ literatura
- ❑ matemáticas
- ❑ música

Tengo mucha tarea en la clase de _____ .

20 Saco una buena nota en la clase de _____ .

Siempre hablo en la clase de _____ .

Nunca hablo en la clase de _____ .

Siempre escucho en la clase de _____ .

Nunca escucho en la clase de _____ .

25 Mi clase más difícil es _____ .

Mi clase más fácil es _____ .

Mi clase favorita es _____ .

Los resultados

Una encuesta a 50 estudiantes

30 Clase con más tarea: matemáticas
(25 estudiantes)

Los estudiantes sacan más buenas notas en la clase de: música
(35 estudiantes)

Los estudiantes hablan más en la clase de: literatura
35 *(30 estudiantes)*

Los estudiantes nunca hablan en la clase de: inglés
(25 estudiantes)

Los estudiantes escuchan más en la clase de: ciencias
(40 estudiantes)

40 Los estudiantes nunca escuchan en la clase de: historia
(20 estudiantes)

La clase más difícil es: ciencias
(35 estudiantes)

La clase más fácil es: arte
45 *(45 estudiantes)*

La clase favorita es: literatura
(30 estudiantes)

READER'S SUCCESS STRATEGY Use a chart like the one below to compare and contrast the courses offered at Ricardo's school with the courses offered at your school.

Ricardo's School

My School

CHALLENGE Look at the results of Ricardo's survey. Note in the heading how many students he surveyed in all. Then convert the number of students listed in each subcategory to the percentage of all students surveyed. **(Calculate)**

Modelo: *Clase con más tarea: matemáticas (25 estudiantes: 50%)*

READER'S SUCCESS STRATEGY

Notes like this one provide ideas to help you read the selection successfully. For example, some notes suggest that you fill in a chart while you read. Others suggest that you mark key words or ideas in the text.

CHALLENGE

This feature asks you to expand upon what you have learned for enrichment.

En voces *continued*

Vocabulario de la lectura
Vocabulary practice follows each reading, reinforcing the *Palabras clave* that appear throughout the selection. Words that appear in blue are *etapa* vocabulary words in *¡En español!*

Vocabulario de la lectura

Palabras clave

la calculadora *calculator*   **la encuesta** *survey*   **el proyecto** *project*
la computadora *computer*   la impresora *printer*   **la respuesta** *response*
el cuaderno *notebook*   el papel *paper*

A. Fill in each blank with the correct form of a **Palabra clave.**

Ricardo prepara una lista de preguntas para su _____ escolar.
(1)

Primero, escribe las _____ de los otros estudiantes en un
(2)

_____. Cuando llega a casa, escribe las respuestas en la
(3)

_____. Usa una _____ para sumar el total de
(4)   (5)

respuestas. El _____ sale de la _____ con los
(6)   (7)

resultados. Ricardo usa los resultados de su encuesta para un _____
(8)

que tiene que hacer en la clase de matemáticas.

B. Choose two **Palabras clave** and write a sentence with each one.

_____
_____
_____
_____
_____
_____
_____

¿Comprendiste?

1. ¿Qué tiene que hacer Ricardo?

_____

2. ¿Qué usa Ricardo para escribir la encuesta?

_____

3. ¿Los estudiantes hablan mucho o poco en la clase de inglés?

_____

4. ¿Es difícil la clase de música o arte en la escuela de Ricardo?

_____

5. ¿Qué clase es la clase favorita de los estudiantes?

_____

Conexión personal

What is your favorite class? Why do you like it? Write your answers in the web below.

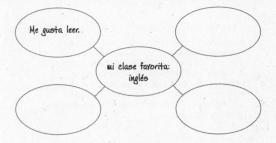

Me gusta leer.

mi clase favorita: inglés

Unidad 2, Etapa 1
Una encuesta escolar   29

¿Comprendiste?
Comprehension questions check your understanding and provide the opportunity to practice new vocabulary words.

Conexión personal
These short writing activities help you see connections between what happens in the selection and in your own life.

Literatura adicional

Notes in the margins make literature from the Spanish-speaking world accessible and help you read works by famous authors such as García Lorca and Cisneros.

Reading Strategy
This feature provides reading tips and strategies that help you effectively approach the material.

What You Need to Know
This section provides a key to help you unlock the selection so that you can understand and enjoy it.

LITERATURA ADICIONAL

Para leer   *Cumpleaños*

Reading Strategy

QUESTION Asking questions about a work of literature as you read is one way to understand the selection better. Use the five W's—who, what, where, when, why—to help you ask your questions. In the chart below, record questions and the answers you discover while reading **"Cumpleaños"** by Carmen Lomas Garza and viewing the illustration.

"Cumpleaños"

Who is the speaker?	a young girl
What	
Where	
When	
Why	

What You Need to Know

"Cumpleaños" is a story from Carmen Lomas Garza's book ***Cuadros de familia***, in which she describes her memories of growing up in Kingsville, Texas, near the border of Mexico. Through illustrated vignettes about family activities from making tamales to picking nopal cactus, ***Cuadros de familia*** relates aspects of Mexican American history and culture. In **"Cumpleaños,"** Carmen Lomas Garza remembers celebrating her sixth birthday.

¡En español! Level 1

¡En español! Level 1

Sobre la autora

Carmen Lomas Garza, artista chicana, nació en Kingsville, Texas, en 1948. Empezó a estudiar arte a la edad de trece años. Sus pinturas, inspiradas en su niñez en el sur de Texas, son escenas típicas de la vida mexicana americana.

~~~~~~~~

Cumpleaños

Ésa soy yo, pegándole[1] a la piñata en la fiesta que me dieron cuando cumplí seis años[2]. Era[3] también el cumpleaños de mi hermano, que cumplía cuatro años. Mi madre nos dio
5 una gran fiesta e invitó a muchos primos, **vecinos** y amigos.

[1]hitting   [2]*cumplí seis años* I turned six   [3]It was

Cumpleaños de Lala y Tudi *by Carmen Lomas Garza, 1989*

PALABRAS CLAVE
el (la) vecino(a)   *neighbor*

READING TIP Review the vocabulary you have learned for family members. Then circle the words in the story that refer to the relatives of the girl who is narrating it.

APUNTES

MÁRCALO > ANÁLISIS
This story contains vivid descriptions, details that help the reader form a strong mental picture. Underline words or phrases in the story that help you visualize in your mind the activity and excitement of the birthday party.

READER'S SUCCESS STRATEGY As you read, look for depictions of the vocabulary in the illustration. First identify the girl who is telling the story and her father. Then find the following: **la cuerda, el palo, el pañuelo, la piñata.**

Sobre la autora
Each literary selection begins with a short author biography that provides cultural context.

MÁRCALO > ANÁLISIS
This feature encourages you to focus on one aspect of literary analysis as you read.

READER'S SUCCESS STRATEGY
Notes like this one provide ideas to help you read the selection successfully. For example, some notes suggest that you fill in a chart while you read. Others suggest that you mark key words or ideas in the text.

Academic and Informational Reading

This section helps you read informational material and prepare for other classes and standardized tests.

VARIED TYPES OF READINGS

The wide variety of academic and informational selections helps you access different types of readings and develop specific techniques for those reading types.

Academic and Informational Reading

In this section you'll find strategies to help you read all kinds of informational materials. The examples here range from magazines you read for fun to textbooks to bus schedules. Applying these simple and effective techniques will help you be a successful reader of the many texts you encounter every day.

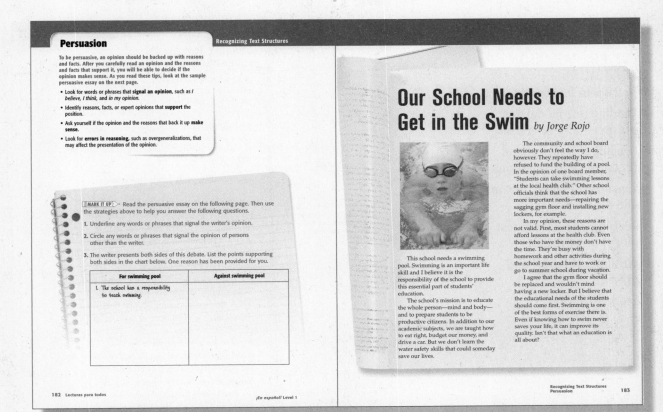

Persuasion

To be persuasive, an opinion should be backed up with reasons and facts. After you carefully read an opinion and the reasons and facts that support it, you will be able to decide if the opinion makes sense. As you read these tips, look at the sample persuasive essay on the next page.

- Look for words or phrases that **signal an opinion**, such as *I believe*, *I think*, and *in my opinion*.

- Identify reasons, facts, or expert opinions that **support** the position.

- Ask yourself if the opinion and the reasons that back it up **make sense**.

- Look for **errors in reasoning**, such as overgeneralizations, that may affect the presentation of the opinion.

MARK IT UP Read the persuasive essay on the following page. Then use the strategies above to help you answer the following questions.

1. Underline any words or phrases that signal the writer's opinion.

2. Circle any words or phrases that signal the opinion of persons other than the writer.

3. The writer presents both sides of this debate. List the points supporting both sides in the chart below. One reason has been provided for you.

For swimming pool	Against swimming pool
1. The school has a responsibility to teach swimming.	

182 Lecturas para todos

¡En español! Level 1

Our School Needs to Get in the Swim *by Jorge Rojo*

This school needs a swimming pool. Swimming is an important life skill and I believe it is the responsibility of the school to provide this essential part of students' education.

The school's mission is to educate the whole person—mind and body—and to prepare students to be productive citizens. In addition to our academic subjects, we are taught how to eat right, budget our money, and drive a car. But we don't learn the water safety skills that could someday save our lives.

The community and school board obviously don't feel the way I do, however. They repeatedly have refused to fund the building of a pool. In the opinion of one board member, "Students can take swimming lessons at the local health club." Other school officials think that the school has more important needs—repairing the sagging gym floor and installing new lockers, for example.

In my opinion, these reasons are not valid. First, most students cannot afford lessons at the health club. Even those who have the money don't have the time. They're busy with homework and other activities during the school year and have to work or go to summer school during vacation.

I agree that the gym floor should be replaced and wouldn't mind having a new locker. But I believe that the educational needs of the students should come first. Swimming is one of the best forms of exercise there is. Even if knowing how to swim never saves your life, it can improve its quality. Isn't that what an education is all about?

Recognizing Text Structures
Persuasion   183

SKILL DEVELOPMENT

These activities offer graphic organizers, Mark It Up features, and other reading support to help you comprehend and think critically about the selection.

Test Preparation for All Learners

Lecturas para todos offers models, strategies, and practice to help you for standardized tests.

TEST PREPARATION STRATEGIES

- Successful test taking
- Reading test model and practice—long selections
- Reading test model and practice—short selections
- Functional reading test model and practice
- Revising-and-editing test model and practice
- Writing test model and practice
- Scoring rubrics

APUNTES

READING STRATEGIES FOR ASSESSMENT

Find the main idea and supporting details. Circle the main idea of this article. Then underline the details that support the main idea.

Use context clues. To discover what a "pack animal" is, study the words and phrases around it. Which phrase helps define it?

Notice important details. Underline the details that explain why alpaca wool is so desirable.

222 Lecturas para todos

Reading Test Model
SHORT SELECTIONS

DIRECTIONS "Warmth from the Andes" is a short informative article. The strategies you have just learned can also help you with this shorter selection. As you read the selection, respond to the notes in the side column.

When you've finished reading, answer the multiple-choice questions. Use the side-column notes to help you understand what each question is asking and why each answer is correct.

Warmth from the Andes

Southeastern Peru and Western Bolivia make up a geographic region called the *Altiplano*, or High Plateau. This largely desolate mountainous area is home to one of the most economically important animals in South America—the alpaca.

The alpaca is related to the camel and looks somewhat like another well-known South American grazing animal, the llama. Alpacas live at elevations as high as 16,000 feet. At such altitudes, oxygen is scarce. Alpacas are able to survive because their blood contains an unusually high number of red blood corpuscles, the cells that carry oxygen throughout the body.

For several thousand years, the Native Americans of the region have raised alpacas both as pack animals for transporting goods and for their most important resource—wool. Alpaca wool ranges in color from black to tan to white. It is lightweight yet strong and resists moisture. Also, it is exceptionally warm. Alpaca wool is much finer than the

¡En español! Level 1

Revising-and-Editing Test Model

DIRECTIONS Read the following paragraph carefully. Then answer the multiple-choice questions that follow. After answering the questions, read the material in the side columns to check your answer strategies.

¹Madrid, the capital of Spain. ²It is home to one of that nations cultural treasures—the Prado museum. ³The building was constructed in the late eighteenth century as a museum of natural science. ⁴Then they decided to change it to an art museum in 1819 and it has more than 9,000 works of art. ⁵The museum is located on a street called the Paseo del Prado. ⁶Their are many famous paintings they're, including works by El Greco, Velázquez, and Goya.

READING STRATEGIES FOR ASSESSMENT

Watch for common errors. Highlight or underline errors such as incorrect spelling or punctuation; fragments or run-on sentences; and missing or misplaced information.

ANSWER STRATEGIES

① Which sentence in the paragraph is actually a fragment, an incomplete thought?

   A. sentence 5
   B. sentence 3
   C. sentence 1
   D. sentence 4

Incomplete Sentences A sentence is a group of words with a subject and a verb that expresses a complete thought. If either the subject or the verb is missing, the group of words is an incomplete sentence.

② In sentence 2, which of the following is the correct possessive form of *nation*?

   A. nation's
   B. nations's
   C. nations'
   D. nations

Possessive Nouns In sentence 2, the word *nation* is singular. So, it takes the singular possessive form.

Writing Test Model

DIRECTIONS Many tests ask you to write an essay in response to a writing prompt. A writing prompt is a brief statement that describes a writing situation. Some writing prompts ask you to explain *what, why,* or *how.* Others ask you to convince someone of something.

As you analyze the following writing prompts, read and respond to the notes in the side columns. Then look at the response to each prompt. The notes in the side columns will help you understand why each response is considered strong.

Prompt A

Some child-rearing experts believe that young people should be kept busy after school and on the weekends with a variety of structured activities, such as music lessons, sports, dance classes, and so on. Others say that young people today have been "overscheduled" and need more time to themselves—to read, think about the future, and even just to daydream.

Think about your experiences and the way your non-school time is structured. Do you think lots of structure, more personal time, or a combination of the two is most beneficial to young people? Remember to provide solid reasons and examples for the position you take.

Strong Response

Today was a typical day for my little brother Jeff. He got up at five o'clock to go to the local ice rink for hockey practice. Then he was off to school. At the end of the school day, Jeff

ANALYZING THE PROMPT

Identify the focus. What issue will you be writing about? Circle the focus of your essay in the first sentence of the prompt.

Understand what's expected of you. First, circle what the prompt asks you to do. Then identify your audience. What kinds of details will appeal to this audience?

ANSWER STRATEGIES

Capture the reader's interest. The writer begins by describing a typical busy day in his younger brother's life.

Para leer *Los latinos de Estados Unidos*

Reading Strategy

PREVIEW GRAPHICS Think about how you read English. Do you check photos or other graphics before reading an article? View the graphics that accompany this reading, then predict what this reading is about. After reading, decide whether your prediction was on target or needs adjustment.

Prediction: _____

_____

_____

_____

How close was your prediction? _____

_____

_____

_____

_____

What You Need to Know

Every ten years—in years ending in zero—the United States government counts the entire population of the United States. This is known as the U.S. Census. The U.S. Constitution requires that every person in the United States, regardless of age, place of birth, or language is counted in the Census, citizens and noncitizens alike. In addition to counting the total population, the Census also captures information such as language spoken at home, place of birth, and national origin. In recent years, people who were born in a Spanish-speaking country or whose family comes from a Spanish-speaking country have become the largest minority group in the United States.

Los latinos de Estados Unidos 🎧

En **Estados Unidos hay** personas de muchos países de Latinoamérica.

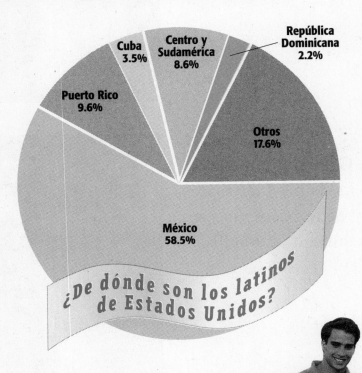

¿De dónde son los latinos de Estados Unidos?

- Cuba 3.5%
- Centro y Sudamérica 8.6%
- República Dominicana 2.2%
- Puerto Rico 9.6%
- Otros 17.6%
- México 58.5%

Francisco: ¿Qué tal? Me llamo Francisco García Flores.
5 Soy de Puerto Rico, pero vivo en Miami. El hombre de México es mi papá. La mujer es mi mamá.

PALABRAS CLAVE
Estados Unidos *United States*
hay *there are*
Centroamérica *Central America*
Sudamérica *South America*

República Dominicana
Dominican Republic
México *Mexico*

APUNTES

A pensar...

A pie chart is a circular chart cut into sections like pie pieces. It divides information and shows parts of a whole. Look at the pie chart on the left. What does the chart tell you about where U.S. Latinos are from? From what two countries are the majority of U.S. residents of Latino descent? Write your answer below. **(Analyze)**

APUNTES

APUNTES

Sra. García: Me llamo
10 Anita García. También soy de Puerto Rico pero trabajo como doctora en Miami.

PUERTO RICO

Sr. García: Buenos días.
15 Yo me llamo Juan García. Soy de México. Vivo en Miami con mi familia.

MÉXICO

Sr. Estrada: Hola. Me llamo Felipe Estrada.
20 Yo soy de Cuba, pero vivo en Miami.

CUBA

Arturo: Hola. Me llamo
Arturo. Soy estudiante
en Miami, pero soy
25 de la República
Dominicana.

REPÚBLICA
DOMINICANA

Alma: Mi nombre es
Alma. Soy de Colombia,
pero también vivo
30 en Miami.

CENTRO Y
SUDAMÉRICA

**READER'S
SUCCESS
STRATEGY** Identify the section
of the chart on page 3 that
corresponds to each person
in the reading. For Alma, first
look at a map to see where
Colombia is located.

Francisco:

Mrs. García:

Mr. García:

Mr. Estrada:

Alma:

Arturo:

APUNTES

_____

_____

_____

_____

_____

_____

_____

_____

_____

CHALLENGE Why do you
think a person would choose
to move to another country?
Write down some ideas below.
(Draw Conclusions)

_____

_____

_____

_____

Vocabulario de la lectura

Palabras clave

Centroamérica *Central America*
el (la) doctor(a) *doctor*
Estados Unidos *United States*
el (la) estudiante *student*
hay *there are*

el hombre *man*
México *Mexico*
la mujer *woman*
República Dominicana *Dominican Republic*
Sudamérica *South America*

A. Complete each sentence with the correct **Palabra clave**.

1. La señora García trabaja de _____.

2. Arturo no es doctor; él es _____.

3. El _____ de México es el papá de Francisco.

4. La _____ de México es la mamá de Francisco.

5. En Estados Unidos _____ muchas personas de México,
   Puerto Rico y Cuba.

B. Fill in each blank with the correct **Palabra clave**.

Los latinos de _____ son de muchos países diferentes.
             (1)
Francisco y su papá son de _____. Arturo es de la
                         (2)
_____. Alma es de Colombia, un país de
      (3)
_____. Muchas otras personas son de Costa Rica, El Salvador,
      (4)
Guatemala, Honduras, Nicaragua o Panamá; ellas son de _____.
                                        (5)

¿Comprendiste?

1. ¿De dónde es la doctora? ¿Cómo se llama?

   _____

2. ¿De dónde es el señor García?

   _____

3. ¿Cómo se llama el señor de Cuba?

   _____

4. ¿De dónde es la chica?

   _____

5. ¿Cómo se llama el estudiante? ¿De dónde es?

   _____

Conexión personal

Choose a person from the reading that you would like to meet. What questions would you like to ask him or her? Write a few questions in Spanish.

Persona: Sra. García

Preguntas:

  ¿Le gusta ser doctora?

Para leer   *Las celebraciones del año*

Reading Strategy

LOOK FOR COGNATES These are words that look alike and have similar meanings in both English and Spanish, such as **europeo** and **artificiales**. What other cognates can you find in **Las celebraciones del año**? List them below.

_____

_____

_____

_____

_____

_____

_____

What You Need to Know

There are many important holidays in Spanish-speaking countries. Some, such as Christmas or Mother's Day, are observed in many parts of Latin America as well as the United States. Many dates of historical significance, such as Mexican Independence Day, are celebrated primarily in one country. Spanish-speaking communities in the United States continue to observe many traditional holidays, such as **el Día de los Muertos** (the Day of the Dead), which is celebrated annually by Mexican Americans.

Las celebraciones del año

Hay muchas fechas importantes durante el año. Los países hispanohablantes celebran estas fechas de varias formas. Algunas[1] celebraciones son **iguales** que las de Estados Unidos, pero también hay tradiciones diferentes.

El Día de la Raza

octubre

12/10 El Día de la Raza En este día no hay trabajo. Hay muchos **desfiles.** El día celebra el encuentro[2] del **indígena** con el europeo y el africano. Hoy esta mezcla[3] de razas[4] y tradiciones forma la cultura latinoamericana.

---

[1] some   [2] meeting   [3] mixture   [4] races

PALABRAS CLAVE
igual   *the same*
el desfile   *parade*

el (la) indígena   *native (Indian)*

READING TIP Remember that, in Spanish, dates are written with the number of the day first, then the number of the month. For example, 4/1 means January 4.

APUNTES

CHALLENGE Why do you think that Mexicans have special holidays for remembering ancestors and deceased relatives and for honoring their families? Write down some notes, then talk about your ideas in small groups. **(Discuss)**

A pensar...

1. Which of the holidays described are the same in both Spanish-speaking countries and the U.S.? Which holidays are celebrated primarily by persons from Spanish-speaking countries? **(Compare and Contrast)**

2. Name two different ways in which **la Nochevieja** is celebrated in Spain and Latin America. Then tell about a custom observed on New Year's Eve that is typical of the United States or of your community. **(Connect)**

noviembre

1/11 El Día de Todos los Santos y

15 **2/11 el Día de los Muertos**[5] En estos días todos honran a las personas de su familia. En México las familias decoran las tumbas de sus **antepasados** con flores bonitas.

La Nochevieja

diciembre y enero

20 **31/12 La Nochevieja y**

1/1 el Año Nuevo Hay **fuegos artificiales**, desfiles o celebraciones en todos los países. En Ecuador los años viejos se representan con figuras grandes de

25 personas famosas de ese año. A **medianoche** los años viejos se queman[6]. En España es tradicional comer doce **uvas** a la medianoche.

---

[5] Dead   [6] are burned

PALABRAS CLAVE

el (la) antepasado(a) *ancestor*   la medianoche *midnight*
la Nochevieja *New Year's Eve*   la uva *grape*
los fuegos artificiales *fireworks*

READER'S
SUCCESS
STRATEGY As you read, pay
attention to the pictures that
accompany the text. They
may help you understand
some of the unfamiliar words.

enero

6/1 El Día de los Reyes Es el día tradicional

30 para dar regalos[7] de Navidad en los países

latinos.

---

[7] give gifts

MÁRCALO GRAMÁTICA
Circle all of the dates that
appear in the article. Then
write each of them below, in
numbers and in words.

Modelo: 13/4, el trece de abril

Vocabulario de la lectura

Palabras clave

el año   *year*

el (la) antepasado(a)   *ancestor*

el desfile   *parade*

la fecha   *date*

los fuegos artificiales   *fireworks*

igual   *the same*

el (la) indígena   *native (Indian)*

la medianoche   *midnight*

la Nochevieja   *New Year's Eve*

la uva   *grape*

A. Complete each sentence with the correct form of a **Palabra clave.**

1. Hay doce meses en un _____.

2. La _____ de hoy es diez de octubre.

3. La _____ es un tipo de fruta.

4. Mis _____ son de España.

5. El treinta y uno de diciembre es la _____.

6. En Estados Unidos, hay _____ el cuatro de julio.

B. Fill in each blank with the correct form of a **Palabra clave.**

Los países hispanohablantes celebran varias _____ durante el año. El
                                                      (1)
Día de la Raza, los latinoamericanos honran el encuentro del _____,
                                                                      (2)
el europeo y el africano. Las familias mexicanas decoran las tumbas de sus

_____ con flores en el Día de los Muertos. En la _____,
       (3)   (4)
los españoles comen doce uvas a la _____. Algunas celebraciones
                                            (5)
de España y Latinoamérica son diferentes de las de Estados Unidos, pero otras,

como la Navidad, son _____.
                            (6)

¿Comprendiste?

1. ¿Cómo celebran los latinoamericanos el Día de la Raza?

_____

2. ¿Cuáles son las fechas en que los mexicanos honran a su familia?

_____

3. Describe dos tradiciones del Año Nuevo.

_____

_____

4. ¿En qué fecha dan regalos de Navidad las personas de los países latinos? ¿Cómo se llama ese día?

_____

Conexión personal

Choose one of your favorite holidays. What words or phrases come to mind when you think of this day? Write them down in the word web.

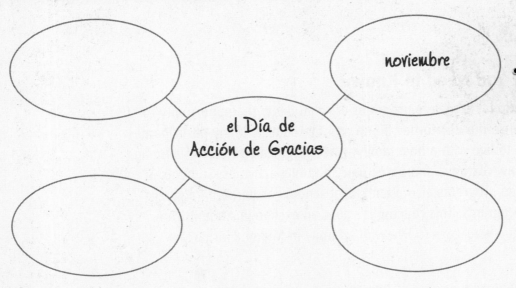

el Día de Acción de Gracias

noviembre

Para leer   *Una estudiante de Nicaragua*

Reading Strategy

LOOK FOR COGNATES Words in Spanish that look like words in
English are called cognates. They will help you understand readings
in Spanish. One example of a cognate in this reading is **estudiante**.
What do you think it means? Scan the reading and jot down all the
other cognates you can find.

_____

_____

_____

_____

What You Need to Know

International exchange programs offer students the opportunity to
experience the day-to-day life of another culture. Many participants
choose to live with a host family, where they can be part of a home,
learn new customs, and participate in family activities. Students in
exchange programs also attend local schools or enroll in language
study programs. This reading is about an exchange student from
Nicaragua who goes to live with a family in Miami, Florida.

Una estudiante de Nicaragua 🎧

U na chica viaja sola[1] en **avión** a Miami. Se llama Eva. Eva es de Nicaragua, pero este año estudia en
5 Estados Unidos. Eva es estudiante del programa del Intercambio Académico Internacional. A Eva le gusta viajar y le gusta practicar el inglés. Pero ahora Eva está un poco tímida.

[1] travels alone

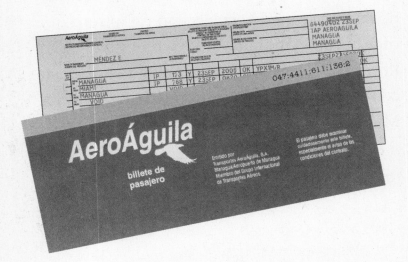

PALABRAS CLAVE
el avión *airplane*

READER'S SUCCESS STRATEGY Often you can understand a story better if you place yourself in the situation of the characters. Imagine that you are going to spend the next year living in another country as an exchange student. How would you feel as you arrived at the airport and were about to meet your host family?

APUNTES

MÁRCALO ✏ GRAMÁTICA
Underline the passage in the reading that tells what country Eva is from. Then write a sentence below saying what country you are from.

1. Why does Eva feel shy as she arrives at the airport in Miami? Mark passages in the text that support your answer. **(Infer)**

_____

_____

_____

_____

_____

2. How does she feel after she sees her host family, and why? **(Infer)**

_____

_____

_____

_____

_____

_____

CHALLENGE Write a dialog between Eva and her new family. Then act it out in small groups. **(Extend)**

_____

_____

_____

_____

_____

_____

_____

_____

_____

10 En el aeropuerto internacional de Miami los **letreros** están en inglés ¡y español! Eva se siente[2] más contenta. Los oficiales de la **aduana** también son **bilingües** y muy simpáticos. Eva ya tiene confianza[3] y va

15 a la **sala de espera**. Una simpática familia norteamericana la espera con un letrero que dice, «¡Bienvenida Eva! Welcome Eva!» Eva llora[4] de gusto y de emoción. «Sí, voy a estar contenta. ¡Voy a pasar un buen año aquí en

20 Miami!»

_____

[2] feels   [3] has confidence   [4] cries

PALABRAS CLAVE

el letrero *sign*   **bilingüe(s)** *bilingual*

la aduana *customs*   **la sala de espera** *waiting room*

¡En español! Level 1

Vocabulario de la lectura

Palabras clave

la **aduana**   *customs*

el **avión**   *airplane*

bilingüe(s)   *bilingual*

la **chica**   *girl*

el (la) **estudiante**   *student*

la **familia**   *family*

el **letrero**   *sign*

la **sala de espera**   *waiting room*

A. Complete each sentence with the best **Palabra clave.** Use each word only once.

Eva, una _____ de Nicaragua, es una _____ del
           (1)   (2)

programa de Intercambio Académico Internacional. Viaja sola en

_____ a Miami. Los oficiales de la _____ del aeropuerto
        (3)   (4)

son _____; hablan inglés y español. En la _____ hay
          (5)   (6)

una _____ norteamericana con un _____ que dice
       (7)   (8)

«¡Bienvenida Eva!»

B. Choose two **Palabras clave** and write a sentence with each one.

_____

_____

_____

_____

¿Comprendiste?

1. ¿Quién es Eva?

_____

2. ¿De dónde es ella?

_____

3. ¿Adónde viaja?

_____

4. ¿Qué le gusta?

_____

Conexión personal

You are going to participate in an international exchange program. Write a letter to your host family introducing yourself. Say what town or city you are from, what kind of home you live in, and what you like to do.

¡Hola! Me llamo...

_____

_____

_____

_____

_____

_____

_____

_____

_____

_____

_____

_____

_____

Para leer *Los Ángeles: Una carta del pasado*

Reading Strategy

PICTURE CLUES Looking at the pictures that accompany
a reading can help you understand the reading better. Look
at the illustrations on these pages. What do you think the
reading will be about? Write your ideas in the space below.

_____

_____

_____

_____

_____

_____

What You Need to Know

In 1769 Gaspar de Portolá, a soldier in the Spanish army, and Juan
Crespi, a Catholic priest, led an expedition up the California coast to
an area that is now part of Los Angeles. They camped by a river, which
they named **El Río de Nuestra Señora la Reina de los Ángeles de
Porciúncula. Porciúncula** was a chapel in Italy. In 1781 the Spanish
government recruited a group of eleven families in northern Mexico
to move to the area and establish a **pueblo,** or town. The settlers, known
as **los pobladores,** consisted of 11 men, 11 women, and 22 children.
They named their new home **El Pueblo de Nuestra Señora la Reina
de los Ángeles de Porciúncula** after the nearby river. The letter you
are about to read is by a boy who lived in the settlement of Los Angeles
just three years after the original founding families arrived there.

READER'S SUCCESS STRATEGY On a world map, locate Mexico; Málaga, Spain; and Los Angeles, California. Imagine what route people coming from Mexico or Spain might have taken to reach Los Angeles in the eighteenth century.

MÁRCALO > GRAMÁTICA Underline the passage in the reading in which Miguel gives his age and his sister's age. Then write sentences that tell your own age and the ages of any brothers or sisters that you have.

APUNTES

Los Ángeles: Una carta del pasado[1]

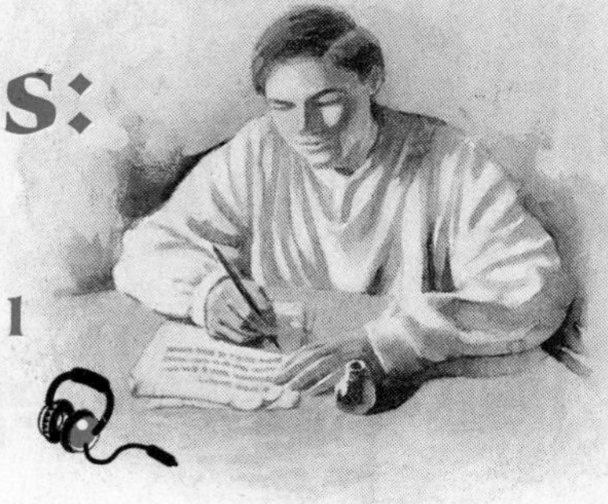

Aquí tienes un fragmento de una carta de Miguel José Guerra, un chico español, que vivía[2] en Los Ángeles en ¡1784!

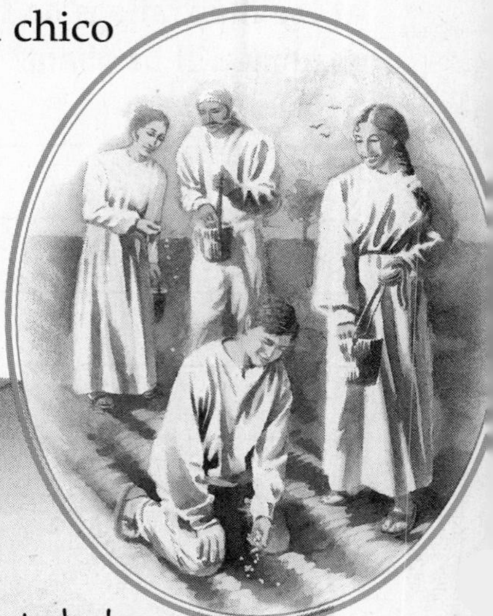

2 de agosto de 1784

Querido primo:

¿Cómo estás? ¿Cómo está toda la familia allá en Málaga? Aquí en el Pueblo de Nuestra Señora de Los Ángeles estamos contentos. ¡Hoy mi familia y yo no trabajamos!

Generalmente, mi hermana y yo trabajamos en el campo[3] con mamá y papá. (Mi hermana ya tiene 15 años y yo tengo 13, pero mi papá es muy viejo —¡él tiene 36 años!) Papá es fuerte y

[1] past [2] lived [3] fields

PALABRAS CLAVE
la carta *letter*
querido(a) *dear*

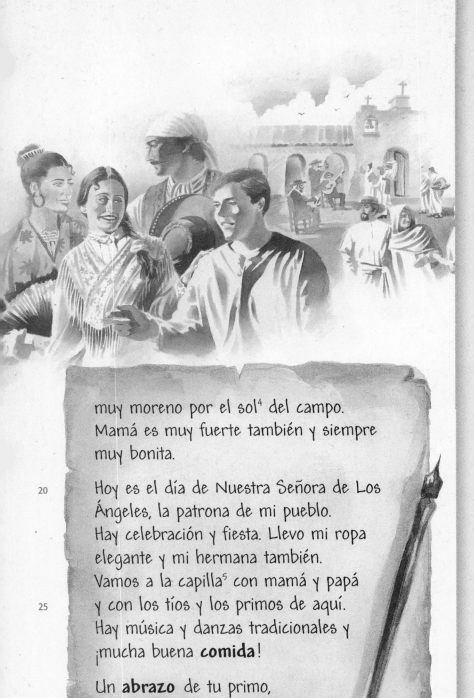

muy moreno por el sol⁴ del campo.
Mamá es muy fuerte también y siempre
muy bonita.

20 Hoy es el día de Nuestra Señora de Los
Ángeles, la patrona de mi pueblo.
Hay celebración y fiesta. Llevo mi ropa
elegante y mi hermana también.
Vamos a la capilla⁵ con mamá y papá
25 y con los tíos y los primos de aquí.
Hay música y danzas tradicionales y
¡mucha buena **comida**!

Un **abrazo** de tu primo,
Miguel José

---

⁴sun   ⁵*Vamos…capilla* We go to chapel

PALABRAS CLAVE
la comida *food*   el abrazo *hug*

READING TIP Some words, such as **ropa** in line 22, are false cognates. False cognates are words that look alike in English and Spanish, but have different meanings. What does **ropa** mean? What English word does it resemble?

A pensar...

1. Why does Miguel have a cousin and other relatives in Spain? **(Infer)**

_____

_____

_____

_____

2. Why do you think that even the children in Miguel's family had to work? **(Draw Conclusions)**

_____

_____

_____

_____

_____

CHALLENGE Why do you think a family would make the decision to leave their own country and move far away to a new, unsettled place? **(Make Judgments)**

_____

_____

_____

Vocabulario de la lectura

Palabras clave

el abrazo *hug*	**la comida** *food*	**querido(a)** *dear*
agosto *August*	**la hermana** *sister*	**los tíos** *uncle(s) and aunt(s)*
la carta *letter*	**el (la) primo(a)** *cousin*	

A. Complete the following letter with the correct **Palabras clave.**

16 de _____
(1)

_____ primo:
(2)

¿Cómo estás? Aquí en Málaga estoy muy contenta. Me gusta esta ciudad. Picasso, el artista, es de aquí. Hoy mis padres y yo vamos a visitar el Museo Picasso. Esta noche, vamos a un restaurante que sirve _____ típica de España. ¡Qué (3) chévere! Te escribo otra _____ pronto. (4)

Un _____ de tu _____, (5)   (6)

Manuela

B. Complete each sentence with the correct form of a **Palabra clave.**

1. El hijo de tus tíos es tu _____.

2. La hija de tus tíos es tu _____.

3. Los padres de tus primos son tus _____.

4. La hija de tus padres es tu _____.

¿Comprendiste?

1. ¿Quién escribe la carta?

_____

2. ¿A quién le escribe? ¿Dónde vive esa persona?

_____

3. ¿Por qué está contento?

_____

4. ¿Cuántos miembros de la familia hay? ¿Quiénes son?

_____

5. ¿Cómo celebran el día?

_____

Conexión personal

Write a letter to a pen pal, real or imaginary, describing yourself and your family.

Querido(a)...

_____

_____

_____

_____

_____

_____

_____

_____

_____

_____

_____

_____

Para leer   *Una encuesta escolar*

Reading Strategy

USE CONTEXT CLUES You can use the context to guess the meaning of unfamiliar words. Context includes what is written before and after the word. Pictures often contribute to the context too. What do you think the highlighted words mean? Write your answers in the chart below.

• Una encuesta **escolar**

• El papel sale de la impresora con los **resultados** de la encuesta.

Word	Definition
escolar	
resultados	

What You Need to Know

In Mexico, children are required to attend public or private school through grade nine. There are six grades of primary education and three grades of secondary education. The school day for the primary grades is usually from 9 A.M. to 12:30 P.M. and for the secondary grades it is from 7:30 A.M. to 2:30 P.M. Most Mexican students attend public schools, although in the cities many attend private schools. Students who wish to continue their education beyond the secondary level take college preparatory classes for three more years or they attend vocational school, after which they may apply to a university. Both public and private universities in Mexico have highly competitive entrance exams, which applicants must pass in order to gain admission.

Una encuesta escolar

READING TIP This article employs chronological order to keep track of the steps Ricardo follows, from preparing his survey to utilizing the results. As you read, ask questions about what happens first, next, and last.

Ricardo tiene que hacer una **encuesta** en la escuela. Él prepara una lista de preguntas. Ricardo habla con los otros estudiantes y escribe sus **respuestas** en un cuaderno. En
5 casa escribe las respuestas en la computadora. Con una calculadora suma[1] el total de respuestas. El papel sale[2] de la impresora con los resultados de la encuesta. Ricardo usa los resultados de la encuesta para hacer un
10 **proyecto** en la clase de matemáticas.

[1] he adds   [2] comes out

▥▥ **MÁRCALO** ⟫ **VOCABULARIO**
Reread the boxed text. How many words name classroom objects? Circle each one.

PALABRAS CLAVE
la encuesta *survey*   el proyecto *project*
la respuesta *response*

APUNTES

A pensar...

1. Reread Ricardo's survey, then take the survey yourself. Fill in the blanks and place checkmarks in the boxes as appropriate. If you have classes not listed on the form, write them in. **(Assess)**

2. In groups, compare your individual responses to the survey. Then prepare the survey results for your group using a format like Ricardo's, as shown on the next page. Were there any questions to which all members of your group had the same response? What did you learn from the results of this survey? **(Tabulate/Summarize)**

APUNTES

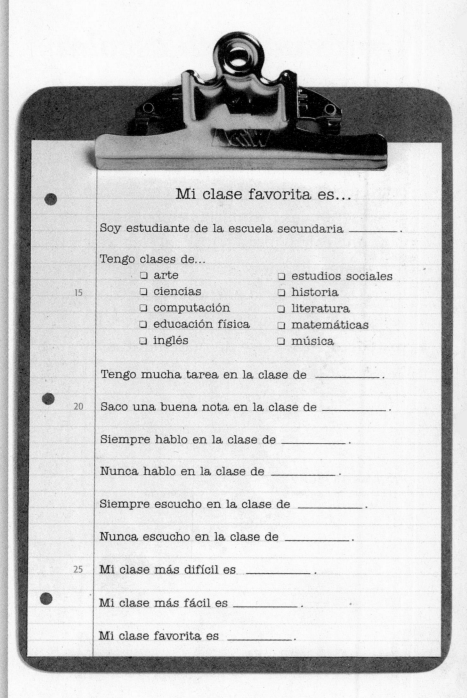

Mi clase favorita es...

Soy estudiante de la escuela secundaria _____ .

Tengo clases de...
- ❑ arte
- ❑ ciencias
- ❑ computación
- ❑ educación física
- ❑ inglés
- ❑ estudios sociales
- ❑ historia
- ❑ literatura
- ❑ matemáticas
- ❑ música

Tengo mucha tarea en la clase de _____ .

Saco una buena nota en la clase de _____ .

Siempre hablo en la clase de _____ .

Nunca hablo en la clase de _____ .

Siempre escucho en la clase de _____ .

Nunca escucho en la clase de _____ .

Mi clase más difícil es _____ .

Mi clase más fácil es _____ .

Mi clase favorita es _____ .

Los resultados

Una encuesta a 50 estudiantes

30 Clase con más tarea: matemáticas
    (25 estudiantes)

    Los estudiantes sacan más buenas notas en la clase de: música
    (35 estudiantes)

    Los estudiantes hablan más en la clase de: literatura
35 *(30 estudiantes)*

    Los estudiantes nunca hablan en la clase de: inglés
    (25 estudiantes)

    Los estudiantes escuchan más en la clase de: ciencias
    (40 estudiantes)

40 Los estudiantes nunca escuchan en la clase de: historia
    (20 estudiantes)

    La clase más difícil es: ciencias
    (35 estudiantes)

    La clase más fácil es: arte
45 *(45 estudiantes)*

    La clase favorita es: literatura
    (30 estudiantes)

READER'S SUCCESS STRATEGY Use a chart like the one below to compare and contrast the courses offered at Ricardo's school with the courses offered at your school.

Ricardo's School

My School

CHALLENGE Look at the results of Ricardo's survey. Note in the heading how many students he surveyed in all. Then convert the number of students listed in each subcategory to the percentage of all students surveyed. **(Calculate)**

Modelo: Clase con más tarea: matemáticas (25 estudiantes: 50%)

Vocabulario de la lectura

Palabras clave

la **calculadora** *calculator*   la **encuesta** *survey*   el **proyecto** *project*

la **computadora** *computer*   la **impresora** *printer*   la **respuesta** *response*

el **cuaderno** *notebook*   el **papel** *paper*

A. Fill in each blank with the correct form of a **Palabra clave**.

Ricardo prepara una lista de preguntas para su _____ escolar.

(1)

Primero, escribe las _____ de los otros estudiantes en un

(2)

_____. Cuando llega a casa, escribe las respuestas en la

(3)

_____. Usa una _____ para sumar el total de

(4)   (5)

respuestas. El _____ sale de la _____ con los

(6)   (7)

resultados. Ricardo usa los resultados de su encuesta para un _____

(8)

que tiene que hacer en la clase de matemáticas.

B. Choose two **Palabras clave** and write a sentence with each one.

_____

_____

_____

_____

_____

_____

¿Comprendiste?

1. ¿Qué tiene que hacer Ricardo?

_____

2. ¿Qué usa Ricardo para escribir la encuesta?

_____

3. ¿Los estudiantes hablan mucho o poco en la clase de inglés?

_____

4. ¿Es difícil la clase de música o arte en la escuela de Ricardo?

_____

5. ¿Qué clase es la clase favorita de los estudiantes?

_____

Conexión personal

What is your favorite class? Why do you like it? Write your answers in the web below.

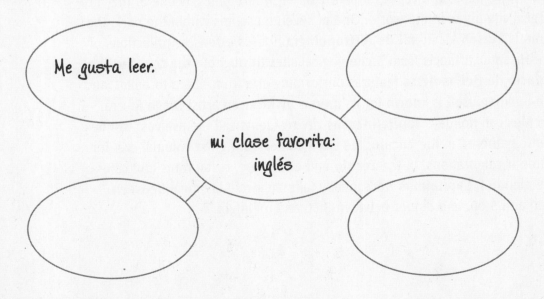

Me gusta leer.

mi clase favorita: inglés

Para leer   *México y sus jóvenes*

Reading Strategy

SKIM Before reading a long passage, it is helpful to read quickly to get a general idea of its content. Skim the paragraphs, noting clues that indicate the central theme or topic. By skimming, you can tell quickly what a reading is about. Then it will be easier to do a more careful reading. After skimming **México y sus jóvenes**, write down some words or phrases below that indicate what it is about.

_____

_____

_____

_____

What You Need to Know

Mexico City offers a variety of attractions for residents and visitors alike. **El Bosque de Chapultepec**, at nearly three square miles, is one of the largest city parks in the world. One of seven museums within the park, the famous **Museo Nacional de Antropología** houses extensive collections of pre-Hispanic artifacts from archeological sites throughout the country. The **Palacio de Bellas Artes** features performing arts from opera to ballet, and the building itself is known for its murals by Mexican artist Diego Rivera. On Mexican holidays **capitalinos**, as city residents call themselves, can be found gathered in the **Zócalo**, the city's center during the colonial era, for outdoor celebrations. In the **Zócalo** and elsewhere, restaurants and cafés are plentiful. **Capitalinos** traditionally take their midday meal between 3:00 and 5:00, and dinner between 8:30 and midnight.

México
y sus jóvenes

¿Qué hacen los mexicanos jóvenes? De lunes a viernes los muchachos que tienen **menos de** 18 años van a la escuela.

5 Tienen muchas materias — a veces tienen hasta ocho clases en un día. Y también tienen mucha tarea. Por eso, después de clases

10 muchos de los estudiantes van a sus casas para hacer la tarea y después descansar.

15 En la Ciudad de México hay muchos teatros, museos, tiendas y parques. En **cada** lugar es posible ver a muchos jóvenes, especialmente los fines de semana.

PALABRAS CLAVE
menos de *less than*   **cada** *every*

READING TIP Cover the definitions of the **Palabras clave** at the bottom of the page, and see if you can determine what the words mean on your own. Clues to meaning are often offered by the context of a sentence. If you guessed a word correctly, ask yourself how you figured out what it meant.

_____

_____

_____

_____

CHALLENGE Imagine that you are interviewing an exchange student from Mexico City. What would you like to know about what life is like in the capital of Mexico? You might want to ask about a typical school day, what teenagers do for fun with their friends, what activities they share with their families, or something else you are interested in. In Spanish, write three interview questions below. (**Connect**)

Preguntas

1. _____

_____

2. _____

_____

3. _____

_____

READER'S SUCCESS STRATEGY Highlight the words in the article that name places visited by young people in Mexico on the weekends.

▥ **MÁRCALO** ⬥ **VOCABULARIO**
You have just learned words and phrases to describe leisure activities. Using this vocabulary, write a caption for each of the photographs on these pages.

APUNTES

A pensar...

Consider what you have learned about how teenagers in Mexico City spend time on the weekends. Do you and your friends enjoy the same types of activities in your free time? Name some activities you have in common with Mexican teenagers and some activities that differ from theirs.
(Compare and Contrast)

Los viernes por la tarde, los sábados y los
20 domingos son los días principales en que los jóvenes mexicanos están **libres.** Los domingos hay mucha gente en los parques. Andan en bicicleta, practican **deportes** o tocan un instrumento. De vez en cuando, para el
25 almuerzo, van a un restaurante con sus familias. El domingo es el día principal para pasear y descansar.

PALABRAS CLAVE
libre *free*   **los deportes** *sports*

¡En español! Level 1

Vocabulario de la lectura

Palabras clave

cada *every*	**menos de** *less than*	**el teatro** *theater*
los deportes *sports*	**el museo** *museum*	**la tienda** *store*
libre *free*	**el parque** *park*	

A. For each **Palabra clave** in the first column, find the sentence in the second column that best describes it. Write the corresponding letter in the blank.

_____ 1. tienda

_____ 2. parque

_____ 3. teatro

_____ 4. museo

_____ 5. deportes

A. Es donde la gente pasea y descansa.

B. Venden cosas aquí.

C. Incluyen patinar, nadar y andar en bicicleta.

D. Tiene cosas muy viejas.

E. Es donde va la gente para ver ballet y escuchar música.

B. Fill in each blank with the correct form of a **Palabra clave**.

1. Julio descansa los sábados y los domingos, los días principales en que

   está _____.

2. Los viernes por la tarde, me gusta practicar _____ en el parque con los amigos.

3. Normalmente hay muchas personas en el museo, pero hoy hay

   _____ diez.

4. A María le gusta hacer ejercicio; anda en bicicleta _____ día.

5. Mamá va a la _____ de ropa para comprar una falda nueva.

¿Comprendiste?

1. ¿Qué hacen los jóvenes de lunes a viernes?

   _____

2. ¿Adónde van muchos jóvenes los fines de semana en la Ciudad de México?

   _____

3. ¿Qué actividades hacen los domingos?

   _____

4. ¿Qué hace a veces una familia los domingos?

   _____

Conexión personal

How would you describe an ideal Saturday? Write some of your favorite weekend activities in the space at the right.

Los sábados, me gusta...

1. andar en bicicleta

2.

3.

4.

Para leer

Una leyenda azteca:
El origen de la Ciudad de México

Reading Strategy

LOOK FOR CONTEXT CLUES At first glance, there may appear to be many words in the reading you can't seem to understand. To improve your comprehension, use this strategy: Read each sentence as a whole rather than translating word for word.

What You Need to Know

It is believed that the people who founded the Aztec capital of Tenochtitlán migrated south from a place called Aztlan in the area of present-day northern Mexico or southern Arizona. The name Aztec comes from the word *Aztlan*. Tenochtitlán, the largest city in the Aztec empire, was built on a lake and linked to the mainland by three large causeways. By the early 1400s, the Aztecs had one of the most advanced civilizations in the world. Although they were met with fierce resistance, the Spanish finally destroyed Tenochtitlán in 1521 and built Mexico City on the site of the Aztec capital. The Mexican flag, which shows an eagle standing on a nopal cactus with a rattlesnake in its mouth, was inspired by the Aztec legend about Tenochtitlán that is the subject of this reading.

Una leyenda azteca

El origen de la Ciudad de México

Los aztecas, una tribu de **guerreros,** deciden dejar[1] su casa en el norte por necesidades económicas. Caminan todos los días por mucho tiempo buscando un lugar nuevo.

5 Pasan por muchos lugares pero no encuentran[2] el lugar perfecto. Esperan ansiosos la señal[3] de su **dios,** Huitzilopochtli.

Pasa mucho tiempo y están los aztecas muy
10 cansados[4]. Llegan a un **lago** donde miran la señal en medio del lago. Está un **águila** sobre un **cacto,** ¡con
15 una **serpiente** en la **boca**! Todos miran y hablan.

[1]leave [2]find [3]sign [4]tired

PALABRAS CLAVE

el guerrero *warrior*	**el cacto** *cactus*	
el dios *god*	**la serpiente** *snake*	
el lago *lake*	**la boca** *mouth*	
el águila (f.) *eagle*		

¡En español! Level 1

A pensar...

1. What do the Aztecs begin to do after they see the eagle on a cactus with a snake in its mouth, and why? **(Clarify)**

_____

_____

—¡Ésta es la señal que esperamos! ¡Ésta es la señal de nuestro dios!

20 —¡Aquí es donde preparamos nuestra ciudad!

Y así, en el lago de Texcoco, los aztecas empiezan a construir su ciudad. Usan tierra y raíces[5] para crear pequeñas **islas.** Construyen sus casas en las islas.

2. Look at the picture of the Mexican flag. What is the symbol on the flag? What is its significance? **(Clarify)**

_____

_____

_____

_____

25 Y así fue la creación, en el año 1325, de la gran Tenochtitlán, que ahora es la maravillosa Ciudad de México.

[5] earth and roots

CHALLENGE What can you infer about the role of religion in Aztec life from reading this legend? Mark any passages that support your ideas. **(Infer)**

_____

_____

_____

_____

PALABRAS CLAVE
la isla *island*

Vocabulario de la lectura

Palabras clave

el **águila** (f.) *eagle*   **esperar** *to wait for, to expect*   el **lago** *lake*

la **boca** *mouth*   el **guerrero** *warrior*   **mirar** *to watch, to look at*

el **cacto** *cactus*   la **isla** *island*   la **serpiente** *snake*

el **dios** *god*

A. Fill in each blank with the correct form of a **Palabra clave.**

Los aztecas _____ una señal de Huitzilopochtli. Huitzilopochtli es el
(1)

_____ de los aztecas. La señal es un _____ sobre un
(2)   (3)

cacto. El águila tiene una _____ en la _____ . Un día,
(4)   (5)

los aztecas _____ la señal en medio de un lago. Usan tierra y raíces
(6)

para crear _____ en el lago. Construyen Tenochtitlán en las islas del
(7)

_____ de Texcoco.
(8)

B. Complete each sentence with the correct form of a **Palabra clave.**

1. Los aztecas son un tribu de _____ .

2. El _____ de los aztecas se llama Huitzilopochtli.

3. En un lago, hay un _____ con una serpiente en la boca.

4. El águila está sobre un _____ .

5. Los aztecas empiezan a construir pequeñas _____ .

6. El _____ en que los aztecas construyen las islas se llama Texcoco.

¿Comprendiste?

1. ¿Quiénes son los aztecas?

_____

2. ¿Qué buscan?

_____

3. ¿Cuál es la señal que reciben?

_____

4. ¿Qué es Tenochtitlán?

_____

Conexión personal

Suppose you are part of an archaeological dig on the site of an Aztec civilization. What would you most like to find? Make a list on the right.

Busco...

casas

Para leer

Una leyenda mexicana: La Casa de los Azulejos

Reading Strategy

FOLLOWING PLOT Use a chart to help you follow what happens in this legend. Show the beginning, middle, and end of the story. What do the father and the son do at each point of the story?

	Beginning	Middle	End
Father			
Son			

What You Need to Know

In 1737, the Count and Countess of Orizaba Valley ordered a reconstruction of their house in Mexico City and covered it with blue and white tiles. Tiled houses were a sign of success in Mexico during the colonial era, and were already popular in the town of Puebla, where the countess had lived before moving to Mexico City. **La Casa de los Azulejos,** or the House of Tiles, as the count and countess's former home is known today, is one of Mexico City's oldest landmarks. Its two-story courtyard is now a restaurant, and the second-floor stairwell contains a mural by the famous Mexican artist Orozco. The following legend gives one account of the history of **La Casa de los Azulejos.**

Una leyenda mexicana

La Casa de los Azulejos 🎧

En la Ciudad de México hay una casa muy famosa. Hay muchas leyendas de esta casa. Una de ellas va así...

5 En la **época colonial**, el señor **conde** de Valle tiene un hijo que no trabaja y no estudia. Sólo va a
10 muchas fiestas de noche y descansa de día. Sólo quiere llevar ropa elegante. Su padre está muy **triste.** Piensa[1] que su hijo nunca va a hacer nada[2]
15 bueno. Por fin, un día dice: —Veo, hijo mío, que tú nunca vas a trabajar, nunca vas a estudiar y nunca vas a hacer tu casa de azulejos como la gente buena de esta ciudad.

---

[1] He thinks   [2] *nunca...nada* is never going to do anything

PALABRAS CLAVE
el azulejo *ceramic tile*
la época colonial *colonial period, the time during which Spain ruled Mexico*
el conde, la condesa *count, countess*
triste *sad*

READER'S SUCCESS STRATEGY In Spanish, dashes are often used to indicate dialog, a conversation between two or more persons. As you read this selection, make note of who is speaking the words that follow the first dash, and who is speaking the words that follow the second dash.

READING TIP Note that the first and last paragraphs of this reading are an introduction and a conclusion to the legend. They describe a building that still stands in Mexico City today.

CHALLENGE How do you think this legend began? Exchange ideas in small groups. **(Make Judgments)**

MÁRCALO ⟩ GRAMÁTICA

Circle the verb in line 25. Then conjugate it in the space below.

_____

_____

_____

_____

_____

_____

_____

A pensar...

1. Why is the count displeased with his son at the start of the story? **(Clarify)**

_____

_____

_____

2. Why does the count's son decide to build a house of tiles? **(Cause and Effect)**

_____

_____

_____

3. Check two sentences below that are _facts_ about **La Casa de los Azulejos.** **(Differentiate)**

☐ There are many legends about its origin.

☐ It has always been a restaurant.

☐ The house is still standing in Mexico City.

El hijo escucha con atención las palabras de su

20 papá por primera vez y contesta: —Lo veo a
usted muy triste por mi culpa³. Quiero
cambiar mi vida. Voy a abandonar mi vida
de perezoso y voy a trabajar.

Entonces, el hijo empieza a trabajar mucho.

25 Hace una casa grande y bonita con azulejos
por dentro y ¡**por fuera**! Es para enseñarle
a su papá que sí escucha sus palabras.

¡Y todavía existe esta
casa! Si vas a la

30 Ciudad de México,
puedes visitarla. Es
un restaurante muy
bonito y famoso.

³ fault

PALABRAS CLAVE
cambiar _to change_
por dentro _inside_

por fuera _outside_

¡En español! Level 1

Vocabulario de la lectura

Palabras clave

el azulejo *ceramic tile*
cambiar *to change*
el conde, la condesa *count, countess*
entonces *then, so*
la época colonial *colonial period, the time during which Spain ruled Mexico*

la gente *people*
por dentro *inside*
por fin *finally*

por fuera *outside*
primero *first*
triste *sad*

A. Complete each sentence with the correct form of a **Palabra clave.**

El señor _____ de Valle vive en la Ciudad de México durante la
　　　　　　　　(1)

_____. Está _____ porque su hijo perezoso no trabaja y
　　　(2)　　　　　　　　　　　(3)

no estudia. El hijo ve a su padre muy descontento y por fin decide

_____ su vida. Hace una casa bonita con _____ por
　　　(4)　　　　　　　　　　　　　　　　　　　　　　(5)

dentro y _____.
　　　　　　　(6)

B. On the line next to each word pair, write whether the words are synonyms or
antonyms. Synonyms are words with the same or similar meaning. Antonyms are
words with opposite meanings.

1. primero–final _____

2. descontento–triste _____

3. por fuera–por dentro _____

4. triste–feliz _____

5. personas–gente _____

¿Comprendiste?

1. ¿Cómo es el hijo del conde?

_____

2. ¿Qué hace todos los días?

_____

3. ¿Qué piensa el padre?

_____

4. Por fin, ¿qué hace el hijo?

_____

Conexión personal

If you were the son or daughter of a wealthy nobleman, how would you spend your time? List some things you would do in the space on the right.

ir al teatro
_____
_____
_____
_____
_____
_____
_____
_____
_____
_____

Para leer   *Bomba y plena*

Reading Strategy

SCAN Reading very quickly to get a specific piece of information, like a football score or a movie time, is called scanning. Scan the poster on page 47 and decide whether you could attend the festival if you had baseball practice on Saturday, October 16, at 2:00 P.M. Write down your answer below.

_____

_____

_____

_____

What You Need to Know

Puerto Rico has developed unique musical traditions reflecting the convergence of indigenous, African, and European cultures. Some instruments still used in Puerto Rican music are believed to have originated with the **taínos.** Most notable among these is the **güiro**, a hollow gourd with grooves carved into its surface used in the forms of Puerto Rican music and dance called **bomba** and **plena. Maracas,** percussive instruments originally made from the fruit of the **higuera** tree, also date to the **taínos** and are an important part of Caribbean **salsa** music. **Conga** drums, also used by salsa bands, trace their roots to African instruments made from hollow logs covered with animal skins. A stringed instrument adapted from the Spanish classical guitar, the four-stringed **cuatro** is unique to Puerto Rico and a central presence in a wide variety of traditional and contemporary Puerto Rican music.

READING TIP As you read, look at the photographs or illustrations to see if you can identify the instruments mentioned in the text.

APUNTES

MÁRCALO ⟩ **GRAMÁTICA**
Find and underline each form of the verb **tener** that appears in the article. Then conjugate **tener** and **venir** below.

A pensar...

The article refers to the musical traditions of three world cultures. What are they? What is their relation to the subject of the reading? **(Analyze)**

Bomba y plena

La bomba y la plena son danzas típicas de Puerto Rico. Tienen sus orígenes en la música africana. Los instrumentos originales para tocar esta música alegre son los **tambores,**
5 las **panderetas,** las maracas y el cuatro. El cuatro es un tipo de guitarra española pequeña, originalmente con cuatro **cuerdas.** Las personas que bailan estas danzas llevan ropa de muchos colores. La música tiene
10 mucho **ritmo** y las personas ¡mueven todo el **cuerpo**!

PALABRAS CLAVE
el tambor *drum*   **el ritmo** *rhythm*
la pandereta *type of tambourine*   **el cuerpo** *body*
la cuerda *string*

¡TODOS A BAILAR!

Concierto espectacular de

BOMBA y PLENA

¡Músicos sensacionales!

Claudio de Mata: maracas

Rubén López: cuatro

Lucio Escobar: tamborín

¡Y la actuación especial de los bailarines

Lilián y Alberto!

Sábado 16 de octubre
a las 5 de la tarde
en el Instituto de Cultura

READER'S SUCCESS STRATEGY While reading the poster for the concert, ask yourself the questions Who? What? When? Where? Look for the answers in the poster and write them down below.

Who?

What?

When?

Where?

CHALLENGE What kind of music or dance do you like? Using the Venn diagram, compare this music or dance to **la bomba** and **la plena**. Where the circles are separate, write in differences. Where they intersect, write in similarities.

Bomba y plena

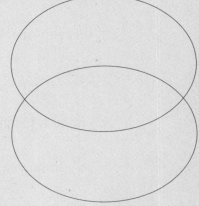

Other music/dance:

PALABRAS CLAVE
el (la) músico(a) *musician*
la actuación *performance*

el (la) bailarín/bailarina *dancer*

Vocabulario de la lectura

Palabras clave

la **actuación**   *performance*

el (la) **bailarín/bailarina**   *dancer*

el **concierto**   *concert*

la **cuerda**   *string*

el **cuerpo**   *body*

el (la) **músico(a)**   *musician*

la **pandereta**   *type of tambourine*

el **ritmo**   *rhythm*

el **tambor**   *drum*

A. For each **Palabra clave** in the first column, find the phrase in the second column that is closest in meaning. Write the corresponding letter in the blank.

_____ 1. cuerdas

_____ 2. ritmo

_____ 3. tambor

_____ 4. bailarín

_____ 5. músico

A. elemento de la música

B. persona que se dedica al baile

C. parte de una guitarra

D. persona que toca un instrumento

E. instrumento de percusión

B. Fill in each blank with the correct form of one of the **Palabras clave.** Then unscramble the boxed letters to complete the sentence below the puzzle.

1. Viernes, 11 de julio, hay un __ __ __ __ __ __ __ __ [ ] de bomba y plena en el teatro.

2. La __ __ __ __ __ __ [ ] __ __ de los bailarines, Silvana y Jaime, va a ser fenomenal.

3. Los [ ] __ __ __ __ __ __ tocan las maracas y el cuatro.

4. También tocan la __ __ __ __ __ __ __ __ [ ] __, un tipo de tamborín.

5. La bomba y la plena son danzas alegres, y las personas ¡mueven todo

   el __ __ __ [ ] __ __!

   La música de bomba y plena tiene mucho __ __ __ __ __.

¿Comprendiste?

1. ¿Cuándo es el concierto?

_____

2. ¿En qué tienen sus orígenes la bomba y la plena?

_____

3. ¿Es una música triste o alegre?

_____

4. ¿Qué es el cuatro?

_____

5. ¿Qué otros instrumentos hay?

_____

6. ¿Qué ropa llevan las personas que bailan?

_____

Conexión personal

Design your own poster in
Spanish advertising a school event
or a local cultural event, either
real or imagined. Your goal is to
try to entice people to attend the
event. Be sure to include the
name of the event, the names of
any performers, and the date,
time, and place.

Para leer *El coquí*

Reading Strategy

DISTINGUISH DETAILS Find out what **coquíes are.** What features do they have? Use the word web to describe a **coquí** and name its identifying characteristics.

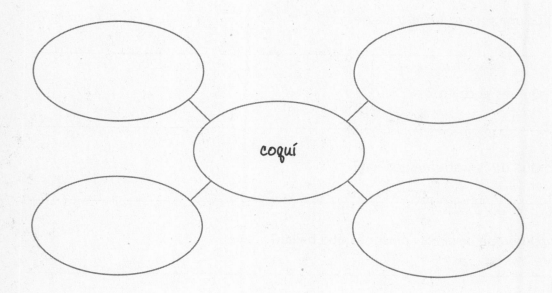

What You Need to Know

The only rain forest in the U.S. National Forest Service is found on the island of Puerto Rico, in the **Sierra de Luquillo,** 25 miles from San Juan. Twenty-eight thousand acres in size, **El Bosque Nacional del Caribe,** commonly called **El Yunque,** is home to 240 species of trees and plants, some of which are found nowhere else in the world. The highly diverse wildlife of **El Yunque** includes 16 types of **coquíes**; 11 types of bats; and the Puerto Rican boa, a snake that can grow to over eight feet in length. Hunting is not allowed at El Yunque, which is a wildlife refuge and the habitat for eight endangered species, including the extremely rare **loro puertorriqueño,** or Puerto Rican Parrot.

El coquí

No muy lejos de[1] San Juan está el Bosque
Nacional del Caribe. En este bosque tropical,
El Yunque, hay animales y plantas que no ves
en ninguna otra parte[2] del mundo. El coquí,
5 el animal más conocido de todo Puerto Rico,
vive **protegido** en El Yunque.

[1] Not far from   [2] any other part

El Yunque, el Bosque Nacional del Caribe

READING TIP As you read
El coquí, use a highlighter to
mark words that help you
visualize the rain forest. Look
for words that appeal to your
senses, especially sight and
hearing.

APUNTES

MÁRCALO VOCABULARIO
Imagine that you are planning
a trip to El Yunque. You know
that the park's daytime
temperature ranges from
approximately 65°F to 78°F, it
rains frequently, and at higher
elevations visitors can swim in
the pools. Make a list of
clothing and accessories you
should bring with you.

APUNTES

PALABRAS CLAVE
protegido(a) *protected*

A pensar...

Why do you think certain species of the **coquí** are in danger of becoming extinct? **(Cause and Effect)**

_____

_____

_____

_____

_____

_____

CHALLENGE Write a brief paragraph about an animal of your own choosing. Describe the animal's appearance, say where it is found, and discuss what the weather is like in the animal's habitat. **(Extend)**

_____

_____

_____

_____

_____

_____

_____

_____

El coquí es una **rana** de **tamaño**

10 pequeño que vive en los árboles. Los coquíes son de diferentes colores. Hay coquíes **grises,**

15 marrones, amarillos y verdes. Reciben su nombre por su **canto** característico. Hay 16 **especies** de coquíes en Puerto Rico, pero sólo dos producen el canto típico «coquí». Dos están en **peligro** de extinción. Casi todos los

20 coquíes empiezan a cantar cuando llega la noche.

Si visitas Puerto Rico, vas a ver imágenes del coquí en muchos lugares — en nombres de tiendas, artículos de promoción y libros. La

25 tradición puertorriqueña es que si ves un coquí vas a tener mucha suerte. Y si quieres tener un bonito recuerdo[3] de Puerto Rico es posible comprar un coquí verde de juguete[4], símbolo de la isla.

_____

[3]souvenir   [4]toy

PALABRAS CLAVE

la rana frog	**el canto** song
el tamaño size	**la especie** species
gris grey	**el peligro** danger

Vocabulario de la lectura

Palabras clave

el **árbol** *tree*	**gris** *grey*	**protegido(a)** *protected*
el **bosque** *forest*	el **peligro** *danger*	la **rana** *frog*
el **canto** *song*	la **planta** *plant*	la **extinción** *extinction*
la **especie** *species*		

A. Fill in the blanks with the most appropriate **Palabra clave**.
Use each word only once.

El Yunque es un _____ tropical de Puerto Rico. Aquí hay
(1)

_____ que no ves en ninguna otra parte del mundo. El coquí,
(2)

una _____ pequeña, vive _____ en los
(3)   (4)

_____ del parque. Los coquíes reciben su nombre por su
(5)

_____ típico «coquí». Hay coquíes marrones, amarillos, verdes y
(6)

_____ . Hay 16 _____ de coquí en Puerto Rico,
(7)   (8)

pero dos están en _____ de _____ .
(9)   (10)

B. What did you learn from the article about **El Yunque**? Use at least two of the
Palabras clave in your answer.

_____

_____

_____

_____

¿Comprendiste?

1. ¿Dónde vive el coquí?

_____

2. ¿Qué es el coquí? ¿Por qué se llama coquí?

_____

3. ¿Cómo es el coquí?

_____

4. ¿Cuándo canta el coquí?

_____

5. ¿Por qué es bueno ver un coquí?

_____

Conexión personal

Describe a national park or wilderness area that you have been to or that you would like to visit. What are its geographical characteristics? What is the weather like there? Why would you like to go to this place?

Me gustaría ir a Yosemite, un
parque nacional de California....
_____

_____

_____

_____

_____

_____

_____

Para leer   *El bohique y los niños*

Reading Strategy

USING CONTEXT You can use context to understand a word's meaning. Context includes what is written before and after the word. Write the words that help you understand what these words mean.

Word	Context
voz	
areito	

What You Need to Know

When Christopher Columbus arrived in Puerto Rico in 1493, the island was inhabited by **taínos. Taíno** villagers lived in round, straw huts (**bohíos**) arranged around a central plaza, where the village chief, or **cacique,** had his headquarters. The chief governed the village with the help of the **bohique,** a respected member of **taíno** society who acted as an oracle, or prophet. The **bohique** knew the medicinal properties of herbs and trees and was also considered to be a healer. Even before the arrival of the Spanish, the survival of the **taínos** had been threatened by the warlike Caribs, an indigenous people of South America. By the mid-1500s, however, the **taínos** had been virtually annihilated by the Europeans.

READING TIP Remember the concept of false cognates, words that look alike in Spanish and English but have different meanings. Can you find the false cognate in line 2 of this reading? What English word does it look like?

A pensar...

1. Which sentence below is *not* true of the **bohique?** Cross it out. **(Clarify)**

He is a respected member of **taíno** society.

He relates his knowledge in writing.

He sings songs that tell stories.

He explains **taíno** history.

2. How are historical knowledge and cultural traditions passed down by the **taíno** people? **(Summarize)**

El bohique[1] y los niños

Hace sol[2] en las islas del Caribe. Unos niños taínos[3] pasan un buen rato en la **playa.** Enseñan a hablar a los **loros.** El bohique está en su casa. El bohique es una persona muy
5 importante. Es la persona que sabe toda la historia de su **pueblo.** Es la persona que comunica la historia a su pueblo. El bohique empieza[4] a contar[5] un areito. Un areito es una **canción,** leyenda o historia.

10 Cuando los niños escuchan la voz del bohique, uno dice[6]: —Vamos a ir a la casa del bohique. ¡Va a contar un areito! ¡Va a contar la historia de nuestra gente!

---

[1] storyteller   [2] It's sunny   [3] original inhabitants of Puerto Rico
[4] begins   [5] to tell   [6] says

PALABRAS CLAVE
la playa   *beach*   el pueblo   *people, civilization*
el loro   *parrot*   la canción   *song*

¡En español! Level 1

—¡Sí! —dicen todos los niños—. ¡Vamos a
15 escucharlo!

—¡Escuchen! Acaba de empezar el bohique.
Escucho los **tambores.**

—Y tocan las maracas también.

—¡Vamos a cantar con el bohique!

20 —A mí me gustan los areitos. Me gusta bailar
cuando canta el bohique.

—¡Escuchen! El bohique empieza a contar el
areito.

El bohique empieza: «Dicen que de las
25 primeras personas, los taínos, el sol crea todo
el mundo...»

Gracias al bohique que cuenta las historias,
los niños aprenden de la vida de su pueblo.

PALABRAS CLAVE
el tambor *drum*

READER'S
SUCCESS
STRATEGY As you have
learned, dashes are often
used in Spanish to indicate
dialog, or conversation. In
addition to dashes, this
selection also contains
Spanish quotation marks
(see lines 24 and 26),
which are used to set off
quoted material.

MÁRCALO GRAMÁTICA
You know how to use the verb
gustar with an infinitive to talk
about what a person likes to
do. In this reading, one of the
children uses a form of **gustar**
with the infinitive **bailar**. Find
this phrase and circle it. Then
write three similar sentences
using **gustar** with an infinitive
to tell three things that you like
to do.

CHALLENGE Why do you
think the **taíno** children
enjoyed hearing the **bohique**
tell his stories through songs?
(Draw Conclusions)

Vocabulario de la lectura

Palabras clave

la canción *song*   **la playa** *beach*   **el tambor** *drum*
el loro *parrot*   **el pueblo** *people, civilization*

A. For each **Palabra clave** in the first column, find the phrase in the second column that is closest in meaning. Write the corresponding letter in the blank.

_____ 1. loro   A. una composición musical

_____ 2. tambor   B. un instrumento musical

_____ 3. playa   C. un grupo de personas que forma una comunidad

_____ 4. canción   D. donde vas para nadar

_____ 5. pueblo   E. un tipo de pájaro

B. Complete each sentence with the correct form of a **Palabra clave.**

1. Un areito es un tipo de _____ taína.

2. El bohique sabe la historia de su _____.

3. En las islas del Caribe hay muchas _____.

4. Los niños taínos enseñan a hablar a los _____.

5. Les gusta bailar cuando oyen los _____.

¿Comprendiste?

1. ¿Dónde están los niños taínos?

_____

2. ¿Qué hacen?

_____

3. ¿Qué hace el bohique?

_____

4. ¿Qué aprenden los niños gracias al bohique?

_____

Conexión personal

Not all teachers are found in school. The children in the reading learn history from the **bohique.** Who are the important teachers in your life? In the boxes below, name two. Describe some things you have learned from each person. An example has been done.

Abuela		
Me dice la historia de nuestra familia. También me enseña canciones.		

Para leer   *Una leyenda taína*

Reading Strategy

SKIM Skimming a reading before you begin can give you valuable information about what you are going to read. Skim this selection and write down what you learn by looking at these things.

Look at	Learn
title	
pictures	
text	

What You Need to Know

When the Spanish explorers arrived in the New World, the **taínos** inhabited Cuba, Jamaica, Puerto Rico, and the island of Hispaniola, which is now Haiti and the Dominican Republic. Religion played a central role in **taíno** culture, and the **taínos** worshipped various gods and spirits. The **taínos** told many myths and legends, such as the one you are about to read, that explained the world around them. After visiting Hispaniola, Christopher Columbus commissioned a Spanish scholar to live with the **taínos** and record their myths. Many **taíno** myths and legends are still a part of Caribbean cultural tradition.

Una leyenda taína

En las islas del Caribe los bohiques cuentan[1] una leyenda de la creación del mundo. Dicen[2] que de las primeras personas, los taínos, el sol crea todo el mundo.

5 Los taínos viven en **cuevas** en las montañas. En una de las cuevas vive un hombre que se llama Marocael. Marocael cuida la cueva de su gente.

Un día el sol le habla a Marocael: —Marocael,
10 Marocael, ¡te invito a mi casa!

Marocael está **aterrorizado** y contesta: —Muchas gracias, pero tengo que cuidar la cueva de mi gente.

El sol habla otra vez y dice:
15 —Por favor, vamos a pasar buen rato.

—No, muchas gracias —contesta Marocael—. Estoy muy contento en mi cueva.

[1] tell   [2] they say

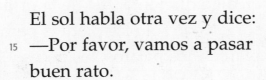

PALABRAS CLAVE
la cueva   *cave*
aterrorizado(a)   *terrified*

READER'S SUCCESS STRATEGY This legend is a myth, an ancient story that serves to explain the origin of natural things. As you read, try to imagine how the story evolved. To what questions does it provide answers?

▌▌▌ **MÁRCALO** ⟩ **GRAMÁTICA**
Circle the direct object pronoun in the boxed sentence on this page and the next page. Then underline the noun that it is replacing.

CHALLENGE What can historians learn about a previous civilization by studying its myths and legends? **(Extend)**

READING TIP Remember the vocabulary you have already learned for animals, **pájaro** and **pez**.

APUNTES

_____

_____

_____

_____

_____

A pensar...

1. Write the numbers 1, 2, 3, 4, and 5 to show the order in which the following things occur. **(Sequence of Events)**

____ The sun turns Marocael into a stone.

____ The sun becomes furious and takes Marocael away.

____ Marocael is terrified and prefers to stay in his cave.

____ The people of the cave become plants, birds, fish, and trees.

____ The sun invites Marocael to its house.

2. What does this legend indicate about the role of the sun in **taíno** culture? **(Infer)**

_____

_____

_____

_____

_____

_____

20 Y Marocael empieza a regresar a su cueva cuando el sol, **furioso,** habla fuerte y dice: —¡Ahora vienes conmigo, Marocael!— Y el sol lleva a Marocael de la cueva a su casa.

Cuando la gente de la cueva se despierta³, 25 busca a Marocael pero no lo encuentra⁴. El sol convierte a Marocael en una de las primeras **piedras** de la **tierra.** Y cuando la gente sale⁵ de la cueva, el sol convierte a cada uno de ellos en algo diferente. Así de la primera gente, el 30 sol crea no sólo las piedras pero también las plantas, los pájaros, los peces y los árboles.

³ wake up   ⁴ find   ⁵ go out

PALABRAS CLAVE
furioso(a) *furious*   **la tierra** *earth*
la piedra *stone*

Vocabulario de la lectura

Palabras clave

el árbol *tree*   **furioso(a)** *furious*   **el sol** *sun*

aterrorizado(a) *terrified*   **la piedra** *stone*   **la tierra** *earth*

la cueva *cave*   **la planta** *plant*

A. For each **Palabra clave** in the first column, find the phrase in the second column that is closest in meaning. Write the corresponding letter in the blank.

_____ 1. sol   A. Significa «enojado».

_____ 2. cueva   B. Es marrón y verde y más alto que una planta.

_____ 3. furioso   C. Es donde vive Marocael.

_____ 4. planta   D. Es grande y amarillo.

_____ 5. árbol   E. Una flor es una...

B. Complete each sentence with the correct form of a **Palabra clave.**

Marocael está _____ cuando el sol lo invita a su casa. Dice que está
$\qquad$ (1)

muy contento en su _____ . Furioso, el sol convierte a Marocael
$\qquad$ (2)

en una _____ . De las otras personas, el sol crea las
$\qquad$ (3)

_____ , los _____ , los pájaros y los peces.
$\qquad$ (4) $\qquad$ (5)

¿Comprendiste?

1. ¿Dónde tiene lugar *(take place)* la leyenda?

_____

2. Según la leyenda, ¿dónde viven los taínos?

_____

3. ¿Quién cuida la cueva?

_____

4. ¿Qué le dice el sol al señor?

_____

5. ¿Qué hace el sol con el señor?

_____

Conexión personal

The sun played an important role in the life of the **taínos.** How does the sun play a part in your life? Using vocabulary you have learned to describe the weather, name some things you like to do when it's sunny outside.

Cuando hace sol, me gusta...

Para leer   *¡Visita Oaxaca! Un paseo a pie*

Reading Strategy

COMBINE STRATEGIES Put together the reading strategies you have practiced.

1. Look at the title, photos, and graphics to predict the reading's theme.
2. Skim the reading to get a general idea of the content.
3. Use context clues to help you make intelligent guesses about new words.

These steps make it easier for you to read Spanish.

Predict	Theme:
Skim	General Idea:
Use context clues	New Words:

What You Need to Know

The city of Oaxaca, in southern Mexico, was founded by Aztec warriors in 1485 and taken over by the Spaniards in 1521. The majority of Oaxaca's present-day population is of Zapotec or Mixtec heritage, and many city residents speak an indigenous language as well as Spanish. Located near some of Mexico's most important archaeological sites, Oaxaca is also known for its examples of European colonial architecture. Of additional interest to travelers are the woodcarvings, textiles, and pottery of local artisans, and Oaxaca's cuisine. **Chapulines**, or fried grasshoppers, are a popular Oaxacan dish available in the city's restaurants and **mercados**. Many types of **mole**, spicy sauces often made with chocolate, also originated in Oaxaca.

▐▐▐ MÁRCALO ◇ GRAMÁTICA
You have just learned how to form affirmative **tú** commands. How many **tú** commands can you find in the article? Underline each one.

_____

_____

_____

_____

APUNTES

_____

_____

_____

_____

_____

_____

_____

¡VISITA OAXACA! UN PASEO¹ A PIE

La ciudad de Oaxaca es un monumento histórico nacional. Hay **arquitectura** colonial, iglesias y museos muy importantes. Para verla mejor tienes que conocer Oaxaca a pie.

5 ❶ Empieza en el Zócalo, el centro de Oaxaca. Es el lugar ideal para ver a los **oaxaqueños**. Hay muchos cafés y restaurantes aquí.

————
¹walk

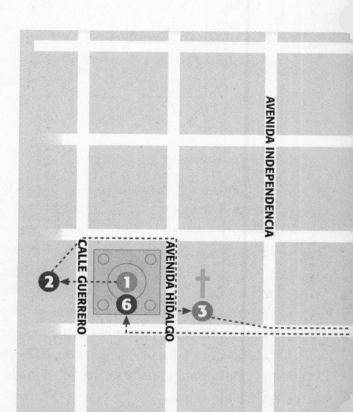

PALABRAS CLAVE
la arquitectura   *architecture*
oaxaqueño(a) n., adj. *Oaxacan*

10 ❷ Ahora cruza la calle
Guerrero y entra en
el Palacio de Gobierno².
Mira el mural sobre la
historia y la cultura
15 de Oaxaca.

❸ Al salir del Palacio,
camina hasta llegar a
la avenida Hidalgo.
Cruza la avenida para
20 ver la catedral. A veces
hay conciertos aquí.

²Government Palace, State Capitol

CALLE IGNACIO ALLENDE

CALLE NICOLÁS BRAVO

CALLE GARCÍA VIGIL

CALLE MACEDONIO ALCALÁ

❹ ❺

APUNTES

A pensar...

1. Based on what you know from the article, which of the following can be found in Oaxaca? Check four. **(Summarize)**

☐ aeropuerto

☐ palacio

☐ centro

☐ metro

☐ iglesias

☐ museos

2. Reread the boxed paragraph. What is Monte Albán? How do you know? **(Infer)**

_____

_____

_____

_____

_____

_____

CHALLENGE You and your family are on vacation in Oaxaca. Choose a place that you would like to visit, and try to persuade a family member to accompany you. **(Convince)**

Reasons to visit_____:

1._____

_____

2._____

_____

3._____

_____

❹ Detrás de la catedral está la avenida Independencia. Sigue
25 por la avenida y dobla a la izquierda en la calle Macedonio Alcalá. Allí hay unas tiendas excelentes y varias casas coloniales. Sigue derecho cuatro cuadras
30 para ver la iglesia de Santo Domingo. Mira el interior.

❺ Al lado de la iglesia queda el Museo Regional de Oaxaca. En el museo hay objetos
35 **arqueológicos** de Monte Albán. También hay ropa, artículos textiles y otros artículos de las primeras culturas de la región.

❻ Regresa al Zócalo.
40 Si hace buen tiempo, hay conciertos aquí a las siete de la tarde. ¿Tienes hambre? Entonces, cena en uno
45 de los restaurantes oaxaqueños. ¡Come algo típico y pasa un rato con tus amigos!

PALABRAS CLAVE
arqueológico(a)   *archaeological*

Vocabulario de la lectura

Palabras clave

a pie *on foot*

arqueológico(a) *archaeological*

la arquitectura *architecture*

el café *restaurant*

la calle *street*

cruzar *to cross*

la cuadra *block*

derecho *straight ahead*

doblar *to turn*

la iglesia *church*

oaxaqueño(a) n., adj. *Oaxacan*

quedar (en) *to be (in a specific place)*

A. Complete the following dialog with the correct **Palabras clave.**

Turista: Perdona, ¿puedes decirme dónde _____ el Palacio
                  de Gobierno?   (1)

Oaxaqueño: ¡Cómo no! Sigue por la calle Macedonio Alcalá y

                  _____ a la derecha en la calle Guerrero.
                         (2)

                  _____ la calle para ver el palacio.
                         (3)

Turista: ¿Queda lejos? No tengo carro. Voy _____ .
                                                            (4)

Oaxaqueño: No queda lejos. Está a solamente tres _____ de aquí.
                                                                (5)

Turista: ¡Tengo hambre! ¿Hay un _____ cerca del palacio?
                                              (6)

Oaxaqueño: Al salir del palacio, cruza la _____ Guerrero y sigue
                                                       (7)

                  _____ para llegar al Zócalo. Allí hay unos cafés
                         (8)

                  excelentes.

B. Fill in each blank with the correct form of a **Palabra clave.**

1. En Oaxaca hay mucha _____ colonial.

2. La _____ de Santo Domingo es un ejemplo de arquitectura europea.

3. En el Museo Regional de Oaxaca, puedes ver objetos _____ de
   Monte Albán.

4. Si quieres comida típica, regresa al Zócalo y cena en un restaurante

   _____ .

¿Comprendiste?

1. ¿Dónde empieza el paseo?

_____

2. ¿Dónde ves un mural sobre la historia y la cultura de Oaxaca?

_____

3. ¿Dónde está la catedral?

_____

4. ¿Qué hay en la calle Macedonio Alcalá?

_____

5. ¿Dónde está el Museo Regional de Oaxaca?

_____

Conexión personal

On the grid below, draw a simple map of your neighborhood or local area. Use the symbols in the key to identify places and landmarks. If you need additional symbols, create your own and add them to the key.

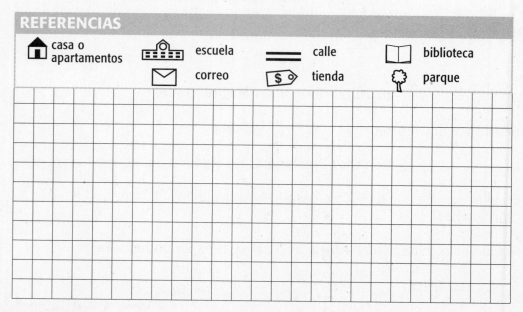

REFERENCIAS

casa o apartamentos · escuela · calle · biblioteca
correo · tienda · parque

Para leer *Andrés, joven aprendiz de alfarero*

Reading Strategy

GATHER AND SORT INFORMATION AS YOU READ Do you and your friends have jobs after school or on weekends? Fill out this chart about jobs by interviewing two people. Then use this chart to gather information about Andrés as you read.

Preguntas	Persona		Andrés
	1	**2**	
¿Dónde trabajas?			
¿Cuándo?			
¿Qué haces?			
¿Trabajas en algo que te puede servir en el futuro?			

What You Need to Know

The distinctive black pottery found in markets and stores throughout Mexico originated in the town of San Bartolo Coyotepec, south of the city of Oaxaca, where in 1953 a woman named doña Rosa discovered a method of firing clay that made it black. The pottery previously produced in the area had been a light grayish brown color. After the pottery was fired, doña Rosa rubbed it with quartz to give it a metallic sheen. Some of doña Rosa's original pieces may be seen at the **Museo del Barro Negro de Coyotepec.** The family of doña Rosa still produces black pottery using her techniques.

APUNTES

☐ jarras
☐ joyas de plata
☐ platos
☐ cerámica
☐ botas
☐ artesanías
☐ artículos de cuero
☐ ollas

CHALLENGE What has changed over the years about the pottery business first started by doña Rosa? What has stayed the same? Underline passages in the text to support your answer. **(Compare and Contrast)**

Andrés, joven aprendiz de alfarero

¡**H**ola! Me llamo Andrés Real. Vivo en San Bartolo Coyotepec, un pueblo cerca de la ciudad de Oaxaca. *Coyotepec* significa[1] «montaña de los coyotes». La verdad es que
5 ya no hay muchos de estos animales. Mi pueblo no es muy grande, pero es muy famoso. La cerámica negra que ves en tiendas y mercados por todo México es de aquí. Si algún día ves una olla de **barro** negro
10 que parece[2] metal, probablemente es de San Bartolo Coyotepec.

---
[1] means   [2] that looks like

PALABRAS CLAVE
el alfarero *potter*
el barro *clay*

READER'S SUCCESS STRATEGY Be aware of time jumps in the article. Use a chart like the one below to keep track of the current action of the reading and the events that occurred at an earlier time.

Past Events	Current Action
Doña Rosa hace la cerámica negra.	Andrés es estudiante de alfarero.

La **Alfarería** *Doña Rosa* es donde yo trabajo después de salir de la escuela. En la alfarería hacemos la cerámica de barro. Esta alfarería se

15 llama *Doña Rosa* en honor a mi abuela doña Rosa Valente Nieto de Real. Ella inventó[3] este tipo de cerámica. Mi abuela murió[4] en 1979, pero mi familia todavía[5] usa su método para hacer la cerámica.

20 Yo soy aprendiz, o estudiante, de alfarero. Mi papá, mi mamá y mis tíos me enseñan este arte. No hago ollas grandes pero hago animalitos, como coyotes. Mis **animalitos** no siempre salen bien porque estoy aprendiendo.

25 Como mi abuela, algún día voy a vender los artículos de barro negro de Coyotepec por todo el mundo.

---

[3] invented [4] died [5] still

A pensar...

1. Write the numbers 1, 2, and 3 to show the order in which the following events occurred. **(Sequence of Events)**

____ Andrés hace animalitos en la alfarería.

____ Los padres de Andrés aprenden el arte de hacer artesanías de barro negro.

____ Doña Rosa inventó la cerámica negra que parece metal.

2. Do you think the tradition of making pottery using the techniques of doña Rosa will continue to be maintained by future generations of her family? Why or why not? **(Predict)**

PALABRAS CLAVE
la alfarería *pottery-making factory; ceramics shop*
el animalito *small animal*

Vocabulario de la lectura

Palabras clave

la alfarería *pottery-making factory; ceramics shop*
el alfarero *potter*
alguno(a) *some*

el animalito *small animal*
el barro *clay*
el pueblo *town, village*

A. For each **Palabra clave** in the first column, find the sentence in the second column that best describes it. Write the corresponding letter in the blank.

_____ 1. animalitos	A. Lo usas para hacer la cerámica.
_____ 2. barro	B. Hacen ollas de barro aquí.
_____ 3. alfarero	C. Son animales pequeños.
_____ 4. alguno	D. Es una persona que hace la cerámica.
_____ 5. alfarería	E. **Algún** es una forma abreviada de esta palabra.

B. Fill in each set of blanks with the correct form of a **Palabra clave**. Then unscramble the boxed letters to complete the sentence below.

1. Andrés Real es aprendiz, o estudiante, de __ __ __ __ __ __ ☐ __.

2. No hace ollas grandes; hace __ ☐ __ __ __ __ __ __ __ __ __ __,
   como coyotes.

3. Andrés vive en el __ __ ☐ __ __ __ de San Bartolo Coyotepec.

4. Después de la escuela, Andrés trabaja en la

   __ __ __ __ __ __ __ __ ☐ Doña Rosa.

5. __ __ ☐ __ __ día, Andrés quiere vender artículos de barro negro,
   como su abuela.

San Bartolo Coyotepec es famoso por la cerámica __ __ __ __ __.

¿Comprendiste?

1. ¿Dónde vive Andrés?

_____

2. ¿Por qué es famoso su pueblo?

_____

3. ¿Quién es su abuela? ¿Por qué es famosa?

_____

_____

4. ¿Qué hace Andrés en la alfarería?

_____

5. ¿Qué quiere hacer Andrés algún día?

_____

Conexión personal

Have you ever had an after-school or weekend job that you enjoyed?
What kind of work have you liked least? In the chart below list jobs you
have liked and disliked. Explain why you feel the way you do.

Trabajo que me gusta	Me gusta porque...
ser mesero(a) en un restaurante	es buen ejercicio.
Trabajo que no me gusta	**No me gusta porque...**

Para leer

Benito Juárez;
un oaxaqueño por excelencia

Reading Strategy

RECOGNIZING SEQUENCE Charts can help you remember the events of a story in the order they happen. For example, when you read a biography, you can list the events in the person's life chronologically. As you read this selection complete a chart like the one below.

Benito Juárez	
Event	**Stage in Life**
loses parents	3 years old
worked as a shepherd	a boy

What You Need to Know

Benito Juárez (1806–1872) was one of Mexico's great political leaders. He fought for the rights of indigenous communities, organized education reform, and issued laws that separated church and state. He was elected governor of the state of Oaxaca in 1847 and president of Mexico in 1861. Born to a poor Zapotec family, Juárez left his native village of San Pablo Guelatao at age 12 and traveled alone to the city of Oaxaca, where he hoped to acquire an education. There he met Antonio Salanueva, a scholar and theologian who made Juárez his godson and sent him to school. Juárez studied at the local seminary in Oaxaca and later attended law school. As a lawyer and throughout his political career he defended the rights of the poor.

Benito Juárez,

un oaxaqueño por excelencia 🎧

READER'S SUCCESS STRATEGY As you read, look for the reasons why things happen. For example, why does Benito leave the village in which he was born? Why does he want to learn Spanish?
_____
_____

En 1806 (mil ochocientos seis), en un pueblo del **estado** de Oaxaca, nace[1] un niño. Se llama Benito. Cuando Benito tiene sólo tres años, su mamá y su papá se mueren[2]. Un tío lleva
5 a Benito a vivir a su casa, pero Benito tiene que trabajar porque la familia es **pobre.** El tío le dice:
—Benito, tienes
10 que cuidar a los corderitos[3] en la montaña.

_____
[1] is born   [2] die   [3] young sheep

📖 **MÁRCALO** ▷ **GRAMÁTICA**
Find and underline the form of **decir** that is used in the article. Then conjugate the verb **decir** in the space below.
_____
_____
_____

READING TIP Like the U.S., Mexico is divided into states. Look at a map that shows the 31 Mexican states. Identify Oaxaca, the state in which Benito Juárez was born.

CHALLENGE In Mexico, Benito Juárez is a national hero. What makes someone a hero? Who are some national heroes of the United States or of other countries? (**Make Judgments**)
_____
_____
_____

PALABRAS CLAVE
el (la) oaxaqueño(a) *Oaxacan*   **pobre** *poor*
el estado *state*

A pensar...

1. In the list below, mark a "T" beside each true statement and an "F" beside each false one. **(Main Idea and Details)**

   ___ Benito came from a wealthy family.

   ___ Orphaned at age three, Benito went to live with his uncle.

   ___ Benito's native language was Zapotec.

   ___ Benito spoke Spanish all his life.

   ___ After serving as governor of Oaxaca, Benito became president of Mexico.

2. How did Antonio Salanueva help Benito? **(Summarize)**

   _____

   _____

   _____

   _____

3. How do you think Benito's childhood influenced his decision to work for the rights of the poor? **(Cause and Effect)**

   _____

   _____

   _____

   _____

   _____

   _____

   _____

Y entonces, Benito trabaja todos los días de **pastorcito.** Un día, decide salir del pueblo

15 porque quiere una vida mejor. Llega a la capital y conoce a un buen hombre, Antonio Salanueva. El señor Salanueva le enseña a Benito a hablar español (antes, sólo hablaba zapoteco, el **idioma** nativo regional).

20 El señor Salanueva también le enseña a leer y a escribir. Después de muchos años de estudio, llega

25 a ser **abogado.** Se dedica a ayudar a la gente pobre.

Los mexicanos conocen a Benito como un hombre bueno, serio y muy trabajador y ¡lo

30 quieren para **gobernador** del estado! Trabaja mucho e, increíblemente, llega a ser presidente de toda la República Mexicana.

¡Así es que el humilde Benito va de pastorcito a presidente!

PALABRAS CLAVE

el pastorcito *shepherd boy* **el (la) abogado(a)** *lawyer*
el idioma *language* **el (la) gobernador(a)** *governor*

Vocabulario de la lectura

Palabras clave

el (la) abogado(a) *lawyer*

decir *to say, to tell*

el estado *state*

el (la) gobernador(a) *governor*

el idioma *language*

el (la) oaxaqueño(a) *Oaxacan*

el pastorcito *shepherd boy*

pobre *poor*

salir *to go out, to leave*

A. For each **Palabra clave** in the first column, find the sentence in the second column that best describes it. Write the corresponding letter in the blank.

_____ 1. estado

_____ 2. idiomas

_____ 3. pobre

_____ 4. abogado(a)

_____ 5. oaxaqueño

A. Es una persona que sabe de cuestiones legales.

B. Un hombre de Oaxaca es un...

C. El español y el inglés son dos.

D. Oaxaca es el nombre de una ciudad y un...

E. Se refiere a una persona que tiene poco dinero.

B. Complete each sentence with a **Palabra clave**.
Use the correct form of the verbs.

Benito Juárez es un niño pobre de un pueblo del _____ de Oaxaca.
(1)

Trabaja todos los días de _____ y quiere una vida mejor. Un día,
(2)

decide _____ de su pueblo a pie para la ciudad. Allí conoce a un
(3)

buen hombre, el señor Salanueva, que le _____ a Benito que le
(4)

enseñe a hablar español. Benito estudia mucho. Primero, llega a ser

_____, luego _____ de Oaxaca, y por fin, presidente
(5)   (6)

de México.

¿Comprendiste?

1. ¿De dónde es Benito?

_____

2. ¿De qué trabaja de niño?

_____

3. ¿Cuál es su profesión de adulto?

_____

4. ¿Qué idiomas habla?

_____

5. ¿Qué llega a ser?

_____

Conexión personal

Benito Juárez overcame many
obstacles to realize his dreams.
What goals or dreams do you
have for yourself, your
community, or your country? List
one important goal, and name
something you would have to do
in order to make it a reality.

> Me gustaría ayudar a los niños de
> mi comunidad que no hablan inglés...
>
> _____
>
> _____
>
> _____
>
> _____
>
> _____
>
> _____

Para leer

*Una leyenda oaxaqueña:
El fuego y el tlacuache*

Reading Strategy

MAKING A STORY MAP To help you remember characters and events in a story, use a story map like the one below. This will help you organize the main ideas in this legend.

Characters:		
1. _mujer vieja_ 2. _____ 3. _____		
Problem: _Los vecinos quieren..._		
Solution: _El tlacuache..._		

What You Need to Know

The Sierra Mazateca, located in northern Oaxaca state, is a beautiful part of Mexico with tall mountain peaks, deep valleys, waterfalls, and lush vegetation including orchids and many other colorful flowers. The **mazatecas**, an indigenous group who make their living mainly by farming and weaving, occupy the Sierra Mazateca region of Oaxaca and parts of the neighboring states of Guerrero and Veracruz. Animals have long played important roles in **mazateca** rites and beliefs. Many **mazateca** textiles are decorated with animal figures. The following legend about an opossum is part of **mazateca** folklore.

READER'S SUCCESS STRATEGY You can remember the meaning of many Spanish words by thinking of English words that are related. In this legend you will notice **calentarse** (related to *calorie*); **frío** (related to *frigid*); **lumbre**, which means fire or light (related to *illuminate*); and **pelado**, which means hairless (related to *peel*).

⫴ MÁRCALO ⟫ GRAMÁTICA
Find and underline the verb **pedir** in the legend. Remember that it is an **e→i** stem-changing verb. Then conjugate **pedir** in the space below.

CHALLENGE In groups, pretend you are characters in the legend. Prepare a version of the action and present it to the class. **(Extend)**

Una leyenda oaxaqueña

El fuego y el tlacuache[1]

La gente mazateca, que vive en la región norte de Oaxaca, les cuenta esta leyenda a sus hijos.

Una noche una mujer vieja atrapa la lumbre[2]
5 al caerse de una **estrella.** Todos sus **vecinos** van a la casa de la vieja a pedir lumbre. Pero la vieja no quiere darle lumbre a la gente.

En ese momento,
llega un tlacuache
10 y les dice
a los vecinos:
—Yo, tlacuache,
voy a darles la
lumbre si ustedes
15 prometen no
comerme.

Todos se ríen[3] cuando oyen las palabras del tlacuache. Pero el tlacuache les repite que él sí va a compartir la lumbre con
20 todo el mundo.

---

[1] opossum   [2] fire, light   [3] laugh

PALABRAS CLAVE
el fuego *fire*   **el (la) vecino(a)** *neighbor*
la estrella *star*

READING TIP **Tlacuache** is a word from the indigenous language of the **mazatecas**. Listen to the audio to see how it is pronounced.

APUNTES

Entonces, el tlacuache va a la casa de la vieja y le dice: —Buenas tardes, señora Lumbre, ¡qué frío hace! Si me permite, quiero estar un rato al lado de la lumbre para calentarme[4].

25 La vieja le permite al tlacuache acercarse[5] a la lumbre porque sabe que sí hace un frío terrible. En ese momento el animalito avanza y pone la **cola** en la lumbre. Entonces, sale rápidamente de la casa y les da la lumbre
30 a todas las casas de la región.

Es por eso que hasta ahora los tlacuaches tienen la cola **pelada**.

―――――――――――――――――――

[4]warm myself   [5]approach

PALABRAS CLAVE
la cola *tail*   **pelado(a)** *hairless*

A pensar...

1. Write the numbers 1, 2, 3, 4, 5, and 6 to show the order in which the events below occurred. (**Sequence of Events**)

___ The opossum puts his tail in the light.

___ The woman's neighbors ask her for light, but she will not give them any.

___ A woman traps the light coming from a star.

___ The opossum gives light from his tail to all the neighbors.

___ The opossum asks the woman if he can come in and get warm.

___ The woman lets the opossum come in.

2. Check the phrase that best completes the following sentence. (**Main Idea**) This legend explains why...

☐ stars shine at night.

☐ the climate is cool in northern Oaxaca.

☐ the opossum has a hairless tail.

☐ the opossum is a generous animal.

Vocabulario de la lectura

Palabras clave

la cola *tail*   **el fuego** *fire*   **pelado(a)** *hairless*

la estrella *star*   **pedir** *to ask for*   **el (la) vecino(a)** *neighbor*

A. For each **Palabra clave** in the first column, find the sentence in the second column that best describes it. Write the corresponding letter in the blank.

_____ 1. estrellas   A. Es alguien que vive cerca.

_____ 2. vecino(a)   B. Las ves por la noche.

_____ 3. colas   C. Se refiere a algo que no tiene pelo.

_____ 4. pelado(a)   D. Es muy caliente.

_____ 5. fuego   E. Los perros y los gatos las tienen.

B. Write two sentences about the legend using two or more of the **Palabras clave.**

_____

_____

_____

_____

_____

_____

_____

_____

_____

_____

¿Comprendiste?

1. ¿Quién atrapa la lumbre?

_____

2. ¿Quiere darle la lumbre a alguien?

_____

3. ¿Qué les dice el tlacuache a los vecinos?

_____

4. ¿Cómo puede el tlacuache entrar a la casa de la vieja? ¿Qué le dice a ella?

_____

5. ¿Cómo es que la gente recibe el fuego?

_____

Conexión personal

Have you ever wondered why some animals look the way they do? Make a list of animals and their physical characteristics that could be the subject of a legend explaining their appearance.

Animales	Características
tigre	rayas

Para leer   *Una exhibición especial de Picasso*

Reading Strategy

SCAN FOR CRUCIAL DETAILS Before you decide to visit the exhibit "Picasso y los retratos" there is some practical information you need to know. Look quickly to pick up certain details. Can you find the answers in the article? If so, write them in below.

¿En qué museo está la exhibición?	¿Cuándo termina?

What You Need to Know

El Museo Picasso occupies five medieval palaces in Barcelona's Gothic Quarter. It contains works from all of Picasso's periods but is best known for its collection of paintings and drawings completed during the artist's early years when he was living in Barcelona. Born in Málaga, Spain, in 1881, Pablo Picasso was painting by the age of fourteen. He worked in a wide range of styles, and over time his art became increasingly abstract. Among his favorite subjects were musical instruments, still-life objects, and people. In 1904 Picasso moved to France, where he remained until his death in 1973.

Una exhibición especial de Picasso

Si te levantas el sábado y tienes ganas de ir a un museo, hay una **exhibición** especial en el Museo Picasso de Barcelona. Es una colección de **retratos** de Pablo Picasso. La exhibición se
5   llama «Picasso y los retratos». Es posible verla hasta el 31 de julio.

Las **pinturas** de la exhibición «Picasso y los retratos» son de varios **estilos.** En algunos retratos, por ejemplo *Retrato de Jaime Sabatés*,
10   usa un estilo **tradicional.** En otros retratos vemos el desarrollo[1] de la pintura **moderna** en la composición de las partes del cuerpo: la cara, las orejas, los brazos y las piernas. Un ejemplo es *Maya con una muñeca.*

———————
[1] development

PALABRAS CLAVE
la exhibición   *exhibit*
el retrato   *portrait*
la pintura   *painting*
el estilo   *style*
tradicional   *traditional*
moderno(a)   *modern*

READING TIP Remember to look for cognates, words that look alike in English and Spanish and have similar meanings. What cognates can you find in **Una exhibición especial de Picasso?** Underline them in the text.

_____

_____

_____

MÁRCALO ⟩ VOCABULARIO
You have just learned vocabulary for parts of the body. How many words for parts of the body do you recognize in the boxed text? Find and underline each one.

_____

A pensar...

1. Check three items in the list below that describe what you can see at the exhibit **"Picasso y los retratos."** (Summarize)

   ☐ portraits of Picasso's friends
   ☐ landscapes by Picasso
   ☐ photographs
   ☐ traditional works
   ☐ modern painting

2. What can we learn about Picasso's life from the subjects he chose for his portraits? (Clarify)

   _____

   _____

   _____

Compare and contrast the two portraits by Picasso. Use the Venn diagram to organize your ideas. Where the circles are separate, write in differences. Where they intersect, write in similarities.

Retrato de Jaime Sabatés

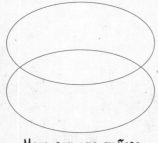

Maya con una muñeca

APUNTES

_____
_____
_____
_____
_____

CHALLENGE What makes _Maya con una muñeca_ an example of what the article calls modern painting? **(Evaluate)**

_____
_____
_____
_____
_____
_____
_____

Retrato de Jaime Sabatés, _1899–1900_
Un retrato de Jaime Sabatés, gran amigo de Picasso. Sabatés le dio⁴ su colección de **obras** _de Picasso al museo._

Maya con una muñeca, _1938_

15 Los retratos de Picasso también nos dan una idea de su vida privada. Hay retratos de sus amigos, sus hijos y las mujeres importantes en su vida.

Si vas a la exhibición, aprovecha² tu visita
20 para ver otras obras de este **pintor** español en nuestro Museo Picasso. ¡Hay más de tres mil³!

_____
²take advantage of   ³thousand   ⁴gave

PALABRAS CLAVE
el (la) pintor(a) _painter_   la obra _work_

¡En español! Level 1

Vocabulario de la lectura

Palabras clave

el estilo *style*   **la obra** *work*   **el retrato** *portrait*

la exhibición *exhibit*   **el (la) pintor(a)** *painter*   **tradicional** *traditional*

moderno(a) *modern*   **la pintura** *painting*

A. For each **Palabra clave** in the first column, find the word or phrase in the second column that is closest in meaning. Write the corresponding letter in the blank.

_____ 1. estilo   A. del período histórico actual; contemporáneo(a)

_____ 2. exhibición   B. clásico(a)

_____ 3. moderno(a)   C. manera de expresarse artísticamente

_____ 4. pintura   D. representación de la cara o la figura entera de una persona

_____ 5. retrato   E. colección de arte que puede ver el público

_____ 6. tradicional   F. creación artística

_____ 7. obra   G. artista

_____ 8. pintor   H. el arte de pintar; obra del que pinta

B. Fill in each blank with the correct form of a **Palabra clave.**
Use each word only once.

El Museo Picasso de Barcelona tiene más de tres mil _____
                                                   (1)

de Picasso, el _____ español. Hay una _____ especial
                      (2)   (3)

en el museo hasta el 31 de julio. Se llama «Picasso y los _____».
                                                          (4)

Picasso usa _____ variados. *Retrato de Jaime Sabatés*
                    (5)

es del estilo _____, pero *Maya con una muñeca* es
                    (6)

un ejemplo de pintura _____. Picasso es más famoso por
                          (7)

sus _____, pero su obra también incluye la escultura y la cerámica.
       (8)

¿Comprendiste?

1. ¿Cómo se llama la exhibición especial del Museo Picasso de Barcelona?

_____

2. ¿Cuáles son dos estilos de retratos de la exhibición?

_____

3. ¿De quiénes son los retratos de la exhibición?

_____

4. ¿Cómo se llama el amigo que Picasso pintó?

_____

5. ¿Cuántas obras de Picasso hay normalmente en el Museo Picasso de Barcelona?

_____

Conexión personal

Imagine that you are a portrait artist. Whom would you choose to paint? Would your subject be real or imaginary? Why would you like to paint this person? How do you imagine your painting would look? Write in your answers on the right.

Yo voy a pintar...

_____

_____

_____

_____

_____

_____

_____

_____

_____

_____

Para leer   *Los favoritos de la cocina española*

Reading Strategy

REORGANIZE INFORMATION TO CHECK UNDERSTANDING A family friend gave you a copy of this recipe from her favorite cookbook. She has asked you to write it down as a recipe for her card file. Read "Los favoritos de la cocina española" and fill out the recipe card for her.

Paso	Ingredientes	Cantidad	Instrucciones
	LA PAELLA VALENCIANA		
1.	Aceite	$\frac{1}{4}$ taza	Pon en la sartén.
2.			
3.			
4.			

What You Need to Know

Paella originated in Valencia, a region of Spain next to Cataluña. It got its name from the pan in which it is prepared, the **paellera.** The traditional iron **paellera** is round and shallow, with handles on either side and a thick, flat base. Historically, Valencians used the **paellera** to cook rice and other locally obtainable ingredients such as tomatoes, onions, snails, rabbit, or duck. Most paella dishes of today contain chicken, sausage, and different types of seafood, typically squid, shrimp, and mussels.

APUNTES

A pensar...

Write the numbers 1, 2, 3, 4, and 5 to show the order in which you should do the following steps according to the recipe. **(Sequence of Events)**

___ Sirve la paella.

___ Cocina el arroz.

___ Fríe el pollo y la salchicha.

___ Pon el aceite en la sartén.

___ Pon las verduras en la sartén.

LOS FAVORITOS
de la cocina española

De la cocina de Maruja Serrat, cocinera[1] del restaurante Tibidabo de Barcelona

Ésta es la receta[2] de un plato muy especial, la paella valenciana. Es importante usar los ingredientes más frescos[3] posibles. Y busca el mejor **azafrán.** El azafrán da sabor[4] y color a
5 la paella. Si no hay azafrán, no hay paella. A todo el mundo le gusta tanto la paella que generalmente no queda[5] nada. Pero si queda algo, ponlo en el frigorífico para mañana.

[1]chef   [2]recipe   [3]freshest   [4]flavor   [5]remains

PALABRAS CLAVE
el azafrán *saffron*

Paella valenciana

10   para cuatro personas

Ingredientes

     1/4 taza de aceite de oliva

     1/2 kilo de pollo

     1/4 kilo de salchicha

15   1 cebolla

     2 **dientes de ajo**

     1 tomate

     1/2 taza de **guisantes**

     1 **pimentón**

20   1/4 kilo de calamares

     200 gramos de **gambas**

     sal y pimienta

     1 1/2 taza de arroz

     1/2 cucharadita de azafrán

25   3 tazas de agua

Instrucciones

Primero pon el aceite de oliva en la sartén[6].
Corta[7] el pollo y la salchicha en pedazos.
Fríelos[8] por diez minutos. Luego corta la
30 cebolla, el ajo, el tomate y el pimentón. Ponlos
en la sartén junto con los guisantes. Ahora
añade[9] los calamares y las gambas, la sal y la
pimienta. En otra sartén o en una **paellera,**
cocina el arroz en el agua. Luego añade el
35 pollo, la salchicha, los calamares, las gambas,
las verduras y el azafrán. Cocínalo otros
veinte minutos. Sirve la paella en la paellera.

[6] frying pan   [7] cut   [8] fry them   [9] add

PALABRAS CLAVE
    los dientes de ajo *cloves of garlic*   **las gambas** *shrimp*
    los guisantes *green peas*   **la paellera** *paella pan*
    el pimentón *sweet red pepper*

READING TIP In the United States we use a different set of units for measuring weight than many other countries, such as Spain, which uses the metric system. In this recipe you will notice that the meats are measured in **kilos** (kilograms) or **gramos** (grams) instead of in pounds or ounces.

APUNTES

◫ **MÁRCALO** ▷ **VOCABULARIO**
Reread the boxed text. Circle the words that name a kind of meat, poultry, or seafood. Underline the names of vegetables or fruits.

CHALLENGE Do you think this is an easy recipe? (Evaluate)

Vocabulario de la lectura

Palabras clave

el aceite *oil*

el azafrán *saffron*

la cebolla *onion*

los dientes de ajo *cloves of garlic*

las gambas *shrimp*

los guisantes *green peas*

la paellera *paella pan*

el pimentón *sweet red pepper*

la salchicha *sausage*

el tomate *tomato*

la verdura *vegetable*

A. Fill in each blank with the correct **Palabra clave.**

Para hacer paella, primero pon el _____ en la sartén. Luego,
              (1)
corta el pollo y la _____ en pedazos, y fríelos. Ahora corta la
                      (2)
_____ , el ajo, el _____ y el pimentón. Ponlos en la
      (3)   (4)
sartén con los guisantes, y añade los calamares y las _____ .
                                                              (5)
Cocina el arroz en una _____ y añade los otros ingredientes.
                              (6)

B. Match the **Palabra clave** in the first column with the sentence that best
describes it in the second column. Write the corresponding letter in the blank.

_____ 1. ajo

_____ 2. pimentón

_____ 3. gambas

_____ 4. azafrán

_____ 5. guisantes

_____ 6. verduras

A. Es una verdura roja.

B. Es algo amarillo.

C. Esta categoría incluye cebollas y zanahorias.

D. Son verdes.

E. Necesitas dos dientes de este ingrediente para
hacer paella.

F. Vienen del mar.

¿Comprendiste?

1. ¿Por qué es importante el azafrán?

_____

2. Si hay demasiada paella, ¿qué debes hacer?

_____

3. ¿Qué haces con el pollo y la salchicha?

_____

4. ¿Qué pones en la segunda sartén?

_____

5. Después de poner el azafrán, ¿cuánto tiempo cocinas la paella?

_____

Conexión personal

Do you have a favorite recipe? Write the ingredients and steps for a simple recipe in the space below. If you don't remember the exact quantities of ingredients, use approximations.

RECETA PARA HACER _____

Paso	Ingredientes	Cantidad	Instrucciones
1.			
2.			
3.			
4.			

Para leer   *La Tomatina: una rara tradición española*

Reading Strategy

PREDICT Look at the title and the illustrations that go with this reading selection. What do you think this piece might be about? Write your predictions in a grid like this. After you've completed the reading, fill out the right side.

Prediction	What I Found Out
1.	1.
2.	2.
3.	3.

What You Need to Know

Spain is famous for its fiestas, observed locally and nationwide. Unlike the majority of Spanish festivals, the tradition of **la Tomatina** has no known religious or historical significance, and no one is exactly sure how it began. **La Tomatina** takes place every year in the town of Buñol, 25 miles west of Valencia. On the morning of the last Wednesday of August, thousands of revelers flock to the town square wearing T-shirts, shorts, and eye goggles. As they wait for a firecracker to begin the festivities, participants shout **"¡Tomate! ¡Tomate! ¡Queremos tomate!"** The article you are about to read explains what happens next.

La Tomatina:
una rara tradición española

¿**Q**ué haces cuando hay demasiados tomates en el **jardín**? A ver... puedes regalárselos a los vecinos. Puedes hacer salsa para la pasta. Tal vez haces salsa ranchera
5 mexicana, ¿verdad?

Pues, en el pueblo español de Buñol, con el exceso de tomates la gente hace la «Tomatina». Llega un
10 **camión lleno** de tomates **maduros** que se depositan en el centro del pueblo. ¡Y todo el mundo se cubre[1] con ellos! Ocurre al final de una fiesta que se celebra cada año a fin de agosto.

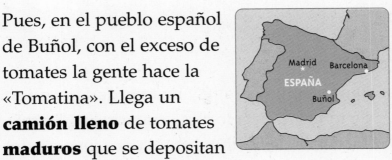

[1] is covered

PALABRAS CLAVE
raro(a) *strange*
el jardín *garden*
el camión *truck*

lleno(a) *full*
maduro(a) *ripe*

MÁRCALO > **GRAMÁTICA**
Imagine you are participating in **la Tomatina**. Write two positive **tú** commands and two negative **tú** commands about things to do or not do during the festival.

CHALLENGE Each year tourists from around the world travel to Buñol to take part in **la Tomatina**. Why do you think this festival is so popular? **(Draw Conclusions)**

APUNTES

A pensar...

1. Cross out the statement that is *not* true about **la Tomatina**. (Clarify)

It takes place in Buñol, Spain.

Thousands of people participate.

The festival is a religious celebration.

Participants throw tomatoes at one another.

Everyone cleans up afterwards.

2. Why do you think this festival takes place in August? (Infer)

---

¹⁵ Durante una hora hay una **verdadera guerra** de tomates. Esta locura² empezó³ en Buñol hace más de 50 años⁴ entre unos jóvenes del pueblo. Pero ahora llega gente de todas partes—¡vienen más de 20.000 personas!

²⁰ ¿Cómo queda el pueblo después de todas estas festividades? Todo el mundo empieza a limpiar y el pueblo queda bonito y limpio como siempre. ¡Olé!

---

²madness   ³began   ⁴*hace... años* more than 50 years ago

PALABRAS CLAVE
verdadero(a)   *true, veritable*   **la guerra**   *war*

Vocabulario de la lectura

Palabras clave

el camión *truck*	**limpiar** *to clean*	**maduro(a)** *ripe*
la guerra *war*	**limpio(a)** *clean*	**raro(a)** *strange*
el jardín *garden*	**lleno(a)** *full*	**verdadero(a)** *true, veritable*

A. Fill in each set of blanks with the correct form of a **Palabra clave**.
Then unscramble the boxed letters to answer the question below the puzzle.

1. Puedes comer la fruta; es __ ☐ __ __ __ __ .

2. Hay tomates y lechuga en el __ __ __ __ __ ☐ .

3. Mi cuarto está muy sucio; lo voy a __ __ __ __ __ __ ☐ .

4. Di si las oraciones son ☐ __ __ __ __ __ __ __ __ __ o falsas.

5. El día de la Tomatina, llega un camión __ __ __ __ ☐ de tomates.

6. Durante la Tomatina, hay una verdadera __ __ ☐ __ __ __ de tomates.

¿En qué estación hacen la Tomatina? __ __ __ __ __ __

B. Pretend you are at **la Tomatina**. Describe what you see using at least four
of the **Palabras clave**.

_____

_____

_____

_____

_____

¿Comprendiste?

1. ¿Dónde se hace la Tomatina?

_____

2. ¿Qué hace la gente del pueblo con los tomates?

_____

3. ¿De dónde vienen los participantes?

_____

4. ¿Cómo está el pueblo después de esta fiesta?

_____

Conexión personal

Do you know of any festivals having to do with food in your town or elsewhere? What foods are featured? Describe the event in the space on the right.

En julio mi comunidad tiene un festival de comida mexicana.. Hay platos típicos de...

Para leer   *Correo electrónico desde Barcelona*

Reading Strategy

NOTING DETAILS The e-mail on page 103 describes **festes**, cultural celebrations that take place in Cataluña. As you read, use a web to note details about the celebrations.

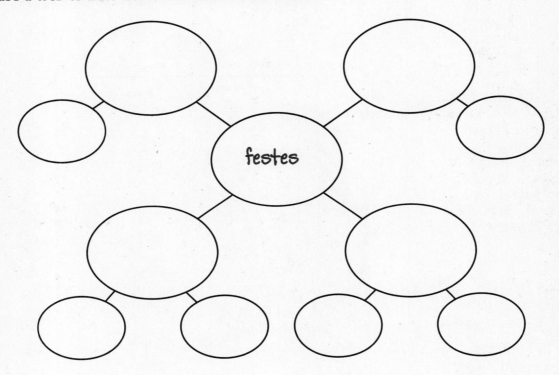

What You Need to Know

Located on the Mediterranean Sea in the northeast of Spain, Barcelona is the capital of the region of Cataluña. One of Europe's oldest cities, Barcelona has celebrated various festivals since the Middle Ages. The city's largest celebration, **Festes de la Mercè**, takes place in September and honors one of the city's patron saints. Festivities last for a week and include a swimming race across the harbor, outdoor music concerts, traditional folk dancing, and spectacular parades. This reading describes some of the exciting elements typical of **Festes de la Mercè** and other **catalán** traditions.

APUNTES

_____

_____

_____

_____

_____

▌▌▌ MÁRCALO ⟩ GRAMÁTICA
You have learned how to form the preterite of regular **-ar** verbs. Read the boxed paragraph and underline the **-ar** preterite verbs. Which of the verbs you underlined is spelled the same in both the present and the preterite?

_____

_____

_____

_____

_____

CHALLENGE Imagine that you are in Barcelona participating in this festival. How would you like to join in? (Connect)

_____

_____

_____

_____

_____

Correo electrónico desde Barcelona 🎧

Aquí tienes un mensaje que escribió un grupo de estudiantes norteamericanos que viajaron a España con su maestra de español.

PALABRAS CLAVE
el correo electrónico *e-mail*

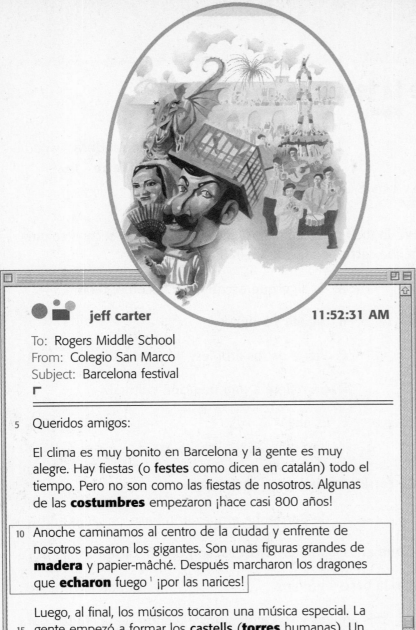

APUNTES

jeff carter   11:52:31 AM

To: Rogers Middle School
From: Colegio San Marco
Subject: Barcelona festival

5   Queridos amigos:

El clima es muy bonito en Barcelona y la gente es muy alegre. Hay fiestas (o **festes** como dicen en catalán) todo el tiempo. Pero no son como las fiestas de nosotros. Algunas de las **costumbres** empezaron ¡hace casi 800 años!

10   Anoche caminamos al centro de la ciudad y enfrente de nosotros pasaron los gigantes. Son unas figuras grandes de **madera** y papier-mâché. Después marcharon los dragones que **echaron** fuego [1] ¡por las narices!

Luego, al final, los músicos tocaron una música especial. La
15   gente empezó a formar los **castells** (**torres** humanas). Un grupo de personas formó la base y otro grupo subió encima del [2] primero. Luego otro grupo subió encima del segundo [3] grupo, etc., etc. Entonces, el niño más **chico** subió hasta lo más alto. Ahora nosotros queremos aprender a hacer los
20   **castells** al regresar a Estados Unidos la semana próxima.

Con el cariño de siempre,

Jeff, Susan, Amy, Emily, Josh, Frank

---

[1] fire   [2] *subió encima del* climbed to the top of   [3] second

PALABRAS CLAVE
la costumbre *custom*   **la torre** *tower*
la madera *wood*   **chico(a)** *small*
echar *to shoot out, emit*

A pensar...

1. Based on what you know from the e-mail, which of the following did the students see in Barcelona? Check three. (**Summarize**)

   ☐ fire-breathing dragons
   ☐ flamenco dancers
   ☐ pâpier-maché figures
   ☐ human towers
   ☐ flower sellers

2. What do the students want to do when they get home? Underline the answer below. (**Clarify**)

   organize a local parade

   study **catalán**

   learn how to make *castells*

3. What is one way in which the fiestas of Barcelona are different from celebrations of the U.S.? (**Compare and Contrast**)

Vocabulario de la lectura

Palabras clave

anoche *last night*	**la costumbre** *custom*	**la madera** *wood*
chico(a) *small*	**echar** *to shoot out, emit*	**la torre** *tower*
el correo electrónico *e-mail*		

A. For each **Palabra clave** in the first column, find the sentence in the second column that best describes it. Write the corresponding letter in the blank.

_____ 1. chico   A. Es algo que escribes en la computadora.

_____ 2. torre   B. Significa pequeño.

_____ 3. costumbre   C. Viene de los árboles.

_____ 4. madera   D. Se refiere a una tradición cultural.

_____ 5. correo electrónico   E. Es alta.

B. Fill in the blanks with the correct form of a **Palabra clave**.

Algunas de las _____ de Barcelona empezaron hace casi 800 años.
(1)

Las _____ humanas, llamadas *castells,* son una tradición catalana.
(2)

Muchas personas forman la base y un niño _____ queda encima de
(3)

todas. _____ mis amigos y yo caminamos al centro de la ciudad para
(4)

ver la fiesta. Primero miramos los gigantes, figuras enormes de _____
(5)

y pâpier-maché. Luego pasaron dragones que _____ fuego por las
(6)

narices.

¿Comprendiste?

1. ¿Quiénes mandaron el mensaje?

_____

2. ¿Cómo es Barcelona?

_____

3. ¿Qué hay en las fiestas de Barcelona?

_____

4. ¿Qué les gustó más de todo a los muchachos?

_____

Conexión personal

Write an e-mail similar to the one in the reading to a real or imaginary pen pal in Spain. Tell your pen pal about a local celebration in your area. The Spanish terms for *From* (**De**), *To* (**Para**), and *Subject* (**Asunto**) have been provided.

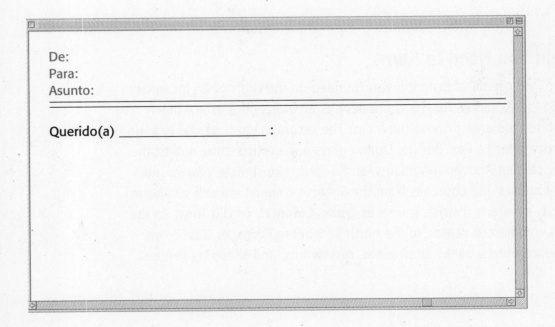

De:
Para:
Asunto: _____
_____

Querido(a) _____ :

Para leer   *Saludos desde Quito*

Reading Strategy

RECOGNIZE PLACE NAMES It is easy to be confused by unfamiliar place names, but often there are simple words nearby to explain them. As you read each of the following place names, identify the word nearby that explains what it is.

NOMBRE	LUGAR
Amazonas	
La Carolina	
La Compañía	
El Ejido	
Pichincha	volcán

What You Need to Know

Quito, the capital of Ecuador, was founded on the ruins of an Incan city in 1534. It is named for the Quitu people, an indigenous group that inhabited the area prior to the Incas. The second highest capital in Latin America after La Paz, Bolivia, Quito enjoys a majestic setting amidst the snow-capped Andean mountains, and a springlike climate year-round. Many houses and churches from the Spanish colonial era still survive in the city's historic district, known as **Quito Colonial,** or Old Town. In the city's commercial center, to the north in modern Quito, or New Town, there are hotels, banks, businesses, restaurants, and shopping centers.

Saludos desde Quito

Un grupo de estudiantes está de visita en Quito, Ecuador. Aquí hay unas tarjetas que ellos les escribieron a sus amigos.

Quito

¡Hola! Hoy llegamos a Quito.
5 ¡Estamos a sólo 24 kilómetros de
la **línea ecuatorial**! Fuimos en taxi
al Cerro[1] Panecillo. Allí fue posible
ver toda la ciudad. La ciudad es
bonita y el **paisaje** es maravilloso.
10 Quito queda al lado del **volcán**
Pichincha. Hoy, la cima se cubrió[2]
de nieve, ¡pero en la ciudad la
temperatura fue de 80 grados!

Alfonso

John Vivas
4231 Avenue M
Galveston, TX 77550
EE.UU.

---

[1] hill   [2] the peak was covered

PALABRAS CLAVE
la línea ecuatorial *equator*   **el volcán** *volcano*
el paisaje *landscape*

READING TIP Remember the vocabulary you have learned for giving addresses and identifying places in the city. You will notice many familiar words in this article.

APUNTES

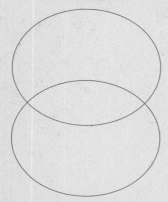

MÁRCALO ⟩ GRAMÁTICA

You have learned that the verbs **ir** and **ser** have the same preterite forms. Look again at the postcards by Alfonso and Lucila. Underline the preterite forms that indicate the verb **ir**, and draw a circle around those that indicate the verb **ser**.

APUNTES

A pensar...

How are **Quito Colonial** and Quito's **sector moderno** the same? How are they different?. Use the Venn diagram to organize your ideas. (**Compare and Contrast**)

Quito Colonial

sector moderno

La Compañía

15   ¡Saludos desde Quito! Ayer paseamos por el Quito Colonial. Fue bonito caminar por las calles estrechas y ver las casas antiguas. Fuimos a la Plaza de la Independencia para ver la
20   Catedral y el Palacio de Gobierno. ¡Allí sacamos muchas fotos! Después fuimos a la iglesia jesuita de la Compañía. Es famosa por su arte y su decoración de oro. Luego, en el Museo
25   Arqueológico aprendí mucho sobre el arte **precolombino**. Mañana vamos al sector moderno. ¡Hasta pronto!
Lucila

ECUADOR
333 98-07-03 09:39
2.600

Elena Martínez
59 Collins Ave.
Corona, CA 91720
EE.UU.

PALABRAS CLAVE
precolombino(a)   *pre-Columbian*

Parque Carolina

Student	Places Visited
Alfonso	Cerro Panecillo,...
Lucila	
Marisa	

APUNTES

CHALLENGE What influences would you expect to see in the architecture of Quito Colonial? (Draw Conclusions)

30 ¿Qué tal? Hoy paseamos por el norte de Quito. ¡Qué diferencia! Las avenidas son anchas y hay parques grandes, como El Ejido y La Carolina. En el sector de la avenida Amazonas está la mayor parte de los hoteles, bancos, restaurantes caros y
35 tiendas finas. Mañana vamos a visitar la Mitad del Mundo, un complejo turístico en la línea ecuatorial. Allí hay un museo, tiendas y restaurantes. Los domingos hay música típica de los Andes. Me encanta
40 escuchar la música andina.

¡Hasta luego!
Marisa

Jennifer Herrera
131 Edgewater Drive
Orlando, FL 32804
EE.UU.

Vocabulario de la lectura

Palabras clave

ancho(a) *wide*

antiguo(a) *old, ancient*

estrecho(a) *narrow*

la línea ecuatorial *equator*

moderno(a) *modern*

el paisaje *landscape*

precolombino(a) *pre-Columbian*

el volcán *volcano*

A. On the line next to each word pair, write whether the words are synonyms or antonyms. Synonyms are words with the same or similar meaning. Antonyms are words with opposite meanings.

1. antiguo–viejo _____

2. estrecho–ancho _____

3. nuevo–antiguo _____

4. moderno-tradicional _____

B. Complete each sentence with the correct form of a **Palabra clave.**

1. Ayer, la cima del _____ Pichincha se cubrió de nieve.

2. La Mitad del Mundo es un complejo turístico en la _____

   _____.

3. Me gusta la ciudad, pero mi hermano prefiere el _____ de las montañas.

4. En el Museo Arqueológico, hay arte de la era _____.

¿Comprendiste?

1. ¿Dónde queda Quito?

_____

2. ¿Cómo es el Quito Colonial?

_____

3. ¿Qué lugares puedes visitar en el Quito Colonial?

_____

_____

4. ¿Dónde está la parte moderna de Quito?

_____

5. ¿Adónde vas para caminar por la línea ecuatorial?

_____

Conexión personal

If you were to visit Quito, what parts would you most like to see? Why do these places interest you? Write your answer in the space on the right.

En Quito, me gustaría ver...

_____

_____

_____

_____

_____

_____

_____

_____

_____

_____

Para leer   *Un paseo por Ecuador*

Reading Strategy

REFLECT ON JOURNAL WRITING Have you ever kept a journal or a diary? How are diaries organized? As you read this article about a bus trip through Ecuador, notice the place and date given for each entry. This diary-style organization of the article helps you experience each day that the writer experiences. Use the chart to record an interesting experience you read from each day.

FECHA	LUGAR	EXPERIENCIA INTERESANTE
17 de abril		
18 de abril		
4 de mayo		
25 de mayo		

What You Need to Know

Buses are the most common means of transportation in Ecuador, where an extensive network of bus routes links towns and cities throughout the country. The most common types of buses are **colectivos** or **busetas,** used for inner-city transportation or small trips, and **autobuses** or **buses grandes,** large coaches that make longer trips. In rural or remote areas, **camionetas** (pick-up trucks) often double as buses, and passengers ride in the back. Along the coast it is common to see **rancheras,** buses with open sides and wooden seats. On buses traveling long distances, baggage is often carried on the roof. On some buses, passengers are permitted to ride on the roof as well.

UN PASEO POR ECUADOR

READING TIP Imagine, or visualize, what the article describes. Don't let unfamiliar words slow you down. Try to focus on the images and feelings.

APUNTES

Para la **mayoría** de los ecuatorianos, el autobús es el transporte más común. Para tener una experiencia muy ecuatoriana, decidí hacer un viaje en autobús.

GUAYAQUIL, 17 de abril:

Guayaquil es el puerto principal y la ciudad más grande del país. Para conocer la costa, decidí viajar a Machala. Compré mi boleto en la terminal moderna. Los buses de larga distancia tienen **cortinas** y televisores con videograbadora. Paseamos por la costa del Pacífico. Hacía[1] mucho calor y mucha humedad. Vi los cultivos de arroz, caña de azúcar y **plátanos.** Por el puerto de Machala pasan más de un millón de toneladas de plátanos y **camarones** por año.

[1] It was

PALABRAS CLAVE
la mayoría   *majority*
la cortina   *curtain*
el plátano   *banana*
los camarones   *shrimp*

Look at the boxed paragraph.
Underline all the preterite
verbs and write them in the
space below. Next to each verb,
write its infinitive.

_____

_____

_____

_____

_____

_____

_____

_____

_____

A pensar...

1. Which of the following
does the narrator see while
traveling through Ecuador?
Check three. (**Main Idea
and Details**)

☐ la costa del Atlántico

☐ volcanes

☐ el océano Pacífico

☐ plantaciones de café

☐ Quito

2. Which of the following are
the names of ports in
Ecuador? Check two. (**Clarify**)

☐ Guayaquil

☐ Amazonas

☐ Machala

☐ Saquisilí

MACHALA, 18 de abril:

Decidí visitar los
pueblitos. Viajé en un
20 bus de transporte
rural de colores muy
alegres con personas
muy animadas.
El bus llevó todas sus
25 posesiones encima. Fuimos a varios pueblos y
plantaciones de café y cacao.

LA SIERRA, 4 de mayo:

Llegué a la sierra de
Ecuador, la región
30 central de los Andes.
Hacía frío en las
montañas. Me levanté
a las cinco y subí a un
antiguo bus de escuela
35 para ir al mercado
indígena de Saquisilí.
Viajamos muy lentamente.

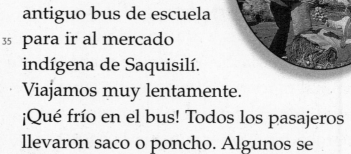

¡Qué frío en el bus! Todos los pasajeros
llevaron saco o poncho. Algunos se
40 durmieron. Muchas personas llevaron
productos al mercado. Vimos los volcanes de
Cotopaxi y Tungurahua. Llegamos al Saquisilí
y todos salieron del bus para trabajar o hacer
compras.

COCA, 25 de mayo:

45

La **carretera** terminó y tuve que seguir en barco por los ríos Napo y Coca, que van al río Amazonas. Vi barcos y canoas con muchos plátanos y pasajeros. En la **selva** vive poca

50 gente, la mayoría son indígenas. Como ven, ¡se puede conocer mucho viajando en autobús!

APUNTES

CHALLENGE What have you learned about the geography or physical features of Ecuador from reading this selection? **(Analyze)**

PALABRAS CLAVE
la carretera *highway*   la selva *jungle*

Vocabulario de la lectura

Palabras clave

los camarones *shrimp*   **la cortina** *curtain*   **el plátano** *banana*
la carretera *highway*   **la mayoría** *majority*   **la selva** *jungle*

A. For each **Palabra clave** in the first column, find the phrase in the second column that is closest in meaning. Write the corresponding letter in the blank.

_____ 1. cortina   A. un camino grande

_____ 2. carretera   B. una fruta amarilla

_____ 3. selva   C. animales del mar

_____ 4. plátano   D. algo para la ventana

_____ 5. camarones   E. un gran número

_____ 6. mayoría   F. un bosque tropical

B. Choose two **Palabras clave** and write a sentence with each one.

_____

_____

_____

_____

_____

_____

_____

_____

¿Comprendiste?

1. ¿Cuál es el transporte más común en Ecuador?

_____

2. ¿En qué región empezó el autor?

_____

3. ¿Qué productos son típicos de la costa?

_____

4. ¿Cómo es el clima de la sierra?

_____

5. ¿Adónde van los ríos Napo y Coca?

_____

Conexión personal

Imagine that you and your family are on vacation in Ecuador. Write a postcard to a friend back home explaining how you spent your day. You might describe a canoe trip through the jungle, a shopping expedition in the mountains, or a visit to a large city.

¡Hola, Mary!

Hoy hicimos un viaje en autobús.

Fuimos a..

Para leer
Un cuento ecuatoriano: El tigre y el conejo

Reading Strategy

FOLLOW THE SEQUENCE It is important to recognize the order of events in a story. The selection you are about to read has three repetitive segments. Scan the reading to try to identify what they are. Look for sequencing words in Spanish such as **un día, una vez más,** and **por última vez** to help you follow the story.

Sequencing Words
un día

What You Need to Know

A fable is a short narrative that conveys a message and features animal characters that talk and act like people. The message in a fable is often a useful piece of wisdom or cautionary advice. Fables are a part of the folklore of many countries. A tiger and a rabbit are the main characters in many fables, with the small, clever rabbit typically outwitting the large, foolhardy tiger. The tiger and the rabbit continue their legendary rivalry in this fable you are about to read from Ecuador.

Un cuento ecuatoriano

El tigre y el conejo

Un día Tío Tigre pasó por el bosque camino a su casa. Tenía[1] una **canasta** de comida muy rica. El amigo conejo lo vio y pensó: «¡Yo tengo hambre! ¡Quiero esa comida!» y saltó[2]
5 por el bosque y se adelantó[3] a Tío Tigre. Se echó como muerto[4]. Cuando llegó Tío Tigre, vio al conejo pero siguió el camino[5].

[1] He had
[2] hopped
[3] got ahead
[4] *Se echó…muerto.*
      He pretended to be dead.
[5] *siguió…camino*
      he continued on his way

PALABRAS CLAVE
el cuento   *story*
ecuatoriano(a)   *Ecuadorian*
el tigre   *tiger*

el conejo   *rabbit*
la canasta   *basket*

READER'S SUCCESS STRATEGY As you read, watch for the sequencing phrases you placed in the chart on the opposite page, such as **una vez más** and **otra vez**. As you come across these phrases, underline them. When you are finished reading, retell the story using these phrases as an aid.

▌▌▌**MÁRCALO** ⟩ **GRAMÁTICA**
This reading is almost entirely in the preterite tense. Look for the preterite verbs and underline all the ones you recognize.

READING TIP In Spanish, quotation marks are often used to indicate thoughts. As you read, underline the rabbit's thoughts.

CHALLENGE Can you think of a saying in English that expresses the same message as one in this fable? (You may find more than one message in the fable.) **(Paraphrase)**

1. Write the numbers 1, 2, 3, 4, and 5 to show the order in which the events below occurred. **(Sequence of Events)**

___ The tiger put down his basket.

___ The rabbit played dead three times.

___ The rabbit stole the tiger's food.

___ The rabbit saw the tiger walking through the forest with a basket of food.

___ The tiger went looking for what he thought were two dead rabbits.

2. Which of the two animals is bigger and stronger? Which one is smarter? What does the fable imply about the relationship between physical strength and intelligence? **(Analyze)**

_____

_____

_____

_____

_____

3. What is your opinion of the tiger and the rabbit? Think of three words to describe each. **(Make Judgments)**

_____

_____

_____

_____

10 El amigo conejo pensó y dijo: «Pues, voy a tratar[6] una vez más» y saltó y se adelantó otra vez a Tío Tigre. Otra vez se echó como muerto. Y una vez más pasó Tío Tigre, vio al conejo y siguió su camino.

15 El amigo conejo pensó: «Bueno, voy a tratar por última vez» y saltó camino adelante y otra vez se echó como muerto. Esta vez Tío Tigre se paró[7]. Decidió que tres conejos muertos en el camino era demasiado bueno para perder. 20 Dejó la canasta y regresó por los otros dos conejos.

Y así el amigo conejo agarró[8] la canasta y le robó al tigre su comida.

---

[6] to try   [7] stopped   [8] grabbed

Vocabulario de la lectura

Palabras clave

   la canasta *basket*   **ecuatoriano(a)** *Ecuadorian*

   el conejo *rabbit*   **el tigre** *tiger*

   el cuento *story*

A. For each **Palabra clave** in the first column, find the sentence in the second column that best describes it. Write the corresponding letter in the blank.

_____ 1. ecuatoriano(a)   A. Es un animal con rayas.

_____ 2. tigre   B. Es algo que puedes decir o leer.

_____ 3. conejo   C. El tigre pone su comida en una...

_____ 4. cuento   D. Se refiere a algo o alguien nativo de Ecuador.

_____ 5. canasta   E. Tiene orejas largas.

B. Choose three **Palabras clave** and write a sentence with each one.

_____

_____

_____

_____

_____

¿Comprendiste?

1. ¿Por dónde pasó el tigre?

_____

2. ¿Qué tenía en la canasta?

_____

3. ¿Qué pensó el conejo cuando vio la canasta?

_____

4. ¿Qué hizo el conejo?

_____

5. ¿Cómo terminó todo?

_____

_____

Conexión personal

Can you think of any memorable tiger or rabbit characters that you have read about in books or seen on TV? Choose several famous tigers, rabbits, or other animals. Write their names and give a Spanish adjective to describe each one.

Animales famosos	Características
Brer Rabbit	inteligente

Para leer   *El murciélago cobarde*

Reading Strategy

USE PICTURES In this legend, the **murciélago** is the main character of the narrative. Skim the reading and look at the pictures to remember what a **murciélago** is. What other characters are part of this reading? Write them in the space below.

_____

_____

_____

_____

What You Need to Know

Ecuador has three distinct land regions: the Pacific coast to the west; the Andes mountains extending north to south down the middle; and a region of tropical forests and rivers to the east. This varied geography supports a large number of habitats, and Ecuador, known for its biodiversity, has thousands of species of flora and fauna. Birdwatchers from all over the world come to Ecuador to see birds typical of the country such as condors and parrots as well as newly discovered species, which are continually being recorded. Many types of mammals are found in Ecuador as well, including monkeys, sloths, and over 100 species of bats. The legend you are about to read, in which a bat is the main character, takes place among the animals of a tropical forest in Ecuador.

READING TIP It may help you remember the word for bat, **murciélago**, to know that it comes from the Latin word **mus,** meaning *mouse*, and the Spanish word **cielo,** meaning *sky*. When spelling **murciélago,** keep in mind that it contains all the vowels.

_____
_____
_____
_____
_____

▥▥▥ MÁRCALO ⟩ **GRAMÁTICA**
You are now familiar with some common irregular preterite verbs, including **decir, hacer,** and **ir.** Underline all the preterite forms of **decir, hacer,** and **ir** that you can find in this legend.

_____
_____
_____

CHALLENGE Do you think the bat was a coward not to take part in the fight? Why or why not? (**Make Judgments**)

_____
_____
_____
_____
_____
_____
_____

El murciélago cobarde

Un día, los animales del bosque y los pájaros del **cielo** decidieron **luchar**. Los animales llamaron al murciélago y le dijeron: «Ven y **pelea** con nosotros contra los pájaros.»
5 Pero el murciélago contestó: «¿No ven ustedes que soy pájaro? ¿No ven que tengo **alas**?»

Entonces, fueron los pájaros al murciélago y le dijeron: «Ven y pelea con nosotros contra los animales.» Pero el murciélago les dijo: «¿No
10 ven que soy animal? Tengo dientes y no tengo **plumas.**»

PALABRAS CLAVE
el murciélago *bat*
cobarde n., adj. *coward, cowardly*
el cielo *sky*
luchar *to fight*

pelear *to fight*
el ala (f.) *wing*
la pluma *feather*

Empezó la lucha y, viendo que ganaban[1] los animales, el murciélago fue con ellos. Pero los animales lo rechazaron[2]. Luego vio que los
15 pájaros ganaban y fue con ellos, pero los pájaros también lo rechazaron.

Por fin, **fatigados** por la lucha, los dos campos pusieron fin[3] al conflicto. Hicieron una fiesta para todos. El murciélago trató de[4] entrar a la
20 fiesta. Cuando todos lo vieron, se pusieron[5] furiosos y lo expulsaron de la fiesta.
Le gritaron: «¡De aquí en adelante vas a vivir en una cueva[6] y sólo vas a salir de noche porque eres un cobarde!»

25 Y así, pues, el murciélago tiene miedo de los animales y los pájaros y por eso no quiere salir de día.

[1] were winning	[2] rejected	[3] *pusieron fin* put an end
[4] *trató de* tried to	[5] became	[6] cave

PALABRAS CLAVE
fatigado(a) *tired*

bat sides with animals
↓

↓

↓

A pensar...

1. What physical characteristic does the bat share with the animals? What physical characteristic does he share with the birds? (**Compare and Contrast**)

2. Why do the birds and animals eject the bat from their party? (**Clarify**)

3. According to the legend, why do bats only come out at night? (**Main Idea**)

Vocabulario de la lectura

Palabras clave

el ala (f.)   *wing*
el cielo   *sky*
cobarde   n., adj.   *coward, cowardly*
fatigado(a)   *tired*

luchar   *to fight*
el murciélago   *bat*
pelear   *to fight*
la pluma   *feather*

A. Complete each analogy with one of the **Palabras clave.** In an analogy, the last two words must be related in the same way that the first two are related.

1. HOMBRE : BRAZO : : pájaro : _____

2. ALEGRE: CONTENTO : : cansado : _____

3. POSTRE : PASTEL : : animal : _____

4. ROJO: TOMATE : : azul : _____

5. TRISTE: DEPRIMIDO : : luchar : _____

B. Fill in the blank with the correct form of a **Palabra clave.**

Un día, los animales del bosque y los pájaros del _____ deciden
                                                            (1)
luchar. Cada campo quiere la ayuda del _____. El murciélago les
                                              (2)
dice a los animales que es pájaro porque tiene _____. Les dice a
                                                      (3)
los pájaros que es animal porque tiene dientes y no tiene _____.
                                                                  (4)
Todos los animales están furiosos con el murciélago porque no quiere

_____. Dicen que sólo sale de noche porque es un _____.
      (5)   (6)

¿Comprendiste?

1. ¿Qué pasó entre los animales y los pájaros?

_____

2. ¿Qué hicieron los animales después de la lucha?

_____

3. ¿Qué hizo el murciélago después de la lucha?

_____

4. ¿Qué le dijeron los animales y los pájaros al murciélago?

_____

_____

Conexión personal

Have you ever wondered why some animals behave as they do? Make a list of animals and their characteristics that could be the subject of a legend explaining their habits.

Animales	Características
pez	Vive en el mar.

Literatura adicional

In this section you will find literary readings in Spanish that range from poems to excerpts from novels, short stories, and other works. Each reading has biographical information about the author and background information about the selection. Like the **En voces** readings, the literary readings have reading strategies, reading tips, reader's success strategies, critical-thinking questions, vocabulary activities, comprehension questions, and a short writing activity to help you understand each selection. There is also a **Márcalo** feature for literary analysis of the readings.

Para leer   *Cumpleaños*

Reading Strategy

QUESTION Asking questions about a work of literature as you read is one way to understand the selection better. Use the five W's—who, what, where, when, why—to help you ask your questions. In the chart below, record questions and the answers you discover while reading **"Cumpleaños"** by Carmen Lomas Garza and viewing the illustration.

"Cumpleaños"

Who is the speaker?	a young girl
What	
Where	
When	
Why	

What You Need to Know

"Cumpleaños" is a story from Carmen Lomas Garza's book *Cuadros de familia*, in which she describes her memories of growing up in Kingsville, Texas, near the border of Mexico. Through illustrated vignettes about family activities from making tamales to picking nopal cactus, *Cuadros de familia* relates aspects of Mexican American history and culture. In **"Cumpleaños,"** Carmen Lomas Garza remembers celebrating her sixth birthday.

Sobre la autora

Carmen Lomas Garza, artista chicana, nació en Kingsville, Texas, en 1948. Empezó a estudiar arte a la edad de trece años. Sus pinturas, inspiradas en su niñez en el sur de Texas, son escenas típicas de la vida mexicana americana.

~~~~~~~~~

Cumpleaños

Ésa soy yo, pegándole[1] a la piñata en la fiesta que me dieron cuando cumplí seis años[2]. Era[3] también el cumpleaños de mi hermano, que cumplía cuatro años. Mi madre nos dio
5 una gran fiesta e invitó a muchos primos, **vecinos** y amigos.

_____

[1]hitting   [2]*cumplí seis años* I turned six   [3]It was

Cumpleaños de Lala y Tudi *by Carmen Lomas Garza, 1989*

PALABRAS CLAVE
  el (la) vecino(a)   *neighbor*

READING TIP Review the vocabulary you have learned for family members. Then circle the words in the story that refer to the relatives of the girl who is narrating it.

APUNTES

_____

_____

_____

_____

_____

MÁRCALO ► ANÁLISIS
This story contains vivid descriptions, details that help the reader form a strong mental picture. Underline words or phrases in the story that help you visualize in your mind the activity and excitement of the birthday party.

_____

_____

_____

_____

_____

READER'S SUCCESS STRATEGY As you read, look for depictions of the vocabulary in the illustration. First identify the girl who is telling the story and her father. Then find the following: **la cuerda, el palo, el pañuelo, la piñata.**

1. Whose birthday is it on the day of the party? **(Clarify)**

_____

_____

_____

2. What details of Mexican American culture are described in the story? **(Main Idea)**

_____

_____

_____

CHALLENGE How is the birthday party described in **"Cumpleaños"** the same as or different from birthday parties you had as a child, or birthday celebrations you attended? Use the Venn diagram to record your answer. Where the circles are separate, write in differences. Where they intersect, write in similarities. **(Compare and Contrast)**

"Cumpleaños"

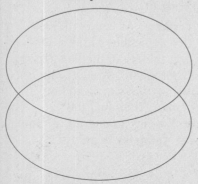

Birthdays I Remember

No puedes ver la piñata cuando le estás dando[4] con el **palo,** porque tienes los ojos cubiertos[5] por un **pañuelo.** Mi padre está
10 tirando[6] de la **cuerda** que **sube** y **baja** la piñata. Él se encargará[7] de que todos tengan[8] por lo menos una oportunidad de pegarle a la piñata. Luego alguien acabará rompiéndola[9], y entonces todos los **caramelos** que tiene
15 dentro caerán[10] y todos los niños correrán a **cogerlos.**

---

[4] _le estás dando_ you're hitting it
[5] covered
[6] is pulling
[7] will make sure
[8] have
[9] _acabará rompiéndola_ will end up breaking it
[10] will fall out

PALABRAS CLAVE
el palo _stick_
el pañuelo _handkerchief_
la cuerda _rope_
subir _to raise_

bajar _to lower_
los caramelos _candies_
coger _to grab_

Vocabulario de la lectura

Palabras clave

bajar *to lower*   **la cuerda** *rope*   **subir** *to raise*

los caramelos *candies*   **el palo** *stick*   **el (la) vecino(a)** *neighbor*

coger *to grab*   **el pañuelo** *handkerchief*

A. Complete the puzzle using forms of the **Palabras clave.**

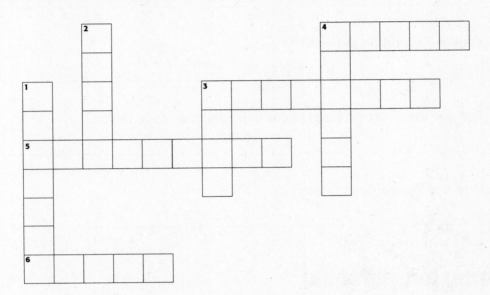

Across

3. En general son blancos.
4. Los niños corrieron a _____ los caramelos.
5. Son dulces.
6. Es lo opuesto *(opposite)* de **bajar.**

Down

1. Estas personas viven en la misma comunidad.
2. Es el opuesto *(opposite)* de **subir.**
3. Rompes una piñata con este objeto.
4. La usas para subir y bajar la piñata.

B. Choose two **Palabras clave** and write a sentence about **"Cumpleaños"** using each one.

_____

_____

_____

_____

¿Comprendiste?

1. ¿Cuántos años tiene la narradora?

_____

2. ¿Cuántos años tiene el hermano de la narradora?

_____

3. ¿Quiénes asistieron la fiesta?

_____

4. ¿Por qué los niños no pueden ver la piñata cuando le pegan?

_____

5. ¿Qué hay dentro de la piñata?

_____

Conexión personal

Do you have vivid recollections of any family celebrations from your childhood? Choose a birthday, holiday, or other celebration you remember and write some details about it in the web below.

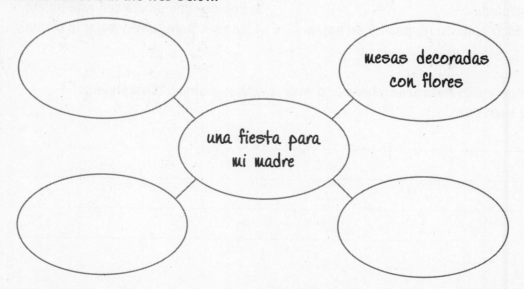

mesas decoradas con flores

una fiesta para mi madre

Para leer   *La exclamación / En Uxmal*

Reading Strategy

CLARIFY THE MEANING OF A POEM The process of stopping while reading to quickly review what has happened and to look for answers to questions you may have is called clarifying.
Complete the chart below by doing the following:

- Read the title and the first two lines of the poem.
- Stop to clarify those lines.
- Paraphrase what the lines are about in one of the boxes.
- Continue to read and clarify the rest of the poem in the same manner.

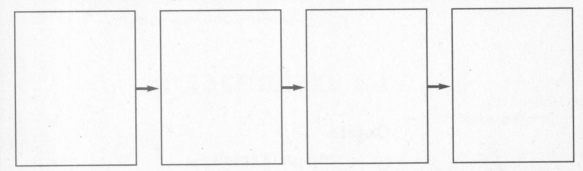

What You Need to Know

In his Nobel lecture, Octavio Paz made the following statements:

In Mexico, the Spaniards encountered history as well as geography. That history is still alive: It is a present rather than a past. The temples and gods of pre-Columbian Mexico are a pile of ruins, but the spirit that breathed life into that world has not disappeared; it speaks to us in the hermetic language of myth, legend, forms of social coexistence, popular art, customs. Being a Mexican writer means listening to the voice of that present, that presence.

. . . .

Poetry is in love with the instant and seeks to relive it in the poem, thus separating it from sequential time and turning it into a fixed present.

Consider how these ideas are reflected in the poems that follow.

A pensar...

1. Form is the placement of a poem's lines on the page. What is the significance of the way the lines are staggered on the page in **"La exclamación"**? (Draw Conclusions)

_____

_____

_____

_____

2. Why does Octavio Paz call this poem **"La exclamación"**? (Analyze)

_____

_____

_____

_____

_____

║MÁRCALO▷ ANÁLISIS
Repetition is a literary technique in which sounds, words, phrases, or lines are repeated for emphasis. Reread **"La exclamación"** and circle each phrase that appears more than once. Why do you think the poet repeats these phrases one after the other?

_____

_____

_____

Sobre el autor

Octavio Paz (1914–1998), poeta y ensayista que ganó el Premio Nóbel de Literatura en 1990, nació en la Ciudad de México. Durante los años cincuenta publicó *El laberinto de soledad (The Labyrinth of Solitude),* una colección de ensayos sobre la identidad mexicana, y *Libertad bajo palabra (Liberty Under Oath),* que contiene el poema «Piedra de sol» («Sunstone»). Inspirado en el calendario azteca, «Piedra de sol» es tal vez su obra más famosa. Desde 1962 hasta 1968 Octavio Paz fue embajador de México en India. Vivió en varios países y su escritura refleja una perspectiva internacional. Paz escribió sobre muchos temas, incluso sobre política, filosofía y amor.

〜〜〜〜〜〜

La exclamación

Quieto
⠀⠀⠀⠀⠀no en la **rama**
en el aire
⠀⠀⠀⠀⠀⠀No en el aire
5⠀en el instante
⠀⠀⠀⠀⠀⠀el **colibrí**

PALABRAS CLAVE
⠀⠀**quieto(a)**⠀⠀*still, motionless*⠀⠀⠀⠀⠀⠀**el colibrí**⠀⠀*hummingbird*
⠀⠀**la rama**⠀⠀*branch*

READING TIP Uxmal, located on the Yucatan Peninsula in Mexico, is the site of an ancient Mayan civilization.

MÁRCALO **ANÁLISIS**
Personification is a figure of speech that gives human characteristics to an object, animal, or idea. Circle the line containing personification in **"En Uxmal."** What is being personified?

_____

_____

A pensar...

1. Consider that this poem was inspired by the ruins of an ancient civilization. What do you think the poet means when he says a bird has stopped in the air? **(Analyze)**

_____

_____

_____

2. What does the poet mean when he says time is transparent? **(Analyze)**

_____

_____

CHALLENGE How are these two poems similar? How are they different? **(Compare and Contrast)**

_____

_____

En Uxmal

Mediodía

La **luz** no **parpadea,**
el tiempo se vacía¹ de minutos,
se ha detenido² un pájaro en el aire.

5 *Pleno³ sol*

La hora es transparente:
vemos, si es invisible el pájaro,
el color de su **canto.**

---

¹empties itself   ²has stopped   ³full

PALABRAS CLAVE
la luz *light*   **el canto** *song*
parpadear *to blink*

Vocabulario de la lectura

el canto *song*   **la luz** *light*   **quieto(a)** *still, motionless*

el colibrí *hummingbird*   **parpadear** *to blink*   **la rama** *branch*

A. Complete each analogy with one of the **Palabras clave.** In an analogy, the last two words must be related in the same way that the first two are related.

1. CABEZA : PELO : : árbol : _____

2. LEER : LIBRO : : cantar : _____

3. PUERTA : CERRAR : : ojo : _____

4. BEBIDA : REFRESCO : : pájaro : _____

5. FELIZ : ALEGRE : : tranquilo : _____

B. Complete each sentence with the correct form of a **Palabra clave.**

1. El _____ puede moverse con extraordinaria rapidez.

2. Apaga la _____, por favor; quiero dormir.

3. Hay un pájaro raro sobre la _____ de ese árbol.

4. No veo el pájaro, pero oigo su _____.

5. _____ significa «cerrar y abrir los ojos».

¿Comprendiste?

1. ¿Qué tipo de pájaro se describe en **«La exclamación»**?

_____

2. ¿En qué tres lugares se encuentra el colibrí?

_____

3. ¿A qué hora empieza el primer verso de **«En Uxmal»**?

_____

4. ¿En el segundo verso de **«En Uxmal»**, ¿qué palabra usa el poeta para describir la hora?

_____

5. ¿Qué palabra usa el poeta para describir el pájaro de **«En Uxmal»**? Si el pájaro es invisible, ¿cómo sabemos que existe?

_____

Conexión personal

If you were a poet, what would you write about? Would it be something in nature, a place you have been, or another subject? In the center of the web write a subject for your poem. Then brainstorm words you associate with it.

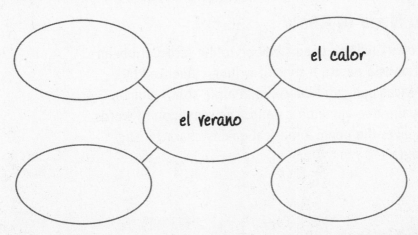

Para leer   *Palma sola*

Reading Strategy

SETTING The setting of a poem or story is the time and place where the action occurs. The setting may be a backdrop, with no effect on what happens, or it may be important to the meaning of the poem. Use the chart below to jot down lines from **"Palma sola"** that indicate setting.

Time/Place	Meaning
bajo la luna y sol	shows the passage of time

What You Need to Know

Many of Nicolás Guillén's poems belong to the Afro-Caribbean genre called **poesía negra,** a style of writing influenced by traditional African song and dance. In **"Palma sola,"** Guillén describes a palm tree alone on a patio. The repetition of words and phrases gives the poem a musical quality characteristic of **poesía negra**.

Sobre el autor

El Poeta Nacional de Cuba, Nicolás Guillén (1902–1989) es uno de los escritores latinos más conocidos. Su poesía celebra la herencia africana de la gente cubana y la historia étnica de la isla. Guillén admiró la literatura española y la poesía clásica española. Sus poemas combinan elementos de la poesía española con el lenguaje común de los cubanos. En muchas de sus obras se puede ver el ritmo de *son,* un tipo de música de origen africano y español.

Palma sola

La palma que está en el patio
nació[1] sola;
creció sin que yo la viera[2],
creció sola;
5   **bajo** la **luna** y el sol,
vive sola.

Con su largo cuerpo fijo[3],
palma sola;
sola en el patio sellado[4],
10   siempre sola,
guardián[5] del atardecer[6],
sueña[7] sola.

---

[1] was born   [2] *sin que yo la viera* without my seeing it
[3] fixed, stationary   [4] sealed, enclosed   [5] watchman
[6] late afternoon   [7] dreams

PALABRAS CLAVE
crecer   *to grow*   la luna   *moon*
bajo(a)   *under*

READING TIP Poetry is like words and music all rolled up into one package. Rhythm, the pattern of heavy and light stresses, is one way poets add this musical quality. As you read **"Palma sola,"** notice how Guillén repeats certain words to give the poem rhythm.

MÁRCALO ANÁLISIS
Remember that **personification** is a literary device that gives human characteristics to something nonhuman. Circle the lines in this poem containing personification.

A pensar...

1. What phrases does the poet use to describe the solitary existence of the palm? (**Clarify**)

2. How is the palm tree in the poem different from a palm tree found in nature? (**Compare and Contrast**)

3. Why do you think the poet repeats the words **palma** and **sola** throughout the poem? (**Analyze**)

READER'S SUCCESS STRATEGY Pay attention to the poem's descriptive details. Draw a sketch of what you imagine the palm tree to look like.

MÁRCALO ANÁLISIS
A **metaphor** is an implied comparison between two things. In **"Palma sola,"** **Guardián del atardecer** is a metaphor: the palm tree is being compared to a watchman. Read the last verse of the poem to find another metaphor. Underline the metaphor and name the two things being compared.

_____

_____

_____

_____

CHALLENGE In what ways is the palm tree captive? In what ways is it free? **(Evaluate)**

_____

_____

_____

La palma sola **soñando,**

palma sola,

15 que va **libre** por[8] el viento,

libre y sola,

suelta[9] de **raíz** y **tierra,**

suelta y sola;

cazadora[10] de las nubes,

20 palma sola,

palma sola,

palma.

_____

[8] through   [9] free   [10] huntress

PALABRAS CLAVE

soñar *to dream*	**el raíz** (pl. **raíces**) *root*
libre *free*	**la tierra** *earth*

Vocabulario de la lectura

Palabras clave

bajo(a) *under*   **la luna** *moon*   **soñar** *to dream*
crecer *to grow*   **el raíz** (pl. **raíces**) *root*   **la tierra** *earth*
libre *free*

A. Complete the puzzle using forms of the **Palabras clave**.

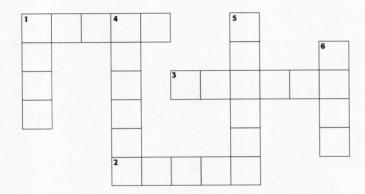

Across
1. ¿Qué haces en tu tiempo _____?
2. Lo haces cuando estás durmiendo.
3. La palma del poema es «suelta de raíz
   y _____».

Down
1. La ves por la noche.
4. Los árboles y las plantas los tienen.
5. Es el proceso de hacerse más grande.
6. Es lo opuesto *(opposite)* de **encima**.

B. Choose three of the **Palabras clave** and write a sentence with each one.

_____

_____

_____

_____

_____

_____

_____

¿Comprendiste?

1. ¿Qué es una palma?

_____

2. ¿Dónde está la palma del poema?

_____

3. ¿Es el patio abierto o sellado?

_____

4. ¿Con qué dos cosas compara la palma Nicolás Guillén?

_____

5. ¿Qué dos palabras se repiten frecuentemente en el poema?

_____

Conexión personal

Nicolás Guillén chose a palm tree on a patio to represent the concept of solitude **(la soledad)**. If you were a poet, what things would you use to illustrate the state of being alone? Use the word web to jot down your ideas. Some words have been provided as examples.

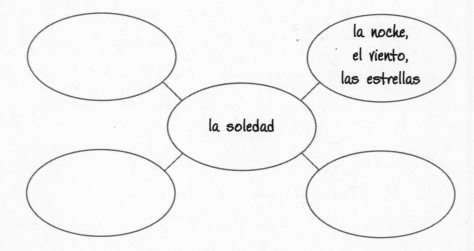

la noche, el viento, las estrellas

la soledad

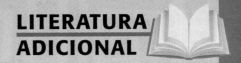

Para leer   *Como agua para chocolate*

Reading Strategy

CONNECT TO YOUR OWN LIFE You can connect the subject
of a reading to your own life. As you read the recipe from
Como agua para chocolate, think about foods and recipes that
have special meaning for you. Compare Laura Esquivel's recipe
for making chocolate to one of your own recipes.

Chocolate	My Recipe
only two ingredients	lots of ingredients

What You Need to Know

This reading is a recipe from the novel *Como agua para chocolate* by
Mexican writer Laura Esquivel. The book is in the form of monthly
installments with food and home remedies used to describe the life and
loves of the main character. The recipe is for chocolate, which is made
from the seeds, or beans, of the cacao tree. The word **cacao** is Spanish,
from the Nahuatl word *cacahuatl*. Cacao was so prized by the Aztecs that
the beans were used as a form of currency. The Aztecs also ground the
beans to produce a rich chocolate beverage.

READING TIP Remember the food and cooking vocabulary you have learned: **libras, azúcar, aceite, caliente, cuchillo.** You can figure out new words like **tostar** and **granos** because they are cognates.

▌▌▌**MÁRCALO** ❯ **ANÁLISIS** This reading contains **sensory details,** descriptive words that have to do with the senses. Reread the recipe and highlight phrases or passages that have to do with sight, taste, and touch. Then write them in the appropriate category in the chart below.

la vista *(sight)*	
el gusto *(taste)*	
el tacto *(touch)*	

APUNTES

_____

_____

_____

_____

_____

_____

_____

_____

_____

_____

_____

Sobre la autora

Laura Esquivel nació en México en 1950. Empezó su carrera de escritora como guionista *(scriptwriter)* de películas. En 1989 publicó la novela *Como agua para chocolate,* que ganó mucha popularidad tanto en Latinoamérica como en Estados Unidos. En 1992, la película basada en la novela tuvo mucho éxito y Esquivel ganó el premio Ariel (de la Academia Mexicana de Ciencias y Artes Cinematográficas) al mejor guión.

〜〜〜〜〜〜〜〜

Como agua para chocolate

Ingredientes chocolate:

2 libras Cacao Soconusco

2 libras Cacao Maracaibo

2 libras Cacao Caracas

Azúcar entre 4 y 6 libras según el gusto

Manaera de hacerse:

La primera operación es tostar el cacao. Para hacerlo es conveniente utilizar una charola de hojalata[1] en vez del comal[2], pues el aceite que se desprende[3] de los granos se pierde entre los
5 poros del comal. Es importantísimo poner cuidado en este tipo de indicaciones, pues la **bondad** del chocolate depende de tres cosas, a saber: de que el cacao que se emplee esté sano[4] y no averiado[5], de que se mezclen[6] en su
10 **fabricación** distintas clases de cacao y, por último, de su **grado** de tueste[7].

El grado de tueste **aconsejable** es el del momento en que el cacao comienza a despedir[8] su aceite. Si se retira[9] antes, aparte de presentar
15 un **aspecto** descolorido y **desagradable,** lo hará indigesto[10]. Por el contrario, si se deja más tiempo sobre el fuego[11], el grano quedará **quemado** en gran parte y contaminará de acrimonia y aspereza al chocolate[12].

(···)

---

[1] *charola de holata* pan made of tin   [2] clay griddle
[3] is given off   [4] in good condition; intact
[5] damaged; spoiled   [6] are mixed
[7] toasting
[8] *comienza a despedir* starts to give off
[9] it is removed
[10] it will be indigestible
[11] flame, heat
[12] *contaminará de acrimonia y aspereza* will make bitter and acrid

PALABRAS CLAVE
  la bondad *goodness*   **el aspecto** *appearance, aspect*
  la fabricación *making, manufacture*   **desagradable** *disagreeable, unpleasant*
  el grado *degree*   **quemado(a)** *burned*
  aconsejable *advisable*

READER'S SUCCESS STRATEGY As you read, make a list below of the kitchen equipment used in the recipe. Then write the verb from the recipe that indicates what each item is used to do.

APUNTES

CHALLENGE Do you think that it would be easy or difficult to use this recipe? Why? (**Evaluate**)

A pensar...

1. Write the numbers 1, 2, 3, 4, or 5 to show the order of steps in the recipe. **(Chronological Order)**

___ Divide the mass into chunks.

___ Separate the hulls with a sieve.

___ Add the sugar and pound the mixture.

___ Toast the beans in a pan made of tin.

___ Grind the beans on a metate.

2. What three things does the goodness of the chocolate depend on? Circle the correct answers. **(Identify Main Idea and Details)**

the bitterness of the cacao beans

the mixing of different kinds of beans

the undamaged condition of the beans

the use of a clay griddle to toast the beans

the degree of toasting of the beans

3. What happens when the cacao is not toasted enough and when it is toasted too much? **(Cause and Effect)**

_____

_____

_____

_____

20 Cuando el cacao ya está tostado como se indicó, se limpia utilizando un cedazo[13] para separar la cáscara[14] del grano. Debajo del metate[15] donde se ha de **moler**[16], se pone un cajete[17] con buena lumbre[18] y cuando ya está

25 caliente el metate, se procede a moler el grano. Se mezcla entonces con el azúcar, **machacándolo** con un mazo[19] y moliendo las dos cosas juntas. En seguida se divide la masa en **trozos.** Con las manos se moldean las

30 tablillas[20], redondas o alargadas[21], según el gusto, y se ponen a orear[22]. Con la punta[23] de un cuchillo se le pueden señalar[24] las divisiones que se deseen[25].

[13] sieve	[14] hull	[15] grinding stone
[16] *se ha de moler* it is to be ground		[17] earthenware bowl
[18] hot fire	[19] mallet, wooden hammer	[20] tablets
[21] round or elongated	[22] to air	[23] tip
[24] to mark	[25] are desired	

PALABRAS CLAVE
moler *to grind*
machacar *to pound*

el trozo *chunk, piece*

Vocabulario de la lectura

aconsejable *advisable*

el aspecto *appearance, aspect*

la bondad *goodness*

desagradable *disagreeable, unpleasant*

la fabricación *making, manufacture*

el grado *degree*

machacar *to pound*

moler *to grind*

quemado(a) *burned*

el trozo *chunk, piece*

A. Complete each sentence with a **Palabra clave.**

1. El _____ de tueste es el del momento en que el cacao empieza a despedir su aceite.

2. El cacao presenta un _____ descolorido si se retira antes.

3. Si se deja más tiempo sobre el fuego, el grano queda _____.

4. Se procede a _____ el grano con un metate.

5. Hay que _____ el grano y el azúcar con un mazo.

B. On the blank line next to each group of words, write the **Palabra clave** that goes with each set of clues.

1. cualidad; bueno _____

2. hacer; productos, comida _____

3. fragmento, porción, pedazo _____

4. feo, horrible _____

5. recomendable, apropiado _____

¿Comprendiste?

1. ¿Cuántas libras de cacao necesitas para preparar la receta?

   _____

2. ¿Cuál es el otro ingrediente?

   _____

3. ¿Qué haces primero?

   _____

4. ¿Cuándo procedes a moler el grano?

   _____

5. ¿Cómo se moldean las tablillas?

   _____

Conexión personal

Do you like chocolate? What other foods do you like? List them in the chart and write a couple of adjectives to describe each one.

Comida	Descripción
chocolate	dulce, marrón

Para leer *Don Quijote de la Mancha*

Reading Strategy

UNDERSTAND CHARACTER'S MOTIVES Motives are the emotions, wants, or needs that cause a character to act or react in a certain way. As you read this retelling of the beginning of *Don Quijote de la Mancha,* use the chart below to understand the actions of don Quijote. Next to each action, describe the reason, or motivation, he had for taking it.

Action	Reason
1. He wants to travel the world in search of adventure.	He wants to be like the knight-errant heroes in books of chivalry.
2. He adds his region's name, *la Mancha,* to his own name.	
3. He polishes the armor that belonged to his great-grandfather.	
4. He names his horse Rocinante.	
5. He imagines that Aldonza Lorenzo is a noble lady.	

What You Need to Know

The following selection is an adaptation of the first chapter of *El ingenioso hidalgo don Quijote de la Mancha,* the famous novel by Miguel de Cervantes. Romances of chivalry, the books that "dried out" don Quijote's brain, were popular reading between the Middle Ages and the Renaissance. Knight-errants, frequent heroes in books of chivalry, wandered in search of adventure to prove their bravery, honor, and gallantry toward women.

APUNTES

Sobre el autor

Miguel de Cervantes Saavedra (1547–1616) nació en Alcalá de Henares, España. Fue soldado y luchó en Lepanto, donde perdió el uso de la mano izquierda. Más tarde fue capturado por piratas y pasó cinco años prisionero. Escribió en todos los géneros. Algunas de sus obras son *Viaje del Parnaso* (poesía); *Comedias y entremeses* (drama); y su obra más famosa, *Don Quijote de la Mancha,* que se publicó en dos partes y puede ser la novela más importante de la literatura universal. Aunque *Don Quijote* fue un éxito inmediato, Cervantes fue pobre toda la vida.

El famoso hidalgo don Quijote de la Mancha

Había una vez[1] un **hidalgo pobre** en un lugar de España que se llama la Mancha. En su casa había[2] muchísimos libros de **caballería** porque el pasatiempo favorito de este señor era[3] leer y leer, especialmente libros de caballería. Se pasaba[4] las noches completas sin dormir, leyendo hasta el **amanecer,** y lo mismo durante el día.

---

[1] Once upon a time there was   [2] there were   [3] was   [4] He spent

PALABRAS CLAVE
el (la) hidalgo(a) *person of noble descent*
pobre *poor*
la caballería *chivalry*
el amanecer *dawn*

Leyó tantos y tantos libros que un día se le

10 secó el **cerebro**[5] y perdió el juicio[6]. Se

imaginó todo tipo de situaciones: batallas,

desafíos[7], encantamientos[8], heridas[9], **amores,**

tormentas[10] y muchas otras cosas imposibles.

Para él todas estas cosas eran[11] reales, tan

15 reales como su casa, el ama[12] de cuarenta

años, su sobrina de diecinueve años, su **rocín**

flaco y el mozo[13].

Un día resuelve **hacerse caballero andante.**

Decide ir por todo el mundo con sus armas y

20 caballo a buscar aventuras. Desea pelear[14] por

la justicia como los caballeros andantes de las

novelas que le gustan. Se va por el mundo a

buscar honra y fama.

Primero limpia las armas que fueron de su

25 **bisabuelo.** Después decide que el rocín de un

caballero andante tiene que tener un nombre

impresionante. «Rocinante te voy a llamar»,

le dice a su rocín. Luego cambia su propio[15]

nombre para incorporar el nombre de su

30 región y hacerla famosa. De esa forma se

convierte en[16] don Quijote de la Mancha.

---

[5] *se le secó el cerebro* his brain dried out	[6] sanity	[7] duels
[8] enchantments	[9] injuries	[10] misfortunes	[11] were
[12] housekeeper	[13] stable boy	[14] to fight	[15] own
[16] *se convierte en* he becomes		

PALABRAS CLAVE

el cerebro *brain*
los amores *love affairs*
el rocín *workhorse*
flaco(a) *thin*

hacerse *to become*
el caballero andante *knight-errant*
el bisabuelo *great-grandfather*

READING TIP This reading contains several plays on words. **Quijote**, the name of the central character, is also the word for a piece of armor. **Rocinante** is made up of two words: **rocín** (*workhorse*), and **ante** (*before*). **Dulcinea**, the name of Quijote's lady, is inspired by the word **dulce**.

MÁRCALO **ANÁLISIS**
Hyperbole is a figure of speech in which exaggeration is used for emphasis or effect, as in *This book weighs a ton*. Find and underline an example of hyperbole in the second paragraph of this reading.

APUNTES

LITERATURA ADICIONAL

A pensar...

1. Write the numbers 1, 2, 3, and 4 to show the order in which Don Quijote does the following things. **(Chronological Order)**

   ___ He names his horse *Rocinante*.

   ___ He decides to call Aldonza Lorenzo *Dulcinea del Toboso*.

   ___ He changes his own name to *Don Quijote de la Mancha*.

   ___ He polishes the armor that belonged to his great-grandfather.

2. Why does Don Quijote want to become a knight-errant? **(Clarify)**

_____

_____

_____

_____

_____

CHALLENGE What does Cervantes suggest about books of chivalry? What evidence can you find in the reading to support your answer? **(Infer)**

_____

_____

_____

_____

_____

Por último, como buen caballero andante, necesita una enamorada [17] a quien dedicarle sus grandes **hazañas.** En Toboso, un lugar
35 cerca de la Mancha, hay una moza labradora [18], Aldonza Lorenzo, de la que antes estuvo **enamorado.** En su imaginación Aldonza se convierte en la **dama** de sus **sueños.** Es así como nace la figura de Dulcinea del Toboso,
40 porque así se llama el lugar donde ella vive.

_____

[17] *girlfriend*   [18] *moza labradora* peasant girl

PALABRAS CLAVE
la hazaña   *feat; heroic deed*   **la dama**   *lady*
enamorado(a) (de)   *in love (with)*   **el sueño**   *dream*

Vocabulario de la lectura

Palabras clave

el amanecer *dawn*

los amores *love affairs*

el bisabuelo *great-grandfather*

la caballería *chivalry*

el caballero andante *knight-errant*

el cerebro *brain*

la dama *lady*

enamorado(a) (de) *in love (with)*

flaco(a) *thin*

hacerse *to become*

la hazaña *feat; heroic deed*

el (la) hidalgo(a) *person of noble descent*

pobre *poor*

el rocín *workhorse*

el sueño *dream*

A. Complete each analogy with one of the **Palabras clave**. In an analogy, the last two words must be related in the same way that the first two are related.

1. CAMINAR : PIERNAS : : pensar : _____

2. CHICO: MUCHACHO : : señora : _____

3. ALTO : BAJO : : gordo : _____

4. HIJO: PADRE : : abuelo : _____

5. MIRAR: VER : : fantasía : _____

B. Complete each sentence with the correct form of a **Palabra clave.**

Don Quijote es un _____ que vive en la Mancha. Tiene pocas
            (1)

posesiones; es _____. También está loco a causa de leer tantos
            (2)

libros de _____. Pasa muchas noches sin dormir, leyendo estos
            (3)

libros hasta el _____. Un día, decide hacerse _____
            (4)   (5)

que se va por el mundo a buscar honra y fama. Primero, limpia las armas de su

_____. Luego, cambia el nombre de su _____ a
        (6)   (7)

Rocinante. Por último, imagina que Aldonza Lorenzo, una moza labradora, es la

_____ de sus sueños y la llama Dulcinea del Toboso.
        (8)

¿Comprendiste?

1. ¿Quién es don Quijote?

_____

2. ¿Qué tipo de libros le gusta leer?

_____

3. ¿Por qué se le secó el cerebro?

_____

4. ¿Qué resuelve hacerse don Quijote?

_____

5. ¿Cómo se llama su caballo?

_____

6. ¿Quién es Aldonza Lorenzo? ¿Qué nombre le da don Quijote?

_____

Conexión personal

Many adventure stories involve a quest, a journey that a character makes to reach a certain goal. Think of characters in books, movies, or television shows that go on quests. List them in the chart below.

Personaje *(Character)*	De	Meta *(Goal)*
don Quijote	Don Quijote de la Mancha	pelear por la justicia

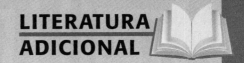
Para leer   *Oda al tomate*

Reading Strategy

WORD CHOICE Writers choose their words with care in order to express their thoughts accurately. Through careful word choice, a writer can make readers feel a certain way or visualize an image. As you read **"Oda al tomate,"** think about how certain words and phrases affect you as a reader. Use the chart below to record interesting words and phrases and what they convey to you.

Words and Phrases	Ideas and Feelings They Convey
"el tomate invade las cocinas"	expresses the abundance of tomatoes
"su color fogoso"	conveys an image of their bright red color

What You Need to Know

This reading is the poem **"Oda al tomate"** from the book *Odas elementales* (1954) by the Chilean poet Pablo Neruda (1904–1973). Odes are long lyric poems, usually of a serious or meditative nature and having an elevated style and formal structure. Unlike most odes, those of Pablo Neruda exalt the ordinary and the everyday, from tomatoes and artichokes to the air and rain.

READING TIP Read the poem aloud. Let punctuation show you where to stop or pause. How many sentences are there in the poem? A capital letter begins each one. Write your answer on the line below.

_____

_____

APUNTES

_____

_____

_____

_____

_____

_____

▌▌▌ **MÁRCALO** ⟩ **ANÁLISIS**
Remember that **personification** is the attribution of human characteristics to an object, animal, or idea. Pablo Neruda uses personification to give life to foods. Find and circle examples of personification in the poem. Which foods are personified? Write your answer on the lines below.

_____

_____

_____

_____

CHALLENGE Why would the street be filled with tomatoes? (Draw Conclusions)

_____

_____

_____

_____

Sobre el autor

Pablo Neruda nació en Parral, Chile. Su verdadero nombre era Ricardo Neftalí Reyes. Estudió pedagogía en francés en la Universidad de Chile. Allí conoció a Albertina Azócar. A ella le dedica los primeros poemas de *Veinte poemas de amor y una canción desesperada* (1924). Para Neruda, todo puede ser poesía. En sus famosas *Odas elementales* escribió versos para el tomate, el átomo, un reloj, la pobreza y la soledad. Pablo Neruda fue diplomático en varios países de Europa y en México. En 1971 obtuvo el Premio Nóbel de Literatura.

〜〜〜〜〜〜〜

Oda al tomate

La calle
se **llenó** de tomates,
mediodía,
verano,
5 la luz
se parte[1]
en dos
mitades
de tomate,
10 corre
por las calles
el jugo.

_____
[1] is split

PALABRAS CLAVE
llenar *to fill*   **la mitad** *half*

¡En español! Level 1

En diciembre
se desata[2]
el tomate,
invade
las cocinas,
entra por los almuerzos,
se sienta[3]
reposado[4]
en los aparadores[5],
entre los vasos,
las mantequilleras[6],
los saleros[7] azules.
Tiene
luz propia,
majestad benigna.
Debemos, por desgracia[8],
asesinarlo:
se hunde[9]
el cuchillo
en su pulpa **viviente,**
en una roja
víscera,
un sol
fresco,
profundo,

[2] breaks loose [3] sits down [4] relaxed
[5] sideboards [6] butter dishes [7] saltcellars
[8] unfortunately [9] sinks

PALABRAS CLAVE
viviente *living*

LITERATURA ADICIONAL

READER'S SUCCESS STRATEGY As you read, highlight the foods that are mentioned in the poem. Sort them into categories of your own choosing and write them below.

APUNTES

CHALLENGE Why is it December and yet it is summertime in the poem? **(Evaluate)**

A pensar...

1. Why do you think the poet compares the tomato to the sun? **(Draw Conclusions)**

2. What do you think the phrase **la cintura del verano** means? **(Analyze)**

APUNTES

inagotable [10],
llena de ensaladas

40 de Chile,
se casa [11] alegremente
con la clara cebolla,
y para celebrarlo
se deja

45 caer [12]
aceite,
hijo
esencial del olivo,
sobre sus hemisferios entreabiertos [13],

50 **agrega**
la pimienta
su fragancia,
la sal su magnetismo:
son las bodas [14]

55 del día,
el perejil
levanta
banderines [15],
las papas

60 hierven [16] vigorosamente,
el **asado**
golpea [17]

---

[10] inexhaustible
[11] it marries
[12] *se deja caer* is dropped
[13] halved
[14] weddings
[15] *perejil levanta banderines* parsley hoists its flag
[16] boil, bubble
[17] beats

PALABRAS CLAVE

agregar *to add*   **el asado** *roasted meat*

con su aroma

en la puerta,

65 es hora!

vamos!

y sobre

la mesa, en la **cintura**

del verano,

70 el tomate,

astro[18] de tierra,

estrella

repetida

y **fecunda,**

75 nos muestra[19]

sus circunvoluciones[20],

sus canales,

la insigne plenitud[21]

y la abundancia

80 sin hueso[22],

sin coraza[23],

sin escamas[24] ni **espinas,**

nos entrega[25]

el regalo

85 de su color **fogoso**

y la totalidad de su **frescura.**

---

[18] star   [19] shows   [20] convolutions, folds
[21] celebrated fullness   [22] stone, pit
[23] shell   [24] scales   [25] delivers

PALABRAS CLAVE
    la cintura *waist, waistline*
    fecundo(a) *fertile*
    la espina *thorn*

    fogoso(a) *fiery*
    la frescura *freshness, coolness*

|||| MÁRCALO ⟩ ANÁLISIS
Parallelism is a literary device in which related ideas are phrased in similar ways. An example is *a time to laugh, a time to weep.* Find and underline an example of parallelism near the end of the poem. What word is used in each line? Write the word on the line below.

_____

_____

APUNTES

Vocabulario de la lectura

Palabras clave

agregar *to add*
el asado *roasted meat*
la cintura *waist, waistline*
la espina *thorn*

fecundo(a) *fertile*
fogoso(a) *fiery*
la frescura *freshness, coolness*

llenar *to fill*
la mitad *half*
viviente *living*

A. On the line next to each word pair, write whether the words are synonyms or antonyms. Synonyms are words with the same or similar meaning. Antonyms are words with opposite meanings.

1. calor—frescura _____

2. adicionar—agregar _____

3. fértil—fecundo _____

4. ardiente—fogoso _____

B. Answer each question by writing one of the **Palabras clave** in the blank.

1. ¿Qué palabra es un tipo de carne? _____

2. ¿Qué palabra significa algo que vive? _____

3. ¿Qué haces con un vaso? _____

4. ¿Qué palabra es una parte del cuerpo humano? _____

5. ¿Qué tiene una rosa? _____

6. ¿Qué palabra significa «una de dos partes»? _____

¿Comprendiste?

1. ¿En qué mes ocurre el poema?

_____

2. ¿Qué tiene el tomate?

_____

3. ¿Qué no tiene el tomate?

_____

4. ¿Cuáles son los ingredientes de la ensalada?

_____

Conexión personal

Of the ordinary and the everyday, what would you write an ode to? Decide on a subject for your ode and write a list of words and phrases you would use to describe it in the notebook at the right. Include at least one example of personification.

Oda a _____

_____

_____

_____

_____

_____

_____

_____

_____

_____

_____

_____

_____

_____

Academic and Informational Reading

In this section you'll find strategies to help you read all kinds of informational materials. The examples here range from magazines you read for fun to textbooks to bus schedules. Applying these simple and effective techniques will help you be a successful reader of the many texts you encounter every day.

Reading a Magazine Article

A magazine article is designed to catch and hold your interest. You will get the most from your reading if you recognize the special features of a magazine page and learn how to use them. Look at the sample magazine article as you read each strategy below.

A Read the **title** to get an idea of what the article is about. Scan any other **headings** to see how information in the article is organized.

B As you read, notice any **quotations.** Who is quoted? Is the person a reliable source on the subject?

C Notice information set in special type, such as **italics** or **boldface.** For example, look at the caption in the article that is set in italic type.

D Study **visuals,** such as charts, graphs, pictures, maps, and bulleted lists. Visuals add important information and bring the topic to life.

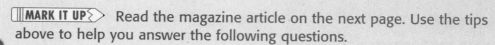 **MARK IT UP** Read the magazine article on the next page. Use the tips above to help you answer the following questions.

1. What is the topic of this article? _____

   _____

2. Underline the name and title of the person who speaks for Marcus Condiments.

3. Do you think the spokesperson for Restivo Tomato Products is a reliable source of information on salsa? Why or why not?

   _____

   _____

4. Circle the caption set in italic type.

5. Draw a box around the visual that compares the sales of ketchup and salsa.

A SALSA AND KETCHUP BATTLE IT OUT FOR TOP SAUCE

When you want to add a little spice to your snack or supper, do you reach for the salsa or the ketchup? Until recently, sales figures showed that more people grabbed the ketchup bottle, slathering the tomato sauce on their hamburgers, hot dogs, French fries, mashed potatoes, scrambled eggs, green beans, and almost anything else you can imagine. Elvis Presley even used it as a topping for sweet potato pie.

In 1996, however, salsa moved into number one position, replacing ketchup as the nation's top tomato sauce. Since then, the two condiments have been battling it out, with ketchup frantically trying to play catch-up. And it seems to have B succeeded. "Salsa's popularity has peaked. Ketchup is back on top," boasts Peter Harrington, chief executive of the world's largest ketchup maker, Marcus Condiments.

Salsa producers do not seem overly concerned, though. Mary Sullivan, a senior marketing manager for a leading salsa maker, Restivo Tomato Products, confidently noted that salsa is perfectly able to keep pace with ketchup. It's every bit as versatile a sauce, she says. "We're not limited to hamburgers and hot dogs." Every day, more people spoon more salsa over a whole alphabet of foods, from avocados to ziti.

To increase their slim lead over salsa, Marcus Condiments is focusing on research that shows families with children use three times more ketchup than childless households.

The salsa-ketchup war probably will not be decided any time soon. And maybe it shouldn't be. After all, to update an old saying, "Variety is the spice of life"—and of tomato sauce, too.

D

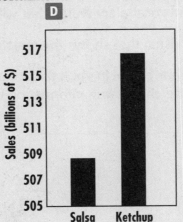

C Ketchup regains lead from salsa.

Reading a Textbook

The first page of a textbook lesson introduces you to a particular topic. The page also provides important information that will guide you through the rest of the lesson. Look at the sample textbook page as you read each strategy below.

A Preview the **title** and other **headings** to find out the lesson's main topic and related subtopics.

B Read the **key ideas** or **objectives** at the top of the page. Keep these in mind as you read. They will help you set a purpose for your reading.

C Look for a list of terms or **vocabulary words** at the start of each lesson. These words will be identified and defined throughout the lesson.

D Study **visuals** such as photographs and illustrations. Read the **captions.** Visuals can add information and interest to the topic.

MARK IT UP Read the sample textbook page. Then use the strategies above to help you answer the following questions.

1. What is the topic of this lesson? _____

_____

2. Circle the key idea of the lesson.

3. Draw a box around the vocabulary words that will be defined in the lesson.

4. Put a star next to the visual that shows the structure of a sea arch.

5. Using a graphic organizer can help you take notes on the textbook material you learn. Complete the chart using information on shoreline features from the lesson.

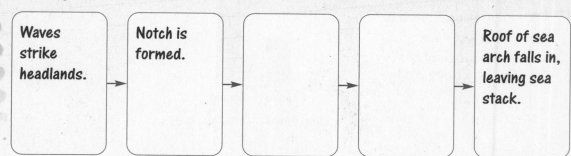

| Waves strike headlands. | → | Notch is formed. | → | | → | | → | Roof of sea arch falls in, leaving sea stack. |

A Shoreline Features

Ocean waves change the shape of a shoreline by eroding rock materials and by depositing sediments.

Waves and Erosion

Breaking storm waves may strike rock cliffs with a force of thousands of kilograms per square meter. Such breakers easily remove large masses of loose sand and clay. Air and water driven into cracks and fissures may split bedrock apart. Sand and pebbles carried by the water abrade the bedrock. Waves pound loose rock and boulders into pebbles and sand. In addition, seawater dissolves minerals from rocks such as limestone.

When waves strike the headlands of a deep-water shoreline, they may cut away the rock up to the high-tide level, forming a notch. If the materials overhanging the notch collapse, a sea cliff results.

Cliffs made of soft materials such as soil and sand wear away very quickly. For example, waves washing up on Cape Cod in Massachusetts are carrying away materials from sand cliffs there so rapidly that the cliffs are receding at a rate of about one meter every year.

In cliffs made of harder rock materials, a notch may deepen until it becomes a sea cave. Waves may cut through the walls of sea caves to form sea arches. Arches may also form when waves cut through vertical cracks in narrow headlands. If the roof of a sea arch falls in, what remains is a tall, narrow rock island called a sea stack.

Sea caves, sea arches, and sea stacks can be seen on the coasts of California, Oregon, Washington, and Maine, on the Gaspé Peninsula of Canada, and in many parts of the Mediterranean Sea.

16.3

B **KEY IDEA**

Waves erode shorelines and deposit sediments in characteristic formations.

C **KEY VOCABULARY**

- beach
- sandbar
- fjord

BAJA PENINSULA Ocean waves have formed this sea stack and sea arch in Mexico.

D

Sea stack

Sea arch

349

Reading a Table

Tables give a lot of information in an organized way. These tips can help you read a table quickly and accurately. Look at the example as you read each strategy in this list.

A Look at the **title** to find out the content of the table.

B Read the **introduction** to get a general overview of the information included in the table.

C Examine the **heading** of each row and column. To find specific information, locate the place where a row and column intersect.

B Water temperatures vary widely along the coasts of North America. This table shows the temperature of the water in March at eight beaches.

A Average March Water Temperature at Eight Beaches (°F)

C

Location	Temperature	Location	Temperature
Newport, RI	37	Oceanside, CA	58
Ocean City, MD	42	Seattle, WA	46
Veracruz, Mexico	75	Honolulu, HI	76
Freeport, TX	62	Juneau, AK	37

MARK IT UP Answer the following questions using the table of March water temperatures.

1. Which two beaches have the same water temperature? Circle the answers in the table.

2. What units are used to measure the water temperatures?

   _____

   _____

3. If you were planning a swimming vacation in March, what two beaches might you consider visiting?

   _____

   _____

Reading a Map

To read a map correctly, you have to identify and understand its elements. Look at the example below as you read each strategy in this list.

A Read the **title** to find out what the map shows.

B Study the **legend**, or **key**, to find out what symbols and colors are used on the map and what they stand for.

C Look at **geographic labels** to understand specific places on the map.

D Look at the **scale** to understand how distances on the map relate to actual distances.

E Locate the **compass rose**, or **pointer**, to determine direction.

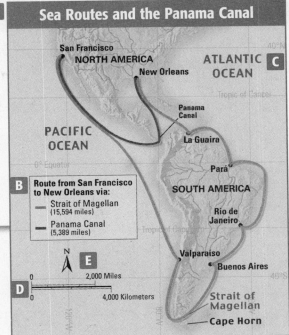

A Sea Routes and the Panama Canal

San Francisco
NORTH AMERICA
New Orleans
ATLANTIC OCEAN **C**
Tropic of Cancer
Panama Canal
PACIFIC OCEAN
La Guaira
0° Equator
Pará
SOUTH AMERICA
Río de Janeiro
Tropic of Capricorn

B Route from San Francisco to New Orleans via:
— Strait of Magellan (15,594 miles)
— Panama Canal (5,389 miles)

Valparaíso
Buenos Aires

N **E**
0   2,000 Miles
D
0   4,000 Kilometers

Strait of Magellan
— Cape Horn

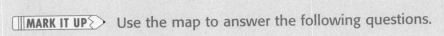

MARK IT UP Use the map to answer the following questions.

1. What does this map show? _____
_____
_____

2. How many miles is the sea route from San Francisco to New Orleans by way of the Strait of Magellan?
_____

3. How many miles would you save by taking the Panama Canal from San Francisco to New Orleans rather than the route through the Strait of Magellan?
_____

4. Draw a straight line from San Francisco to New Orleans. About how many miles apart are these cities by land?
_____

Reading a Diagram

Diagrams combine pictures with a few words to provide a lot of information. Look at the example on the opposite page as you read each of the following strategies.

A Look at the **title** to get an idea of what the diagram is about.

B Study the **images** closely to understand each part of the diagram.

C Look at the **captions** and the **labels** for more information.

MARK IT UP Study the diagram, then answer the following questions using the strategies above.

1. What does this diagram illustrate? _____

_____

_____

2. What is one example of a composite volcano? _____

_____

_____

3. What is one difference between cinder cones and composite volcanoes?

_____

_____

4. Circle the name of the layer of the earth that lies under the continental crust.

5. Draw a box around the part of the diagram that shows the internal structure of a composite volcano.

A Volcanic Landforms

The shape and structure of a volcano are determined by the nature of its eruptions and the materials it ejects. A cinder cone, perhaps the simplest form of volcano, forms when molten lava is thrown into the air from a vent. Cinder cones, which tend to be smaller than other types of volcanoes, typically form in groups and on the sides of larger volcanoes. Composite volcanoes develop when layers of materials from successive eruptions accumulate around a vent. The diagram shows the structure of these two types of volcanoes.

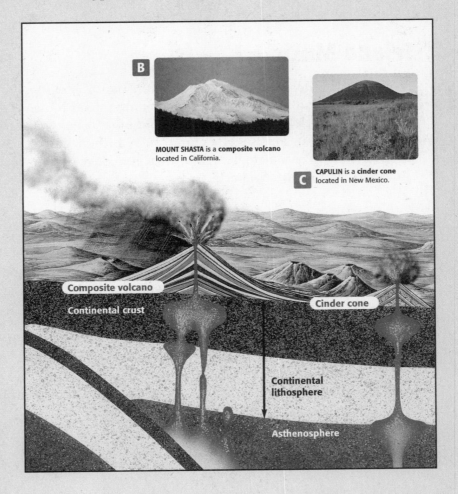

B

MOUNT SHASTA is a **composite volcano** located in California.

C

CAPULIN is a **cinder cone** located in New Mexico.

Composite volcano

Continental crust

Cinder cone

Continental lithosphere

Asthenosphere

Main Idea and Supporting Details

The *main idea* in a paragraph is its most important point. *Details* in the paragraph support the main idea. Identifying the main idea will help you focus on the main message the writer wants to communicate. Use the following strategies to help you identify a paragraph's main idea and supporting details.

- Look for the **main idea,** which is often the first sentence in a paragraph.

- Use the main idea to help you **summarize** the point of the paragraph.

- Identify specific **details,** including facts and examples, that support the main idea.

Tejano Music

Main idea

Tejano music reflects a harmonious combination of Mexican and American lifestyles. Also known as Tex Mex or conjunto music, it blends elements of jazz, country, rock 'n' roll, and rhythm and blues. The typical tejano band, **Details** or conjunto tejano, consists of a guitar, an accordion, and a *bajo sexto*, or large Spanish twelve-stringed guitar. The performers often wear colorful sombreros and fringed jackets.

 MARK IT UP Read the following paragraph. Circle the main idea. Then underline the details that support the main idea.

San Antonio, Texas, is a hub of tejano music. Many radio stations compete to bring listeners the latest recording artists and songs. On any given day, articles in numerous newspapers and magazines keep fans informed about who and what is hot. A San Antonio native, Flaco Jiminez, played an important role in spreading this lively art form around the world.

Problem and Solution

Does the proposed solution to a problem make sense? In order to decide, you need to look at each part of the text. Use the following strategies to read the text below.

- Look at the beginning or middle of a paragraph to find the **statement of the problem.**

- Find **details** that explain the problem and tell why it is important.

- Look for the **proposed solution.**

- Identify the **supporting details** for the proposed solution.

- Think about whether the solution is a good one.

Lunchroom Language Tables Can Beef Up Students' Skills

by Tara Blum

Statement of problem

Teachers, parents, administrators, and school board members are concerned that foreign language students are not getting enough practice actually using the language in conversation.

Details about the problem

In their foreign language classes, students read dialogs from their textbooks and respond to questions, but rarely get a chance to just communicate their thoughts.

Proposed solution

One way to address this problem would be to establish language tables in the lunchroom. Students taking a specific language would eat their lunch at a designated table one day a week. The only rule would be that they must speak no English, just the foreign language.

Details about the solution

This plan has several advantages. First, it doesn't require any additional equipment or materials. Second, it wouldn't take time away from other classes or activities. Language students have to eat lunch just like everyone else. Finally, it would be a lot of fun.

Language tables would let students supplement their language skills while nourishing their bodies. And that's a recipe for success!

[[MARK IT UP]] Use the text and strategies above to answer these questions.

1. Underline the proposed solution.

2. Circle at least one reason that supports this solution.

3. Explain why you think this is or is not a good solution to the problem.

_____

_____

_____

Sequence is the order in which events happen. Whether you read a story or a social studies lesson, it is important for you to understand *when* things happen in relation to one another. The tips below can help you identify sequence in any type of text.

- Look for the **main steps** or **events** in the sequence.

- Look for **words and phrases that signal time**, such as *in 1845, two days later,* and *by fall of that year.*

- Look for **words and phrases that signal order**, such as *after, first,* and *meanwhile.*

MARK IT UP Read the passage about the war with Mexico on the next page. Then use the information from the article and the tips above to answer the questions.

1. Underline two words or phrases that signal time.

2. Circle two words or phrases that signal order.

3. A time line can help you identify and understand a sequence of events. Use the information from the passage to complete this time line.

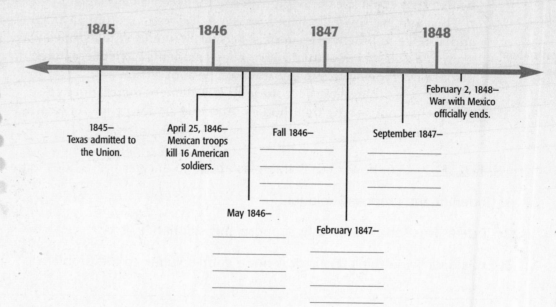

1845

1846

1847

1848

February 2, 1848—
War with Mexico
officially ends.

1845—
Texas admitted to
the Union.

April 25, 1846—
Mexican troops
kill 16 American
soldiers.

Fall 1846—
_____
_____
_____

September 1847—
_____
_____
_____

May 1846—
_____
_____
_____
_____

February 1847—
_____
_____

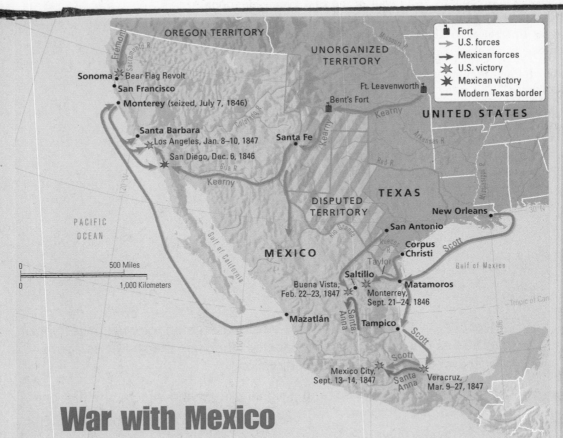

Map legend:
- **Fort**
- **U.S. forces**
- **Mexican forces**
- **U.S. victory**
- **Mexican victory**
- **Modern Texas border**

OREGON TERRITORY

UNORGANIZED TERRITORY

UNITED STATES

Sonoma — Bear Flag Revolt
San Francisco
Monterey (seized, July 7, 1846)
Santa Barbara
Los Angeles, Jan. 8–10, 1847
San Diego, Dec. 6, 1846

Ft. Leavenworth
Bent's Fort
Santa Fe

Kearny

TEXAS

DISPUTED TERRITORY

New Orleans
San Antonio
Corpus Christi

MEXICO

Taylor

Buena Vista, Feb. 22–23, 1847
Saltillo
Monterrey, Sept. 21–24, 1846
Matamoros

Mazatlán
Tampico

Mexico City, Sept. 13–14, 1847
Veracruz, Mar. 9–27, 1847

PACIFIC OCEAN

Gulf of California

Gulf of Mexico

500 Miles
1,000 Kilometers

War with Mexico

In 1845, Congress admitted Texas to the Union as a slave state, despite Northern objections to the spread of slavery. However, Mexico still claimed Texas as its own. Mexico angrily viewed this annexation as an act of war.

In a diplomatic gesture, President Polk sent an ambassador to Mexico offering $25 million for Texas, California, and New Mexico. After Mexico refused, the U.S. sent troops to the northern bank of the Rio Grande. The Mexicans responded with troops on the southern bank. On April 25, 1846, a Mexican cavalry unit crossed the Rio Grande, ambushing an American patrol and killing 16 American soldiers. Two days later, Congress declared war.

U.S. troops entered Mexico in May 1846. About the same time, troops marched toward New Mexico. They took the territory without firing a shot. They then moved westward, and by fall of that year, Americans controlled all of New Mexico and California.

The defeat of Mexico proved far more difficult. The Mexican army was much larger, but the U.S. troops were led by well-trained officers. American forces invaded Mexico from two directions. First, General Taylor battled his way south from Texas toward Northern Mexico. In February 1847, his 4,800 troops met General Santa Anna's 15,000 Mexican forces at Buena Vista. Santa Anna retreated.

Meanwhile, a fierce battle for southern Mexico was raging. Seven months after Taylor's victory in the North, Mexico City fell to U.S. troops led by General Winfield Scott.

The war officially ended on February 2, 1848 with the signing of the Treaty of Guadalupe Hidalgo. This treaty gave the U.S. the present-day states of California, Nevada, Utah, most of Arizona, and parts of New Mexico, Colorado, and Wyoming. In return, the U.S. offered Mexico $15 million and protection of the 80,000 Mexicans living in the newly acquired territories.

Cause and Effect

A *cause* is an event that brings about another event. An *effect* is something that happens as a result of the first event. Identifying causes and effects helps you understand how events are related. Use the tips below to find causes and effects in any kind of reading.

- Look for an action or event that answers the question, "What happened?" This is the **effect.**

- Look for an action or event that answers the question, "Why did this happen?" This is the **cause.**

- Look for words or phrases that **signal** causes and effects, such as *because, as a result, therefore, consequently,* and *since.*

||MARK IT UP⟩ Read the cause-and-effect passage on the next page. Notice that the first cause and effect are labeled. Then use the strategies above to help you answer the following questions.

1. Circle words in the passage that signal causes and effects. The first one has been done for you.

2. Some causes may have more than one effect. What are two effects of the mosquito's saliva on the body of the victim?

_____

_____

3. Complete the following diagram showing the cause and effects of mosquito bites.

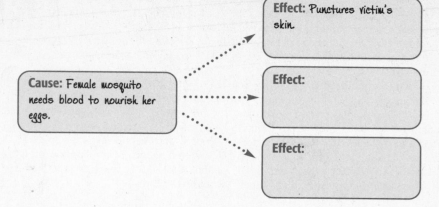

Effect: Punctures victim's skin

Cause: Female mosquito needs blood to nourish her eggs.

Effect:

Effect:

Bzz! Slap!

Cause

Signal
Word

Effect

If you spend any time outdoors in the summer, at some point you will probably find yourself covered with mosquito bites. The word *mosquito* means "little fly" in Spanish, but the impact these pesky insects have on people is anything but small.

Mosquitoes can transmit serious diseases such as yellow fever, encephalitis, and malaria. Usually, though, mosquito bites just (cause) people to develop raised, red bumps that itch like crazy.

This is what happens. Female mosquitoes need blood to nourish the eggs developing in their bodies. Consequently, they zero in on living things whose blood they can suck. Once they find a likely victim, the attack begins.

This attack is not really a bite, since a mosquito isn't able to open her jaws. Instead, she punctures the victim's skin with sharp stylets inside her mouth. The mosquito's saliva then flows into these puncture wounds. Because the saliva keeps the victim's blood from clotting, the mosquito can drink her fill. This can sometimes amount to 150 percent of the mosquito's weight.

Meanwhile, the mosquito's saliva sets off an allergic reaction in the

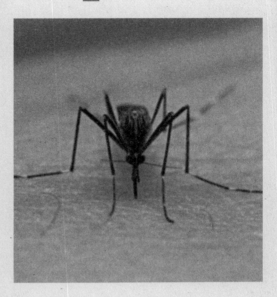

victim. As a result, the person develops the itchy swelling we call a mosquito bite. Ironically, if the mosquito finishes eating before the victim slaps or drives her off, there will be less saliva left in the skin. Therefore, the allergic reaction and itching will not be so severe.

Here are some steps you can take to help prevent mosquito bites or lessen their effect if you do get bitten.
- Don't go out at prime mosquito time—from dusk to dawn.
- Use insect repellent at all times.
- If you do get bitten, DON'T SCRATCH. Scratching just increases the allergic reaction.

Comparison and Contrast

Comparing two things means showing how they are the same. *Contrasting* two things means showing how they are different. Comparisons and contrasts are important because they show how things or ideas are related. Use these tips to help you understand comparison and contrast in reading assignments such as the article on the opposite page.

• Look for **direct statements** of **comparison and contrast.** "These things are similar because…" or "One major difference is…"

• Pay attention to **words and phrases that signal comparisons**, such as *also, both, is the same as,* and *in the same way.*

• Notice **words and phrases that signal contrasts**. Some of these are *however, still, but,* and *in contrast.*

MARK IT UP Read the article on the next page. Then use the information from the article and the tips above to answer the questions.

1. Circle the words and phrases that signal comparisons. A sample has been done for you.

2. Underline the words and phrases that signal contrast. Notice the sample that has been done.

3. A Venn diagram shows how two subjects are similar and how they are different. Complete this diagram, which uses information from the article to compare and contrast *la quinceañera* and a sweet sixteen party. Add one or more similarities to the center of the diagram and one or more differences to each outer circle.

La Quinceañera
takes place on girl's fifteenth birthday

Both
mark a girl's passage to adulthood

Sweet Sixteen Party
takes place on girl's sixteenth birthday

La Quinceañera and Sweet Sixteen

¡FELICIDADES!

Almost every culture has a ceremony to mark the passage of young people from childhood to adulthood. In the Latin culture, this rite of passage for girls is *la quinceañera*. For American girls, it is the sweet sixteen birthday party. Although both *la quinceañera* and the sweet sixteen birthday party commemorate a girl's passage to adulthood, they differ in when, where, and how the occasion is celebrated. *Quinceañera* means "fifteenth birthday," and that's when the celebration is held. In contrast, a sweet sixteen party takes place when, as the name suggests, a girl is a year older.

The origin of *la quinceañera* is uncertain, although it may have roots in the Aztec, Maya, or Toltec cultures. It generally involves celebration of a thanksgiving Mass followed by a lavish party for the extended family and friends. The *quinceañera* often dances a waltz with her father and other male relatives. In Mexico, girlfriends may give the celebrant a rag doll symbolizing her leaving childhood and its toys behind.

Sweet sixteen parties, on the other hand, do not include the religious component of *la quinceañera*. They also tend to be designed for the girl's friends rather than for her family. Like *quinceañeras*, however, they often are held in hotels or reception halls and include live bands, plentiful food, and many-tiered birthday cakes.

Both *quinceañeras* and sweet sixteeners take advantage of the opportunity to look as adult as possible. They generally deck themselves out in long dresses. *Quinceañeras* often choose frilly frocks in white or pastel colors topped by hats or headdresses. Sweet sixteen dresses can run the gamut from frothy and frilly to sleek and sophisticated.

So whether a girl celebrates *la quinceañera* or her sweet sixteen, the message is the same—"Welcome to adulthood!"

Persuasion

To be persuasive, an opinion should be backed up with reasons and facts. After you carefully read an opinion and the reasons and facts that support it, you will be able to decide if the opinion makes sense. As you read these tips, look at the sample persuasive essay on the next page.

• Look for words or phrases that **signal an opinion**, such as *I believe, I think,* and *in my opinion.*

• Identify reasons, facts, or expert opinions that **support** the position.

• Ask yourself if the opinion and the reasons that back it up **make sense.**

• Look for **errors in reasoning**, such as overgeneralizations, that may affect the presentation of the opinion.

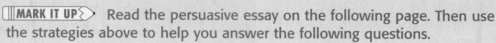 Read the persuasive essay on the following page. Then use the strategies above to help you answer the following questions.

1. Underline any words or phrases that signal the writer's opinion.

2. Circle any words or phrases that signal the opinion of persons other than the writer.

3. The writer presents both sides of this debate. List the points supporting both sides in the chart below. One reason has been provided for you.

For swimming pool	Against swimming pool
1. The school has a responsibility to teach swimming.	

Our School Needs to Get in the Swim *by Jorge Rojo*

This school needs a swimming pool. Swimming is an important life skill and I believe it is the responsibility of the school to provide this essential part of students' education.

The school's mission is to educate the whole person—mind and body—and to prepare students to be productive citizens. In addition to our academic subjects, we are taught how to eat right, budget our money, and drive a car. But we don't learn the water safety skills that could someday save our lives.

The community and school board obviously don't feel the way I do, however. They repeatedly have refused to fund the building of a pool. In the opinion of one board member, "Students can take swimming lessons at the local health club." Other school officials think that the school has more important needs—repairing the sagging gym floor and installing new lockers, for example.

In my opinion, these reasons are not valid. First, most students cannot afford lessons at the health club. Even those who have the money don't have the time. They're busy with homework and other activities during the school year and have to work or go to summer school during vacation.

I agree that the gym floor should be replaced and wouldn't mind having a new locker. But I believe that the educational needs of the students should come first. Swimming is one of the best forms of exercise there is. Even if knowing how to swim never saves your life, it can improve its quality. Isn't that what an education is all about?

Social studies class becomes easier when you understand how your textbook's words, pictures, and maps work together to give you information. Following these tips can make you a better reader of social studies lessons. As you read the tips, look at the sample lesson on the right-hand page.

A Read the **title** of the lesson and other **headings** to find out what the lesson is about. Smaller headings may introduce subtopics that are related to the main topic.

B Read the **main ideas** or **objectives** listed on the first page of the lesson. These items summarize the lesson and help set a purpose for your reading.

C Look at the **vocabulary terms** listed on the lesson's first page. These terms will be boldfaced or underlined where they appear in the text.

D Notice **how information is organized.** In social studies lessons, ideas are often presented using sequence, cause and effect, comparison and contrast, and main idea and supporting details.

E Carefully examine **visuals** such as photographs, boxed text, maps, charts, bulleted lists, time lines, and diagrams. Think about how the visuals and the text are related.

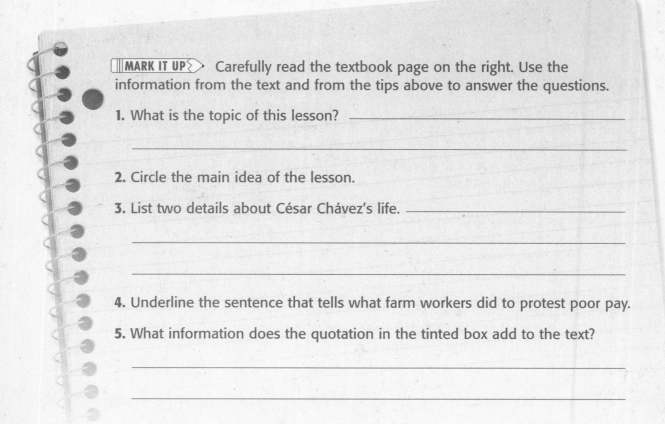

MARK IT UP Carefully read the textbook page on the right. Use the information from the text and from the tips above to answer the questions.

1. What is the topic of this lesson? _____

_____

2. Circle the main idea of the lesson.

3. List two details about César Chávez's life. _____

_____

_____

4. Underline the sentence that tells what farm workers did to protest poor pay.

5. What information does the quotation in the tinted box add to the text?

_____

_____

The Equal Rights Struggle Expands

TERMS & NAMES
César Chávez
National Congress of American Indians
Betty Friedan
NOW
ERA

B | MAIN IDEA | WHY IT MATTERS NOW |

The African-American struggle for equality inspired other groups to fight for equality.

Nonwhites and women continue to fight for equality today.

ONE AMERICAN'S STORY

César Chávez was born in Yuma, Arizona, in 1927. In the 1940s, he and his family worked as migrant laborers in the California fields. (Migrant workers travel from place to place in search of work.) One time, they found work picking peas. The whole family, parents and six children, worked. Chávez described the poor pay for such hard work.

A VOICE FROM THE PAST

They [the managers] would take only the peas they thought were good, and they only paid you for those. The pay was twenty cents a hamper, which had to weigh in at twenty-five pounds. So in about three hours, the whole family made only twenty cents.

César Chávez, *César Chávez: Autobiography of* La Causa

César Chávez, head of the National Farm Workers Association, marches with striking grape pickers in the 1960s. (*Huelga* is the Spanish word for strike.)

In 1962, Chávez decided to start a union for farm workers. But the owners refused to recognize the union. Chávez used the example set by Martin Luther King, Jr., to change their minds.

D Responding to Chávez's call, workers went on strike. Then Chávez asked people not to buy produce harvested by nonunion workers. The tactics worked. In 1970, 26 major California growers signed a contract with the union. It gave the workers higher wages and new benefits. The victory of Chávez and his union showed how the fight for equal rights spread beyond African Americans, as you will read in this section.

A Mexican Americans Organize

The farm workers' struggle inspired other Mexican Americans. By the 1960s, most Mexican Americans lived in cities in the Southwest and California. In 1970, Mexican Americans formed *La Raza Unida* (lah RAH•sah oo•NEE•dah)—"the united people." *La Raza* fought for better jobs, pay, education, and housing. It also worked to elect Mexican Americans to public office.

Mexican-American students also began to organize. They wanted reform in the school system. The students demanded such changes as

Reading a science textbook becomes easier when you understand how the explanations, drawings, and special terms work together. Use the strategies below to help you better understand your science textbook. Look at the examples on the opposite page as you read each strategy in this list.

A Preview the **title** and any **headings** to see what scientific concepts you will learn about.

B Read the **key ideas** or **objectives.** These items summarize the lesson and help set a purpose for your reading.

C Read the list of **vocabulary terms** that will be introduced and defined in the lesson.

D Notice the **boldfaced** and **italicized** terms in the text. Look for the definitions of these terms.

E Carefully examine any **pictures** or **diagrams.** Read the **captions** to see how the graphics help to illustrate the text.

MARK IT UP Use the strategies above and the science lesson on the next page to answer these questions.

1. Underline the title of the lesson.

2. Circle the list of vocabulary words that will appear in the lesson.

3. Draw a box around one boldfaced term in the lesson.

4. Examine the graph and read the text directly above it. What idea does the graph illustrate?

_____

_____

5. At what latitude is the elevation of the snow line lowest?

_____

_____

15.1

B KEY IDEAS

Glaciers are huge ice masses that move under the influence of gravity.

Glaciers form from compacted and recrystallized snow.

C KEY VOCABULARY

• glacier
• snow line
• firn
• valley glacier
• continental glacier
• ice cap

A # What Is a Glacier?

About 75 percent of Earth's fresh water is frozen in glaciers. A **glacier** is a large mass of compacted snow and ice that moves under the force of gravity. A glacier changes Earth's surface as it erodes geological features in one place and then redeposits the material elsewhere thus altering the landscape.

Where Glaciers Form

Glaciers form in areas that are always covered by snow. In such areas, more snow falls than melts each year; as a result layers of snow build up from previous years. Climates cold enough to cause such conditions may be found in any part of the world. Air temperatures drop as you climb high above sea level and as you travel farther from the equator.

Even in equatorial areas, however, a layer of permanent snow may exist on high mountains at high elevation. Farther from the equator, the elevation need not be so high for a layer of permanent snow to exist. In the polar areas, permanent snow may be found even at sea level. The lowest elevation at which the layer of permanent snow occurs in summer is called **D** the **snow line.** If a mountain is completely covered with snow in winter but without snow in summer, it has no snow line.

In general, the snow line occurs at lower and lower elevations as the latitudes approach the poles. The snow line also changes according to total yearly snowfall and the amount of solar exposure. Thus, the elevation of the snow line is not the same for all places at a given latitude.

E

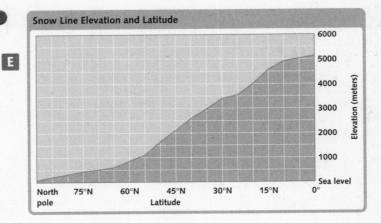

Snow Line Elevation and Latitude

How Glaciers Form

Except for bare rock cliffs, a mountain above the snow line is always buried in snow. Great basins below the highest peaks are filled with snow that can be hundreds of meters thick. In these huge snowfields, buried snow becomes compressed and recrystallizes into a rough, granular ice material called **firn** (feern) or névé (nay-VAY).

Mathematics

Reading in mathematics is different from reading in history, literature, or science. A math lesson has few words, but instead illustrates math concepts using numbers, symbols, formulas, equations, diagrams, and word problems. Use the following strategies, and the lesson on the next page, to help you better understand your math textbook.

A Scan the **title** and **headings** to see which math concepts you will learn about.

B Look for **goals, objectives** or **key ideas**. These help focus your reading.

C Read **explanations** carefully. Sometimes a concept is explained in more than one way to make sure you understand it.

D Look for **special features** such as study or technology tips or connections to real life. These provide more help or information.

E Study any **worked-out solutions** to sample problems. These are the key to understanding how to do the homework assignment.

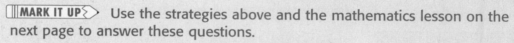 Use the strategies above and the mathematics lesson on the next page to answer these questions.

1. What is this lesson about? _____

_____

2. Put a star next to the goals of the lesson.

3. Underline the definition of scientific notation.

4. Circle the explanations of how to rewrite numbers in decimal form.

5. What practical application does scientific notation have in the real world?

_____

_____

8.4

Scientific Notation A

What you should learn

GOAL 1 Use scientific notation to represent numbers.

GOAL 2 Use scientific notation to describe **real-life** situations, such as the price per acre of the Alaska purchase in **Example 6**.

D *Why you should learn it*

▼ To solve **real-life** problems, such as finding the amount of water discharged by the Amazon River each year in **Example 5**.

REAL LIFE

GOAL 1 USING SCIENTIFIC NOTATION

A number is written in **scientific notation** if it is of the form $c \times 10^n$, where $1 \le c < 10$ and n is an integer. **C**

ACTIVITY
Developing Concepts

Investigating Scientific Notation

❶ Rewrite each number in decimal form.

   a. 6.43×10^4 **b.** 3.072×10^6 **c.** 4.2×10^{-2} **d.** 1.52×10^{-3}

❷ Describe a general rule for writing the decimal form of a number given in scientific notation. How many places do you move the decimal point? Do you move the decimal point left or right?

EXAMPLE 1 *Rewriting in Decimal Form*

Rewrite in decimal form.

   a. 2.834×10^2 **b.** 4.9×10^5 **c.** 7.8×10^{-1} **d.** 1.23×10^{-6}

SOLUTION **E**

   a. $2.834 \times 10^2 = 283.4$ Move decimal point right 2 places.

   b. $4.9 \times 10^5 = 490,000$ Move decimal point right 5 places.

   c. $7.8 \times 10^{-1} = 0.78$ Move decimal point left 1 place.

   d. $1.23 \times 10^{-6} = 0.00000123$ Move decimal point left 6 places.

EXAMPLE 2 *Rewriting in Scientific Notation*

   a. $34,690 = 3.469 \times 10^4$ Move decimal point left 4 places.

   b. $1.78 = 1.78 \times 10^0$ Move decimal point 0 places.

   c. $0.039 = 3.9 \times 10^{-2}$ Move decimal point right 2 places.

   d. $0.000722 = 7.22 \times 10^{-4}$ Move decimal point right 4 places.

   e. $5,600,000,000 = 5.6 \times 10^9$ Move decimal point left 9 places.

Reading an Application

To get a part-time job or to register for summer camp or classes at the local community center, you will have to fill out an application. Being able to understand the format of an application will help you fill it out correctly. Use the following strategies and the sample on the next page to help you understand any application.

A **Begin at the top.** Scan the application to understand the different sections.

B Look for special **instructions for filling out** the application.

C Note any **request for materials** or **special information** that must be included with the application.

D Watch for **sections you don't have to fill in** or **questions you don't have to answer.**

E Look for difficult or confusing words or abbreviations. Look them up in a dictionary or ask someone what they mean.

 **MARK IT UP** Use the warranty application on the following page and the strategies above to answer the questions.

1. Why is it important to fill out and mail this warranty application?

_____

_____

2. Underline the phrase that tells when the application must be mailed.

3. What information about the product do you have to supply?

_____

4. Circle the part of the application that you do not have to fill out.

5. What purchase document must you use to fill out this application?

_____

6. ASSESSMENT PRACTICE Circle the letter of the correct answer.
What amount should you include in the box marked "retail price paid"?
A. the total amount you paid for the product
B. the total amount you paid minus the cost of the maintenance agreement
C. the price marked on the product
D. the cost of extra charges, such as delivery and installation

A Congratulations on investing in a Calvo product. Your decision will reward you for years to come. Please complete your Warranty Registration Card to ensure that you receive all the privileges and protection that come with your purchase.

Your completed Warranty Registration Card serves as confirmation of ownership in the event of theft.

Returning the attached card guarantees you'll receive all the special offers for which your purchase makes you eligible.

- - - - - - - - - - - - - - - - - **DETACH AND MAIL PORTION BELOW.** -

USA Limited Warranty Registration	
123456 XXXX	A B C D E F G 7 6 5 4 3 2 1
MODEL NUMBER	SERIAL NUMBER

Registering your product ensures that you receive all of the benefits you are entitled to as a Calvo customer. Complete the information below in ink, and drop this card in the nearest mailbox.

B █ IMPORTANT - RETURN WITHIN TEN DAYS █

Date of Purchase

Your Name

First   Initial   Last

Address

Street   Apt. #

City   State   ZIP Code

C **Retail Price Paid** $ ⬜ .00

(Excluding sales tax, maintenance agreement, delivery, installation, and trade-in allowance.) **E**

D **Your Phone Number** (optional)

Area Code   Phone Number

CALVO

Public notices can tell you about events in your community and give you valuable information about safety. When you read a public notice, follow these tips. Each tip relates to a specific part of the notice on the next page.

A Read the notice's **title,** if it has one. The title often gives the main idea or purpose of the notice.

B See if there is a logo, credit, or other way of telling **who created the notice.**

C Ask yourself, **"Who should read this notice?"** If the information in it might be important to you or someone you know, then you should pay attention to it.

D Look for **contact information** that indicates where to get answers to questions.

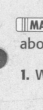

MARK IT UP Use the public notice on the next page and the strategies above to answer the questions.

1. What is the purpose of this notice?

_____

2. Circle the name of the organization that created the notice.

3. Who does this notice apply to?

_____

4. Make a star next to the contact information.

5. Who should get a flu shot earliest—health care workers or healthy people 50–64 years old?

_____

6. ASSESSMENT PRACTICE Circle the letter of the correct answer.
The best time to get a flu shot is
A. your doctor's decision
B. October or November
C. October
D. December

When should *YOU* get your flu shot?

	OCT | NOV	DEC or later
People at high risk of severe illness ✓ **65 years old or older**—Even in you're in great health ✓ **Children 6–23 months old**—Children younger than 2 years old have one of the highest rates of hospitalizations from influenza ✓ **Adults and children with a chronic health condition**—Such as heart disease, diabetes, kidney disease, asthma, cancer, and HIV/AIDS ✓ **More than 3 months pregnant during flu season**—Typically November through March	**Best Time**	**Not too late!**
People who can give the flu to those at high risk ✓ **Household contact or caregiver of someone at high risk** ✓ **Health care workers** ✓ **Household contact or caregiver of a child under 2 years old**—Infants younger than 6 months old can't get a flu shot, but they can get the flu	**Best Time**	**Not too late!**
Your child's very first flu shot ✓ **Children 6 months–8 years old** getting the very first flu shot need a booster shot one month after the first dose of vaccine	**Best Time**	**Not too late!**
Healthy people 50–64 years old	**Best Time**	**Not too late!**
Anyone who wants to prevent the flu	**Best Time**	**Not too late!**

A flu shot is your best protection against the flu.

For more information: Ask your health care provider or call the CDC Immunization Hotline.

English: 1-800-232-2522   Español: 1-800-232-0233   www.cdc.gov/nip/flu

DEPARTMENT OF HEALTH & HUMAN SERVICES • USA

CDC Immunization   SAFER • HEALTHIER • PEOPLE

Fight the Flu

Reading a Web Page

When you research information for a report or project, you may use the World Wide Web. Once you find the site you want, the strategies below will help you find the facts and details you need. Look at the sample Web page on the right as you read each of the strategies.

A Notice the page's **Web address,** or URL. Write down the Web address or bookmark it if you think you might return to the page at another time or if you need to add it to a list of sources.

B Read the **title** of the page. The title usually tells you what topics the page covers.

C Look for **menu bars** along the top, bottom, or side of the page. These guide you to other parts of the site that may be useful.

D Notice any **links** to other parts of the site or to related pages. Links are often highlighted in color or underlined.

E Many sites have a link that allows you to **contact** the creators with questions or feedback.

F Use a **search feature** to find out quickly whether the information you want to locate appears anywhere on the site.

MARK IT UP Look at the Web page on the right. Then use the information from the Web page and the tips above to answer the questions.

1. Circle the Web address of this site.

2. Draw boxes around two places you can search the site to see if it contains the information you need.

3. What is the name of the president of NLN? _____

4. Put a star by the link you should click on to make an online contribution to NLN.

5. **ASSESSMENT PRACTICE** Circle the letter of the best answer.
   This site is designed to give information about
   A. issues of interest to Latinos
   B. Latino education
   C. raising Latino children
   D. politicians Latinos should vote for

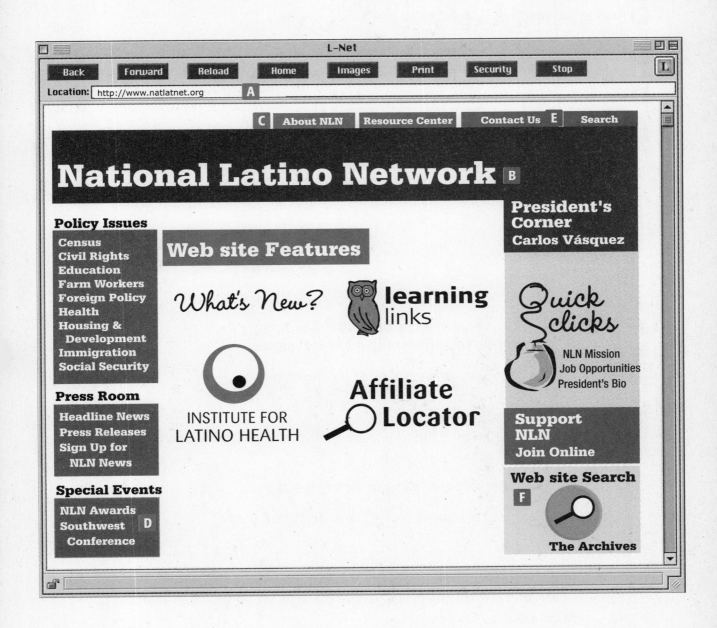

L-Net

Back   Forward   Reload   Home   Images   Print   Security   Stop   L

Location: http://www.natlatnet.org   A

C   About NLN   Resource Center   Contact Us   E   Search

National Latino Network   B

Policy Issues

Census
Civil Rights
Education
Farm Workers
Foreign Policy
Health
Housing &
   Development
Immigration
Social Security

Press Room

Headline News
Press Releases
Sign Up for
   NLN News

Special Events

NLN Awards
Southwest   D
   Conference

Web site Features

What's New?

learning
links

INSTITUTE FOR
LATINO HEALTH

Affiliate
Locator

President's Corner
Carlos Vásquez

Quick
Clicks

NLN Mission
Job Opportunities
President's Bio

Support NLN
Join Online

Web site Search
F

The Archives

Reading technical directions will help you understand how to use the products you buy. Use the following tips to help you read a variety of technical directions.

A Look carefully at any **diagrams** or **other images** of the product.

B **Read all the directions** carefully at least once before using the product.

C Notice **headings** or **lines** that separate one section from another.

D Look for **numbers, letters,** or **bullets** that give the steps in sequence.

E Watch for **warnings** or **notes** with more information.

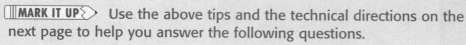

MARK IT UP Use the above tips and the technical directions on the next page to help you answer the following questions.

1. What kind of battery do you need for the clock?

   _____

2. How do you know if the time displayed is AM or PM? Circle the answer on the next page.

3. Underline the steps to follow in setting the alarm.

4. How long will the alarm sound if you don't turn it off?

   _____

5. **ASSESSMENT PRACTICE** Circle the letter of the correct answer.
   Which of the following is NOT a safe place to set up the clock radio?
   A. on a stable, flat desk
   B. in the bathroom
   C. away from open windows
   D. on a bedside table

B

Alarm Clock Radio
INSTRUCTIONS FOR USE

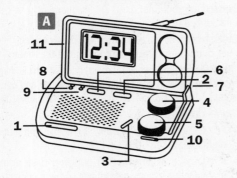

A

11
8
9
1
3
12:34
6
2
7
4
5
10

1. SNOOZE/LIGHT BUTTON
2. FUNCTION SWITCH
3. BAND SWITCH
4. TUNING CONTROL
5. VOLUME CONTROL
6. TIME/ALARM SET SWITCH
7. BATTERY DOOR (RADIO)
8. HOUR BUTTON
9. MINUTE BUTTON
10. EJECT BUTTON
11. BATTERY HOLDER (CLOCK)

BATTERIES
FOR RADIO:
To insert batteries, remove the BATTERY DOOR (7) and insert 2 AAA batteries, observing the correct position of the polarity.

FOR CLOCK:
Pull out the BATTERY HOLDER (11). Use a 1.5 volt battery and place with positive electrode facing front. Reinsert battery holder.

C HOW TO PLAY THE RADIO
- Press the EJECT BUTTON (10) to open lid.
- Turn the FUNCTION SWITCH (2) TO "ON" position.
- Use the BAND SWITCH (3) to select broadcasting band (AM or FM).
- Turn the TUNING CONTROL knob (4) to select the listening station.

D TO SET THE TIME
- Slide the TIME/ALARM SET SWITCH (6) to the "T.SET" position.
- Depress the HOUR BUTTON (8) until the correct hour is displayed. Be careful to set time to AM or PM as required. When PM time is registered, a "P" will apppear on the display.
- Depress the MINUTE BUTTON (9) until the correct minute is reached.

TO SET THE ALARM
- Slide the TIME/ALARM SET SWITCH (6) to the "AL.SET" position. "AL" indicator will appear on the display.
- Depress the HOUR BUTTON (8) until the desired alarm hour is displayed. Be careful to correctly set alarm to AM or PM as required. When PM time is registered, a "P" will appear on the display.
- Depress the MINUTE BUTTON (9) until the desired alarm time is reached.

WAKE TO ALARM
- Set the FUNCTION SWITCH (2) TO "ALARM" position. When the desired alarm time is reached, you will hear a sequential "BEEP" alarm for 60 seconds.
- To shut the alarm off temporarily, press the SNOOZE/LIGHT BUTTON (1) once. The alarm will stop for 4 minutes, then come on again.
- To stop the alarm completely, set the FUNCTION SWITCH (2) to "OFF" position.

WAKE TO MUSIC
- Set the FUNCTION SWITCH (2) TO "AUTO" position.
- The radio will turn on automatically at your desired alarm time.

SAFETY PRECAUTIONS **E**
- Do not place the unit near a moisture environment, such as a bathtub, kitchen, sink, etc. The unit should be well protected from rain, dew, condensation, or any form of dampness.
- Do not place the unit on surfaces with strong vibration. Place the unit only on flat, stable, and level surfaces.

Product Information: Directions for Use

Many of the products you buy come with instructions that tell you how to use them correctly. Directions for use may appear on the product itself, on its packaging, or on a separate insert. Learning to read and follow directions for use is important for your safety. As you read each strategy below, look at the sample.

A Read any **headings** to find out what kinds of information are given with the product.

B Read the directions, which usually tell you *why, how, when,* and *where* to use the product, *how much to use, how often,* and *when* to stop using it.

C Carefully read any **warnings** given with the product. The manufacturer will usually tell you what to do if you experience any problems.

D Look for any **contact information** that tells you where to call or write if you have a question about the product.

Solution of Hydrogen Peroxide 3% U.S.P.

Active ingredient: Hydrogen peroxide 3% **A**

Inactive ingredients: 0.001% Phosphoric Acid as a stabilizer and purified water

Indications: For topical use to help prevent infection in minor cuts, burns, and abrasions, or to cleanse the mouth.

Directions: Apply locally to affected areas. To cleanse the mouth, dilute with an equal amount of water and use as a gargle or rinse. Do not use in excess of ten consecutive days. **B**

Warnings: C

• FOR EXTERNAL USE: Topically to the skin and mucous membranes. KEEP OUT OF EYES.

• If redness, irritation, swelling, or pain persists or increases or if infection occurs, discontinue use and consult a physician.

• KEEP THIS AND ALL DRUGS OUT OF THE REACH OF CHILDREN. **In case of accidental ingestion, seek professional assistance or contact a Poison Control Center immediately**.

Storage: Keep bottle tightly closed and at controlled room temperature 59°–86° F (15°–30° C). Do not shake bottle.

Questions? (888) 555-1234 **D**

MARK IT UP Use the product directions to help you answer these questions.

1. How do you use the product to cleanse your mouth? _____

_____

2. Circle the active ingredient in this product.

3. What should you do if someone accidentally swallows this product? Underline the answer.

4. Draw a box around the number you should call if you have questions about the product.

5. **ASSESSMENT PRACTICE** Circle the letter of the correct answer. When should you stop using this product?

A. when the temperature drops below 59° F

B. if pain and swelling increase

C. if you have a minor abrasion

D. ten days after you buy it

Reading a Bus Schedule

Knowing how to read a bus schedule accurately can help you get where you need to go–on time. Look at the sample bus schedule as you read the tips below.

A Look at the **title** to know what the schedule covers.

B Identify **labels** that show **dates** or **days of the week** to help you understand how the daily or weekly schedule works.

C Look at **place labels** to know what stops are listed on the schedule.

D Look for **expressions of time** to know what hours or minutes are listed on the schedule.

E Pay attention to the **organization** of the information. Read across the row to see when a bus will reach each location.

A Route 238   Quincy Center Station - Holbrook/Randolph Commuter Rail Station via Crawford Sq.

WEEKDAY MORNINGS **B**

C Leave Quincy Station	Leave S. Shore Plaza	Leave Crawford Square	Arrive Holb./Rand. Commuter Rail Sta.	Leave Holb./Rand. Commuter Rail Sta.	Leave Crawford Square	Leave S. Shore Plaza	Arrive Quincy Station
D 5:25A	5:43A	5:58A	...	6:25A	6:29A	6:42A	7:08A
6:10	6:28	6:43	6:47A	6:50	6:54	7:07	7:35
6:25	6:43	6:58	7:03	7:20	7:25	7:38	8:06
6:45	7:03	7:19	7:24	7:50	7:55	8:08	8:36
7:05	7:25	7:41	7:46	8:25	8:30	8:43	9:11	**E**
7:30	7:50	8:06	8:11	8:55	9:00	9:13	9:41
7:55	8:15	8:31	8:36	9:25	9:30	9:46	10:14
8:15	8:35	8:51	8:56	10:05	10:10	10:26	10:54
9:10	9:30	9:46	9:51	11:00	11:05	11:21	11:49
10:05	10:25	10:41	10:46				
10:55	11:15	11:31	11:36				

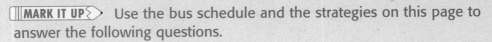 **MARK IT UP**   Use the bus schedule and the strategies on this page to answer the following questions.

1. Circle the name of one stop on this route.

_____

_____

2. What time does the last bus leave Quincy Station for Holb./Rand. Commuter Rail Station on weekday mornings?

_____

3. If you took the 7:25 AM bus from Crawford Square, when would you arrive at Quincy Station?

4. ASSESSMENT PRACTICE Circle the letter of the correct answer. If you have a 10:15 meeting at S. Shore Plaza on Tuesday, what's the latest bus you can take from Holb./Rand. Commuter Rail Station?

A. 8:25   **B.** 8:55   **C.** 9:25   **D.** 10:05

Test Preparation Strategies

In this section you'll find strategies and practice to help you with many different kinds of standardized tests. The strategies apply to questions based on long and short readings, as well as questions about charts, graphs, and product labels. You'll also find examples and practice for revising-and-editing tests and writing tests. Applying the strategies to the practice materials and thinking through the answers will help you succeed in many formal testing situations.

Test Preparation Strategies

You can prepare for tests in several ways. First, study and understand the content that will be on the test. Second, learn as many test-taking techniques as you can. These techniques will help you better understand the questions and how to answer them. Following are some general suggestions for preparing for and taking tests. Starting on page 206, you'll find more detailed suggestions and test-taking practice.

Successful Test Taking

 Study Content Throughout the Year

1. **Master the content of your class.** The best way to study for tests is to read, understand, and review the content of your class. Read your daily assignments carefully. Study the notes that you have taken in class. Participate in class discussions. Work with classmates in small groups to help one another learn. You might trade writing assignments and comment on your classmates' work.

2. **Use your textbook for practice.** Your textbook includes many different types of questions. Some may ask you to talk about a story you just read. Others may ask you to figure out what's wrong with a sentence or how to make a paragraph sound better. Try answering these questions out loud and in writing. This type of practice can make taking a test much easier.

3. **Learn how to understand the information in charts, maps, and graphic organizers.** One type of test question may ask you to look at a graphic organizer, such as a spider map, and explain something about the information you see there. Another type of question may ask you to look at a map to find a particular place. You'll find charts, maps, and graphic organizers to study in your textbook. You'll also find charts, maps, and graphs in your science, mathematics, literature, and social studies textbooks. When you look at these, ask yourself, What information is being presented and why is it important?

4. **Practice taking tests.** Use copies of tests you have taken in the past or in other classes for practice. Every test has a time limit, so set a timer for 15 or 20 minutes and then begin your practice. Try to finish the test in the time you've given yourself.

☑ **Reading Check** In what practical way can your textbook help you prepare for a test?

5. Talk about test-taking experiences. After you've taken a classroom test or quiz, talk about it with your teacher and classmates. Which types of questions were the hardest to understand? What made them difficult? Which questions seemed easiest, and why? When you share test-taking techniques with your classmates, everyone can become a successful test taker.

 ## Use Strategies During the Test

1. Read the directions carefully. You can't be a successful test taker unless you know exactly what you are expected to do. Look for key words and phrases, such as *circle the best answer, write a paragraph,* or *choose the word that best completes each sentence.*

2. Learn how to read test questions. Test questions can sometimes be difficult to figure out. They may include unfamiliar language or be written in an unfamiliar way. Try rephrasing the question in a simpler way using words you understand. Always ask yourself, What type of information does this question want me to provide?

3. Pay special attention when using a separate answer sheet. If you accidentally skip a line on an answer sheet, all the rest of your answers may be wrong! Try one or more of the following techniques:

- Use a ruler on the answer sheet to make sure you are placing your answers on the correct line.

- After every five answers, check to make sure you're on the right line.

- Each time you turn a page of the test booklet, check to make sure the number of the question is the same as the number of the answer line on the answer sheet.

- If the answer sheet has circles, fill them in neatly. A stray pencil mark might cause the scoring machine to count the answer as incorrect.

4. If you're not sure of the answer, make your best guess. Unless you've been told that there is a penalty for guessing, choose the answer that you think is likeliest to be correct.

5. Keep track of the time. Answering all the questions on a test usually results in a better score. That's why finishing the test is important. Keep track of the time you have left. At the beginning of the test, figure out how many questions you will have to answer by the halfway point in order to finish in the time given.

☑ **Reading Check** What are at least two good ways to avoid skipping lines on an answer sheet?

Understand Types of Test Questions

Most tests include two types of questions: multiple choice and open-ended. Specific strategies will help you understand and correctly answer each type of question.

A **multiple-choice question** has two parts. The first part is the question itself, called the stem. The second part is a series of possible answers. Usually four possible answers are provided, and only one of them is correct. Your task is to choose the correct answer. Here are some strategies to help you do just that.

1. Read and think about each question carefully before looking at the possible answers.

2. Pay close attention to key words in the question. For example, look for the word *not*, as in "Which of the following is not a cause of the conflict in this story?"

3. Read and think about all of the possible answers before making your choice.

4. Reduce the number of choices by eliminating any answers you know are incorrect. Then, think about why some of the remaining choices might also be incorrect.

- If two of the choices are pretty much the same, both are probably wrong.

- Answers that contain any of the following words are usually incorrect: *always, never, none, all,* and *only.*

5. If you're still unsure about an answer, see if any of the following applies:

- When one choice is longer and more detailed than the others, it is often the correct answer.

- When a choice repeats a word that is in the question, it may be the correct answer.

- When two choices are direct opposites, one of them is likely the correct answer.

- When one choice includes one or more of the other choices, it is often the correct answer.

- When a choice includes the word *some* or *often*, it may be the correct answer.

- If one of the choices is *All of the above*, make sure that at least two of the other choices seem correct.

- If one of the choices is *None of the above*, make sure that none of the other choices seems correct.

☑ **Reading Check** What words in a multiple-choice question probably signal a wrong answer?

An **open-ended test item** can take many forms. It might ask you to write a word or phrase to complete a sentence. You might be asked to create a chart, draw a map, or fill in a graphic organizer. Sometimes, you will be asked to write one or more paragraphs in response to a writing prompt. Use the following strategies when reading and answering open-ended items:

1. If the item includes directions, read them carefully. Take note of any steps required.

2. Look for key words and phrases in the item as you plan how you will respond. Does the item ask you to identify a cause-and-effect relationship or to compare and contrast two or more things? Are you supposed to provide a sequence of events or make a generalization? Does the item ask you to write an essay in which you state your point of view and then try to persuade others that your view is correct?

3. If you're going to be writing a paragraph or more, plan your answer. Jot down notes and a brief outline of what you want to say before you begin writing.

4. Focus your answer. Don't include everything you can think of, but be sure to include everything the item asks for.

5. If you're creating a chart or drawing a map, make sure your work is as clear as possible.

☑ **Reading Check** What are at least three key strategies for answering an open-ended question?

Reading Test Model
LONG SELECTIONS

DIRECTIONS Following is an excerpt from an article entitled "The Empire of the Aztecs." Read the excerpt carefully. The notes in the side columns will help you prepare for the types of questions that are likely to follow a reading like this. You might want to preview the questions on pages 212–213 before you begin reading.

from The Empire of the Aztecs

When the Spanish explorer Hernán Cortés marched into the Aztec capital of Tenochtitlán in 1519, he was amazed at what he found. Tenochtitlán, the site of present-day Mexico City, was built on two islands in the middle of Lake Texcoco. Tenochtitlán was connected to the mainland by causeways, or raised earthen roads. The city was much larger and more populous than any city in Spain. The people enjoyed a sophisticated lifestyle fueled by a prosperous economy. In fact, life in the Aztec empire five hundred years ago was remarkably similar to life in Mexico today.

Family Life The family was at the center of Aztec society. An Aztec family usually consisted of a husband and wife, their unmarried children, and some of the husband's relatives. Everyone had a role to play that contributed to the family's well-being. The husband supported the family by farming or working at a craft. His wife tended to the home. She cooked and wove cloth, which she used to make the family's clothing. Each family belonged to a larger social group

READING STRATEGIES FOR ASSESSMENT

Find the author's main idea. Think about the focus of the article. What has the author set out to do?

called a *calpolli*. The *calpolli* was made up of closely related families who shared farmland. Its structure was similar to a small village.

Boys were taught by their fathers until around age 10. Then they attended schools established by their *calpolli*, where they received a general education and military training. Some children, especially the children of noble families, attended temple schools. There they received the religious training necessary to become priests or community leaders.

Housing The type of house an Aztec family occupied depended on where the family lived. At higher elevations, the climate required houses made of adobe, a mixture of sun-dried earth and straw. In the lowlands, where the climate was milder, houses were constructed with branches or reeds cemented together with clay. They were then topped with thatched roofs. Most homes consisted of several buildings: the main dwelling where the family lived and worked, a sweathouse for taking steam baths, and a storehouse.

Clothing In Aztec society, most people wore similar types of clothing. Men wore a piece of cloth that encircled their hips and a cape that was knotted over one shoulder. Women wore a wraparound skirt topped by a loose, sleeveless blouse.

Draw conclusions How are Aztec families similar to families today? How are they different?

Notice topic sentences. A topic sentence reveals the purpose of a paragraph by telling you what the paragraph is about.

As in many societies today, clothing was an indicator of social and economic status. The clothing most ordinary Aztecs wore was woven from the coarse fibers of the maguey plant. Nobles, however, enjoyed clothing made from soft cotton cloth. In addition, their clothing was often decorated with feathers and other ornaments to signal their status in society.

Diet The Aztecs dined on meat and vegetables, and some of their dishes remain popular to this day. Hunters brought home ducks, geese, rabbits, and deer. The farms of the *calpolli* provided corn, avocados, squashes, papayas, sweet potatoes, beans, and tomatoes.

A staple of the Aztec diet was the *tlaxcalli*, a thin pancake made from corn. We know it today by its Spanish name—*tortilla*. *Tlaxcallis* often were used to scoop up other foods. When the Aztecs wrapped *tlaxcallis* around bits of meat or vegetables, they called the result *tacos*.

The favorite beverage of the Aztecs was a drink made from chocolate. Because chocolate was made from expensive cacao beans, only wealthy nobles could enjoy it regularly.

Economy As in modern societies, the success of the Aztec empire was largely due to its economy. The Aztec economy was based on agriculture. In addition to fruits and vegetables, the Aztecs grew cotton and cacao beans and harvested latex to make rubber.

Aztec agricultural methods were similar to methods still in use today. In heavily forested areas, farmers used a technique called "slash-and-burn." They would cut down the trees and burn them, making a clearing in which crops could be planted. Where the landscape was hilly, farmers cut terraces into the hills. These terraces greatly increased the acreage of level land that could be farmed. In wetland areas, farmers created islands, called *chinampas*, by scooping and piling up the fertile mud of the wetland.

The bounty from the Aztec farmlands, along with the works of artists and craftspeople, found its way to marketplaces throughout the empire. The largest market anywhere in the Americas was in the city of Tlatelolco. Cortés himself estimated that this market attracted over 60,000 traders each day. The Aztecs traded because they had no money in the modern sense of that word. Instead, they offered one type of good in exchange for another type—cacao beans for a richly decorated blouse, for example, or a jaguar pelt for brightly colored bird feathers.

Language The language the Aztec spoke, *Nahuatl*, belonged to a family of languages called Aztec-Tanoan. This language family included languages spoken by Native

Notice supporting details. What three types of farming methods did the Aztecs use? Where did they use each type?

Think about the author's purpose. Is this article meant to inform, persuade, entertain, or describe?

Americans, including the Comanche and the Shoshone.

The Aztecs had a written language, but it was based on pictures, not unlike the hieroglyphs of ancient Egypt. Each picture represented either an idea or the sound of a *Nahuatl* syllable. Because their written language was limited, the Aztecs used it mainly for government and religious purposes.

The Arts Artistic expression was important to the Aztecs. They created monumental sculptures to decorate their temples and other important buildings. Craft workers produced beautiful metalware, pottery, wood carvings, and weavings.

The Aztecs valued music and literature as well. Flutes, rattles, and drums provided a musical background for religious ceremonies. Poetry and historical accounts were handed down orally through the generations.

Religion The central focus of Aztec life was religion, and this is where Aztec society differed greatly from societies today. Hundreds of Aztec gods and goddesses presided over every aspect of human life: farming, the weather, war, fertility, the sun, the wind, and fire, to name just a few. In addition to a 365-day solar calendar, the Aztecs also had a 260-day religious calendar.

This calendar helped Aztec priests decide the best time of the year to plant crops, go to war, or build new temples.

The Aztec gods demanded a great deal of attention from their followers. To appease their gods, the Aztecs held many religious ceremonies. The centerpiece of these ceremonies was human sacrifice. The Aztecs believed that the gods drew strength and bravery from the blood of sacrificial victims. Most of the victims were slaves or prisoners of war. In fact, the Aztecs sometimes went to war just to get prisoners for their religious ceremonies.

Now answer questions 1–6. Base your answers on the excerpt from "The Empire of the Aztecs." Then check yourself by reading through the Answer Strategies in the side columns.

Understand the meaning of *purpose*. An author's purpose is his or her reason for writing. Just because a selection is entertaining doesn't necessarily mean entertainment was the author's reason for writing.

1 Which of the following best describes the author's purpose?

   A. to entertain

   B. to inform

   C. to describe

   D. to persuade

Read foreign words and phrases carefully. This excerpt uses many foreign words and phrases. Be sure you locate the one asked for in the question before you choose an answer.

2 What is a *tlaxcalli*?

   A. a thin corn pancake

   B. a drink made from cacao

   C. a *tortilla* wrapped around meat or vegetables

   D. a social group

Find main ideas. Remember that the main idea of a piece of writing describes what the author will talk about throughout the *entire* selection and not just one part of it.

3 Which of the following best expresses the author's main idea?

   A. Hernán Cortés was amazed when he first saw the Aztec city of Tenochtitlán.

   B. The Aztecs enjoyed a sophisticated lifestyle.

   C. Life in the Aztec empire was similar in many ways to life today.

   D. The family was at the center of Aztec society.

4 Which of the following is NOT a conclusion you can draw about how Aztec and modern families are alike?

   A. Children went to school for their education.

   B. Parents provided for their families.

   C. Families are part of larger social groups.

   D. Relatives of the husband live with the husband's family.

Note key words. Pay attention to the key word or words in the question. The key word here is *not*.

5 Which method of farming involved clearing the forest?

   A. slash-and-burn

   B. crop rotation

   C. cutting terraces

   D. creating islands

Don't rely on memory. Each of the responses to this question is a type of farming. One of them, however, is never mentioned in the excerpt. Before answering, look back at the excerpt and find the types that *are* mentioned.

6 In what ways is the Aztec religion similar to and different from modern religions?

Plan your response. Read the question carefully. This question asks you to compare and contrast. Look for similarities and differences and state them in your own words.

Sample short response for question 6:

The Aztec religion shares many similarities with modern religions. The Aztecs recognized the existence of gods. They believed these gods would protect them if they respected and worshipped the gods. Also, the Aztecs held regular religious services and ceremonies. The most important difference between the Aztec religion and modern religions is human sacrifice. Today, people pray to their god or gods and make offerings, but no religions practice human sacrifice.

Study your response. Notice how the writer follows the same organization as the question—similarities first and then differences.

Answers:
1. B, 2. A, 3. A, 4. C, 5. A

Reading Test Practice
LONG SELECTIONS

DIRECTIONS Now it's time to practice what you've learned about reading test items and choosing the best answers. Read the following selection, "The Gauchos of the Pampa." Use the side columns to make notes about the important parts of this selection: the setting, important ideas, comparisons and contrasts, difficult vocabulary, interesting details, and so on.

The Gauchos of the Pampa

In the mythology of Argentina, no one sits taller in the saddle than the gauchos. Part expert horsemen and part outlaws, these free spirits of the Pampas played a brief but crucial role in the development of cattle ranching and agriculture in Argentina. Although the gaucho era lasted barely a century, it remains an essential part of Argentina's culture, celebrated in literature and song.

La Pampa Stretching across central Argentina from the Atlantic coast to the foothills of the Andes, *la Pampa*, the Pampa, is a nearly flat plain. It is bordered to the north by the Gran Chaco and to the south by Patagonia. The Quechuas gave the Pampa its name. In their language it means "flat surface." Today, the region is commonly known as "the Pampas." It was onto this great plain that the Spanish introduced both cattle and horses. Soon, great herds of these animals were running wild throughout the eastern Pampas.

The Rise of the Gauchos Portuguese, Dutch, British, and French traders were eager to exploit the resources provided by the herds, namely hides and tallow, a waxy white fat used to make soap and candles. In turn, the horsemen of the Pampas were eager to help the traders because cattle and horse rustling was a profitable, if illegal, business. Thus were born the gauchos, who soon established their own culture on the plains of Argentina.

The gauchos lived simply, in mud huts with thatched roofs, sleeping on piles of hides. They formed families and had children, but their marriages were rarely officially recognized by the state or the church. Favorite pastimes of the gauchos included horseback riding and guitar playing.

Tools of the Gaucho Trade Everything about the gaucho lifestyle was geared to existence on the plains, including their clothing. Typically, a gaucho wore long, accordion-pleated trousers called *bombachas* that were tucked securely into high leather boots. A wide silver belt was cinched at the waist. A warm woolen poncho and a brightly colored scarf completed the costume.

The gaucho's weapons were simple and effective: a lasso, a sharp knife, and, most importantly, a *boleadora*, or *bola*. The bola consisted of three long leather cords attached at one end. At the other end of each cord was a stone or iron ball. Galloping after a stampeding herd of horses or cattle, the gaucho would twirl the bola in the air and then release it, parallel to the ground, at the legs of a fleeing animal. The bola would wrap itself around the animal's legs and send it crashing to the ground.

The End of an Era Toward the end of the 18th century, many of the gauchos had become legitimate animal handlers. They were hired by businessmen who had acquired large herds of wild cattle and horses. Then, during the 19th century, large tracts of the Pampas were carved into vast ranches called *estancias* or estates. The wild animals of the Pampas were slowly replaced with purebred stock from Europe. Railroads were built across the Pampas to transport livestock and tractors replaced horses on the ranches. The gaucho lifestyle had come to an end, and the remaining gauchos were now *peones*, or farmhands.

Celebrating the Gaucho Although the gaucho lifestyle ended, the gaucho legend lives on. During the heyday of the gaucho, a rich literary tradition had begun chronicling their exploits. In 1872, José Hernández wrote his epic poem *El gaucho Martín Fierro (The Gaucho Martin Fierro)*. Fifteen years later, the celebrated gaucho minstrel Santos Vega was the subject of three poems by Rafael Obligado. As late as 1926, Argentinian writer Ricardo Güiraldes added to the body of gaucho literature with *Don Segundo Sombra: Shadows in the Pampas*.

Like the age of the American cowboy, the gaucho era was a colorful time in the history of the Pampas. Even today, the legend and spirit of the gaucho is kept alive through traveling gaucho shows, reminders of a time when the Pampas and the proud, independent people who lived there shaped the future of Argentina.

Now answer questions 1–7. Base your answers on the selection "The Gauchos of the Pampa."

1 Which of the following best describes the main idea of this selection?

A. The gauchos were free spirits.

B. The gauchos played a crucial role in the development of cattle ranching and agriculture.

C. The gaucho era lasted barely a century.

D. The gauchos were expert horsemen and outlaws.

2 Patagonia lies in which direction from the Pampas?

A. north

B. west

C. east

D. south

3 Why did the gauchos agree to help the European traders?

A. Cattle rustling was illegal.

B. Cattle rustling was profitable.

C. Cattle rustling was an outlaw's trade.

D. Cattle rustling was not profitable.

4 Which of the following does NOT describe the gaucho lifestyle?

A. The gauchos lived on large ranches.

B. The gauchos lived in mud huts.

C. The gauchos enjoyed playing the guitar.

D. The gauchos slept on piles of hides.

5 Why was the bola an effective weapon?

    A. It had long leather cords attached at one end.

    B. It was easy to twirl and throw.

    C. It had three heavy stone or iron balls.

    D. It tripped the animal being hunted so the animal could no longer run.

6 Why does the author describe the gauchos as "proud, independent people"?

    A. because they were outlaws

    B. because they endured harsh conditions on the Pampas

    C. because they made a living successfully by their own rules

    D. because they agreed to work for others

7 Explain why the era of the gauchos came to an end.

THINKING IT THROUGH

The notes in the side columns will help you think through your answers. See the answer key at the bottom of the next page. How well did you do?

Each answer lists a detail from the opening paragraph. However, since the main idea tells about the focus of the *entire* selection, you can easily eliminate three of the four choices.

1 Which of the following best describes the main idea of this selection?

  A. The gauchos were free spirits.

  B. The gauchos played a crucial role in the development of cattle ranching and agriculture.

  C. The gaucho era lasted barely a century.

  D. The gauchos were expert horsemen and outlaws.

Skim the reading looking for the key word *Patagonia*.

2 Patagonia lies in which direction from the Pampas?

  A. north

  B. west

  C. east

  D. south

Notice that answer choices A and C say the same thing. Answer choices B and D are opposites—a good clue that either B or D is the correct answer.

3 Why did the gauchos agree to help the European traders?

  A. Cattle rustling was illegal.

  B. Cattle rustling was profitable.

  C. Cattle rustling was an outlaw's trade.

  D. Cattle rustling was not profitable.

Read the question carefully. A word printed in capital letters is important to understanding the question correctly.

4 Which of the following does NOT describe the gaucho lifestyle?

  A. The gauchos lived on large ranches.

  B. The gauchos lived in mud huts.

  C. The gauchos enjoyed playing the guitar.

  D. The gauchos slept on piles of hides.

5 Why was the bola an effective weapon?

    A. It had long leather cords attached at one end.

    B. It was easy to twirl and throw.

    C. It had three heavy stone or iron balls.

    D. It tripped the animal being hunted so the animal could no longer run.

> Notice that the first three choices just describe properties of the bola. Only the last choice describes how the bola worked to bring down prey.

6 Why does the author describe the gauchos as "proud, independent people"?

    A. because they were outlaws

    B. because they endured harsh conditions on the Pampas

    C. because they made a living successfully by their own rules

    D. because they agreed to work for others

> This question asks you to infer meaning. What do "proud" and "independent" mean? Which answer choice reflects the meaning of the two words?

7 Explain why the era of the gauchos came to an end.

The gaucho era came to an end because Argentina was changing. First, the once wild herds were acquired by people who wanted to manage them and profit from them. The gauchos were hired by these people. Then, the Pampas was "carved into vast ranches." These ranches meant that the gauchos could no longer roam freely. Railroads were built to transport the cattle, making cattle drives unnecessary. Soon, the only way the gauchos could make a living was to work as farmhands.

> This is considered a strong response because it
> - directly addresses the question and stays focused on the topic.
> - uses supporting details from the selection, including a quotation, to make its point.
> - is written clearly, using correct spelling, grammar, and punctuation.

READING STRATEGIES FOR ASSESSMENT

Find the main idea and supporting details. Circle the main idea of this article. Then underline the details that support the main idea.

_____

_____

_____

_____

_____

_____

_____

Use context clues. To discover what a "pack animal" is, study the words and phrases around it. Which phrase helps define it?

_____

_____

Notice important details. Underline the details that explain why alpaca wool is so desirable.

Reading Test Model
SHORT SELECTIONS

DIRECTIONS "Warmth from the Andes" is a short informative article. The strategies you have just learned can also help you with this shorter selection. As you read the selection, respond to the notes in the side column.

When you've finished reading, answer the multiple-choice questions. Use the side-column notes to help you understand what each question is asking and why each answer is correct.

Warmth from the Andes

Southeastern Peru and Western Bolivia make up a geographic region called the *Altiplano*, or High Plateau. This largely desolate mountainous area is home to one of the most economically important animals in South America—the alpaca.

The alpaca is related to the camel and looks somewhat like another well-known South American grazing animal, the llama. Alpacas live at elevations as high as 16,000 feet. At such altitudes, oxygen is scarce. Alpacas are able to survive because their blood contains an unusually high number of red blood corpuscles, the cells that carry oxygen throughout the body.

For several thousand years, the Native Americans of the region have raised alpacas both as pack animals for transporting goods and for their most important resource—wool. Alpaca wool ranges in color from black to tan to white. It is lightweight yet strong and resists moisture. Also, it is exceptionally warm. Alpaca wool is much finer than the wool from sheep. In fact, it is so luxurious that when the Inca civilization dominated the *Altiplano* region, garments made from Alpaca wool could be worn only by royalty.

Alpacas are usually sheared once each year by herders in Bolivia and Peru. Some of the wool is sold to manufacturers in the United States and Europe to be woven into cloth as soft and sought after as cashmere. The herders sell the rest to local weavers, who use it to produce beautiful shawls and other fine garments.

ANSWER STRATEGIES

1 Which of the following best describes the main idea of the article?

  A. Alpacas can survive at high altitudes.

  B. The *Altiplano* is a high plateau.

  C. The alpaca is related to the camel.

  D. The Alpaca is one of the most economically important animals of South America.

> **Identify the focus.** Each answer choice offers information from the article, but only one choice explains what the entire article is about.

2 Which of the following best describes what pack animals do?

  A. transport goods

  B. survive at high altitudes

  C. provide wool for clothing

  D. graze on the *Altiplano*

> **Pay attention to the context of unfamiliar words.** Find the sentence in the article where *pack animals* is used. Notice that only one answer choice is a phrase found right next to *pack animals*.

3 Why is alpaca wool highly prized?

  A. It resembles the fur of camels.

  B. It has been woven for thousands of years.

  C. It is lightweight, warm, strong, and resists moisture.

  D. It can be worn only by royalty.

> **Evaluate details.** Something "highly prized" has important qualities. Which answer choice talks about the qualities of alpaca wool?

Answers: 1.D, 2.A, 3.C

Read the title. What does the title tell you the chart is about?

Read the labels What do the labels on the left side of the chart tell you? What about the labels at the top of the chart?

ANSWER STRATEGIES

Read the question carefully. Notice that the questions asks for depth in feet, not meters.

Read the labels carefully. Be sure you understand which column represents square miles and which represents square kilometers.

Follow rows and columns carefully. If necessary, use your finger to trace across a row or down a column so that you don't accidentally wind up in the wrong place with the wrong information.

DIRECTIONS Some test questions ask you to analyze a visual rather than a reading selection. Study this chart carefully and answer the questions that follow.

Largest Lakes of Central and South America

	Surface Area (sq. mi./sq. km.)	Depth (feet/meters)	Elevation (feet/meters)
Lake Maracaibo, Venezuela	5,200/13,468	197/60	sea level
Lake Titicaca, Bolivia and Peru	3,200/8,288	990/302	12,500/3,810
Lake Nicaragua, Nicaragua	3,150/8,159	230/70	102/31

4 What is the depth, in feet, of the deepest lake?

A. 990

B. 12,500

C. 302

D. 13,468

5 What is the surface area of Lake Titicaca in square kilometers?

A. 3,200

B. 302

C. 8,288

D. 3,810

6 At what altitude is Lake Maracaibo?

A. 197 feet

B. sea level

C. 12,500 feet

D. 31 sq. km.

Answers: 4. A, 5. C, 6. B

Reading Test Practice
SHORT SELECTIONS

DIRECTIONS Use the following to practice your skills. Read the paragraphs carefully. Then answer the multiple-choice questions that follow.

During the 1990's, Spanish opera singer Placido Domingo teamed up with two other singers, Italy's Luciano Pavarotti and Portugal's José Carreras, to form a wildly popular singing group known as The Three Tenors. They enjoyed worldwide success, touring and appearing on television. Domingo's musical career, however, got its start much earlier—mid-century, in fact.

Born in Madrid in 1941, Domingo and his parents moved to Mexico City in 1950 where he began studying singing at the National Conservatory of Music. Ten years later, Domingo made his opera debut in a production of *La Traviata* in Monterrey, Mexico. After a three-year stint with the Israeli National Opera, Domingo joined the New York City Opera in 1966. Two years later, he made his debut with the Metropolitan Opera of New York.

Over the next three decades, Domingo dazzled audiences with his technical skill and virtuoso acting. Thirty-six years after his debut in Monterrey, Domingo became the artistic director of the Washington (D.C.) Opera. Then, in 2000, he assumed the same post at the Los Angeles Opera.

1. What was the author's purpose in writing this selection?

   A. to persuade readers that Placido Domingo is a great opera singer

   B. to explain who The Three Tenors were

   C. to inform readers about the career of Placido Domingo

   D. to describe the roles Placido Domingo has sung during his career

2. Which of the following is NOT a conclusion you can draw from the selection?

   A. Domingo is the greatest opera singer of his generation.

   B. Domingo has had a successful career as an opera singer.

   C. Domingo, Pavarotti, and Carreras captivated audiences with their singing.

   D. Domingo is widely respected in the opera world as a singer and an artist.

DIRECTIONS Use the graph below to answer the questions that follow.

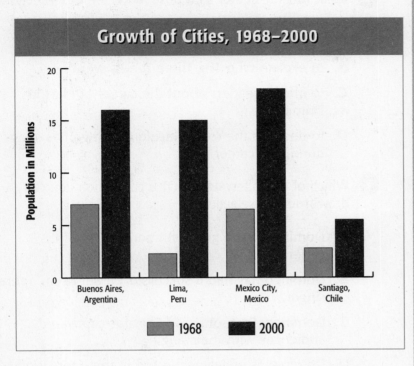

Growth of Cities, 1968–2000

Population in Millions

Buenos Aires, Argentina Lima, Peru Mexico City, Mexico Santiago, Chile

■ 1968 ■ 2000

3 Which city had the SMALLEST population in 1968?

A. Lima

B. Buenos Aires

C. Santiago

D. Mexico City

4 Which city had the LARGEST population in 2000?

A. Lima

B. Buenos Aires

C. Santiago

D. Mexico City

5 Which city had the SMALLEST increase in population between 1968 and 2000?

A. Lima

B. Buenos Aires

C. Santiago

D. Mexico City

THINKING IT THROUGH

1 What was the author's purpose in writing this selection?

   A. to persuade readers that Placido Domingo is a great opera singer

   B. to explain who The Three Tenors were

   C. to inform readers about the career of Placido Domingo

   D. to describe the roles Placido Domingo has sung during his career

2 Which of the following is NOT a conclusion you can draw from the selection?

   A. Domingo is the greatest opera singer of his generation.

   B. Domingo has had a successful career as an opera singer.

   C. Domingo, Pavarotti, and Carreras captivated audiences with their singing.

   D. Domingo is widely respected in the opera world as a singer and an artist.

3 Which city had the SMALLEST population in 1968?

   A. Lima

   B. Buenos Aires

   C. Santiago

   D. Mexico City

4 Which city had the LARGEST population in 2000?

   A. Lima

   B. Buenos Aires

   C. Santiago

   D. Mexico City

5 Which city had the SMALLEST increase in population between 1968 and 2000?

   A. Lima

   B. Buenos Aires

   C. Santiago

   D. Mexico City

Answers: 1. C, 2. A, 3. A, 4. D, 5. C

Functional Reading Test Model

DIRECTIONS Study the following nutrition label from a jar of tomatillo salsa. Then answer the questions that follow.

Nutrition Facts

Serving Size 2 TBSP (30 g)
Servings Per Container 15

Amount Per Serving	
Calories 10	
Calories from Fat 0	

	% Daily Value*
Total Fat 0 g	0%
Saturated Fat 0 g	0%
Cholesterol 0 mg	0%
Sodium 230 mg	10%
Total Carbohydrate 2 g	
Dietary Fiber 0 g	0%
Sugars 1 g	
Protein 0 g	

Vitamin A 6% • Vitamin C 8%
Calcium 4% • Iron 0%

* Percent Daily Values are based on a 2,000 calorie diet.

1 How many calories does this whole bottle of salsa contain?

A. 10

B. 150

C. 15

D. 30

2 If you ate two servings of salsa, how many mg. of sodium would you consume?

A. 460

B. 10

C. 230

D. 690

3 Is salsa a smart food choice for people trying to limit their fat intake?

A. No, because it has 230 mg. of sodium per serving.

B. Yes, because the serving size is just 2 TBSP.

C. No, because it has ten calories per serving.

D. Yes, because each serving has 0 g. of fat.

READING STRATEGIES FOR ASSESSMENT

Examine the structure of the label. Notice the type of information included in each of the four parts of the label.

Do the math. Remember that the "% Daily Value" and vitamin and mineral numbers on the label are for just a single serving.

ANSWER STRATEGIES

To find the correct answer, multiply the number of calories per serving by the number of servings in the bottle.

Again, multiplication is the key to finding the correct answer.

To answer this question, just look at that part of the label that tells how much fat each serving contains.

Answers:
1. B, 2. A, 3. D

Functional Reading Test Practice

DIRECTIONS Study the following travel advertisement for a vacation package to Puerto Rico. Circle the information that you think is the most important. Then answer the multiple-choice questions that follow.

EXPERIENCE THE EXCITEMENT OF PUERTO RICO!

Snorkeling! Windsurfing! Sailing! Golf!
First-Class Entertainment!

4 days/3 nights at the
San Juan Adventure Resort

only $479 per person
airfare included *

Adventure Resort Package also includes
continental breakfast, two beach passes,
two spa treatments

* Price based on double occupancy. Airfare from
New York City only. From Chicago add $175. From
Los Angeles add $350. Single travelers add $200.

---

1. Which of the following is NOT included in the $479 price?

   A. beach passes

   B. windsurfing

   C. spa treatments

   D. continental breakfast

2. How much will this vacation package cost a single traveler from Los Angeles?

   A. $479

   B. $654

   C. $679

   D. $1,029

3. For which of the following is this vacation package the LEAST expensive per person?

   A. two sisters from New York

   B. a stockbroker from Los Angeles

   C. a single traveler from New York

   D. a college student from Chicago

THINKING IT THROUGH

The notes in the side column will help you think through your answers. Check the answer key at the bottom of the page. How well did you do?

Although the ad mentions windsurfing prominently, it does not indicate that this activity is included in the price.

1 Which of the following is NOT included in the $479 price?

  A. beach passes

  B. windsurfing

  C. spa treatments

  D. continental breakfast

To answer this question, read the small type at the bottom of the ad and add the extra charges to the advertised price.

2 How much will this vacation package cost a single traveler from Los Angeles?

  A. $479

  B. $654

  C. $679

  D. $1,029

Read each answer choice carefully. How many people are traveling? Where are they coming from? Then use the information in the ad to determine who will get the best deal.

3 For which of the following travelers is this vacation package the LEAST expensive per person?

  A. two sisters from New York

  B. a stockbroker from Los Angeles

  C. a single traveler from New York

  D. a college student from Chicago

Revising-and-Editing Test Model

DIRECTIONS Read the following paragraph carefully. Then answer the multiple-choice questions that follow. After answering the questions, read the material in the side columns to check your answer strategies.

¹Madrid, the capital of Spain. ²It is home to one of that nations cultural treasures—the Prado museum. ³The building was constructed in the late eighteenth century as a museum of natural science. ⁴Then they decided to change it to an art museum in 1819 and it has more than 9,000 works of art. ⁵The museum is located on a street called the Paseo del Prado. ⁶Their are many famous paintings they're, including works by El Greco, Velázquez, and Goya.

READING STRATEGIES FOR ASSESSMENT

Watch for common errors. Highlight or underline errors such as incorrect spelling or punctuation; fragments or run-on sentences; and missing or misplaced information.

1. Which sentence in the paragraph is actually a fragment, an incomplete thought?

   A. sentence 5

   B. sentence 3

   C. sentence 1

   D. sentence 4

2. In sentence 2, which of the following is the correct possessive form of *nation*?

   A. nation's

   B. nations's

   C. nations'

   D. nations

ANSWER STRATEGIES

Incomplete Sentences A sentence is a group of words with a subject and a verb that expresses a complete thought. If either the subject or the verb is missing, the group of words is an incomplete sentence.

Possessive Nouns In sentence 2, the word *nation* is singular. So, it takes the singular possessive form.

Pronoun References Avoid unclear or inaccurate pronoun references. In sentence 4, *they* has no antecedent at all and so must be replaced with the noun *government*. The antecedent for *it* is unclear and must be replaced with *the natural science museum*.

3 What is the best way to rewrite the first part of sentence 4?

   A. Then he decided to change it to an art museum

   B. Then the government decided to change it to an art museum

   C. Then the government decided to change the natural science museum to an art museum

   D. Then he decided to change the natural science museum to an art museum

Run-on Sentences A run-on sentence is two or more complete thoughts joined without correct punctuation. Often the word *and* is used instead of a period to connect the two complete thoughts—a clue that the sentence is a run-on.

4 Which sentence in the paragraph is a run-on sentence?

   A. sentence 2

   B. sentence 5

   C. sentence 1

   D. sentence 4

Spelling Errors Words that sound the same may be spelled differently and have different meanings. Check to be sure that the spelling you use carries the meaning you intend.

5 What is the best way to rewrite the first part of sentence 6?

   A. They're many famous paintings their

   B. There are many famous paintings they're

   C. There are many famous paintings there

   D. Their are many famous paintings there

Logical Organization The order of the sentences in a paragraph should be logical. The location of the Prado logically should come before the sentence that discusses the museum's construction.

6 Sentence 5 is out of place. Where should sentence 5 occur?

   A. after sentence 2

   B. before sentence 2

   C. after sentence 5

   D. after sentence 3

Answers:
1. C, 2. A, 3. C, 4. D, 5. C, 6. A

234 Lecturas para todos

¡En español! Level 1

Revising-and-Editing Test Practice

DIRECTIONS Read the following paragraph carefully. As you read, circle each error that you find and identify the error in the side column—for example, *misspelled word* or *incorrect punctuation*. When you have finished, circle the letter of the correct choice for each question that follows.

¹On December, 17, 1830, one of the most greatest leaders in South American history died. ²He was born in Venezuela, which was ruled by Spain. ³As a young man, Simón Bolívar tours Europe, and he vows to free Venezuela from Spanish rule. ⁴After a series of setbacks. ⁵Bolívar began winning his fight to oust the Spanish from South America. ⁶By 1824, Spanish rule in South America was over and Bolívar is now known as *El Libertador* and the "George Washington of South America."

1 Which sentence in the paragraph is a fragment?

A. sentence 4

B. sentence 2

C. sentence 6

D. sentence 7

2 What is the correct way to write the date in sentence 1?

A. Dec./17/1830

B. December 17 1830

C. December 17, 1830

D. December, 17 1830

3 In sentence 1, which of the following is the correct form of the superlative adjective?

A. greatest

B. greater

C. more great

D. more greatest

4 Which of the following errors occurs in sentence 2?

A. unclear pronoun reference

B. incorrect capitalization

C. incorrect punctuation

D. incorrect verb tense

5 Which of the following is the correct way to rewrite the first part of sentence 3?

A. As a young man, Simón Bolívar tours Europe, and he vowed

B. As a young man, Simón Bolívar toured Europe, and he vows

C. As a young man, Simón Bolívar is touring Europe, and he vows

D. As a young man, Simón Bolívar toured Europe, and he vowed

6 Which of the following is the best way to punctuate the middle of sentence 6?

A. Spanish rule in South America was over: and Bolívar is now

B. Spanish rule in South America was over. Bolívar is now

C. Spanish rule in South America was over; and Bolívar is now

D. Spanish rule in South America was over—and Bolívar is now

THINKING IT THROUGH

Use the notes in the side columns to help you understand why some answers are correct and others are not. Check the answer key on the next page. How well did you do?

1 Which sentence in the paragraph is a fragment?

   A. sentence 4

   B. sentence 2

   C. sentence 6

   D. sentence 7

> Remember that a sentence has a subject and a verb and expresses a complete thought. Which sentence is lacking either a subject or a verb?

2 What is the correct way to write the date in sentence 1?

   A. Dec./17/1830

   B. December 17 1830

   C. December 17, 1830

   D. December, 17 1830

> When writing a date, the name of the month should be spelled out, and the day and year should be separated by a comma.

3 In sentence 1, which of the following is the correct form of the superlative adjective?

   A. greatest

   B. greater

   C. more great

   D. more greatest

> A superlative adjective is formed by adding –*est* to the adjective or placing the word *most* before the adjective. Never do both at the same time.

First check to be sure that words are capitalized correctly, that the sentence is punctuated correctly, and that the verb has the same tense as other verbs in the paragraph. Then ask, "Who is *he*?" Unless you can answer that question with a proper name, the pronoun reference is unclear.

Remember that all the verbs in a paragraph should agree—that is, have the same tense. So both verbs in sentence 3 must agree.

Remember that a run-on sentence is two or more sentences strung together with either no punctuation or incorrect punctuation. The solution is to create separate sentences.

4. Which of the following errors occurs in sentence 2?

   A. unclear pronoun reference

   B. incorrect capitalization

   C. incorrect punctuation

   D. incorrect verb tense

5. Which of the following is the correct way to rewrite the first part of sentence 3?

   A. As a young man, Simón Bolívar tours Europe, and he vowed

   B. As a young man, Simón Bolívar toured Europe, and he vows

   C. As a young man, Simón Bolívar is touring Europe, and he vows

   D. As a young man, Simón Bolívar toured Europe, and he vowed

6. Which of the following is the best way to punctuate the middle of sentence 6?

   A. Spanish rule in South America was over: and Bolívar is now

   B. Spanish rule in South America was over. Bolívar is now

   C. Spanish rule in South America was over; and Bolívar is now

   D. Spanish rule in South America was over—and Bolívar is now

Writing Test Model

DIRECTIONS Many tests ask you to write an essay in response to a writing prompt. A writing prompt is a brief statement that describes a writing situation. Some writing prompts ask you to explain *what, why,* or *how.* Others ask you to convince someone of something.

As you analyze the following writing prompts, read and respond to the notes in the side columns. Then look at the response to each prompt. The notes in the side columns will help you understand why each response is considered strong.

Prompt A

Some child-rearing experts believe that young people should be kept busy after school and on the weekends with a variety of structured activities, such as music lessons, sports, dance classes, and so on. Others say that young people today have been "overscheduled" and need more time to themselves—to read, think about the future, and even just to daydream.

Think about your experiences and the way your non-school time is structured. Do you think lots of structure, more personal time, or a combination of the two is most beneficial to young people? Remember to provide solid reasons and examples for the position you take.

Strong Response

Today was a typical day for my little brother Jeff. He got up at five o'clock to go to the local ice rink for hockey practice. Then he was off to school. At the end of the school day, Jeff

ANALYZING THE PROMPT

Identify the focus. What issue will you be writing about? Circle the focus of your essay in the first sentence of the prompt.

Understand what's expected of you. First, circle what the prompt asks you to do. Then identify your audience. What kinds of details will appeal to this audience?

ANSWER STRATEGIES

Capture the reader's interest. The writer begins by describing a typical busy day in his younger brother's life.

State the position clearly. The last sentence of the first paragraph makes the writer's position clear to the reader. Now the writer can spend the rest of the essay developing his argument.

Address opposing views. The writer brings up an opposing view—that busy kids are less likely to get into trouble—and admits that it might sometimes be true.

Use good examples to support the position. Here, the writer uses an example to make the point that not all busy kids stay out of trouble.

Use logical reasoning to further develop the position. The writer offers logical reasons why free time is important.

Restate the position in the conclusion. Using another concrete example, the writer restates his position that kids need some time to themselves.

had a piano lesson followed by a meeting of his Cub Scout troop. After a quick dinner, he did homework for two hours. He finally got to bed at ten o'clock. That's a lot to pack into a single day, especially since Jeff is just seven years old! I think that in addition to sports, music, and other activities, kids like Jeff need some time to themselves.

Many parents, mine included, think a busy kid is a safe kid. They believe that the less time a kid has on his hands, the less likely he'll wind up doing something he shouldn't be doing or being with people he shouldn't be with. That's probably true for many kids. After all, it's hard to get into trouble when you spend every day being carpooled from one activity to another.

But some busy kids do get into trouble anyway. Jeff's friend Mark got caught trying to shoplift a CD last weekend, and he's involved in just as many activities as Jeff is. So having a busy schedule is no guarantee that a kid won't get into trouble.

Plus, I think kids benefit from having free time to go to the movies, play video games, read, or even just be by themselves. Growing up isn't always easy, and kids need some time alone to figure things out, think about what's important to them, and decide what they really want to do.

Last Saturday afternoon, Jeff's soccer practice was canceled because of thunderstorms. We went to see a movie and later spent some time talking and listening to music in my room. It was the first time in months that we had time just to hang out together, and we really enjoyed it. Jeff said it was like having a day off. I think more kids like Jeff could use a day off too.

Prompt B

Depending on where you live, each season of the year can be very different than it is in other parts of the country. Which season do you enjoy the most—summer, autumn, winter, or spring? What is that season like in your part of the country? What makes it special to you?

Strong Response

Here in the upper Midwest, the seasons seem as different from one another as night and day. Summer usually arrives suddenly. The temperatures soar, the humidity rises, and fierce thunderstorms add drama and sometimes destruction to the season. Autumn brings a crisp, cool, and colorful change as the leaves turn golden and the air turns chilly. Winter can be bitterly cold, and heavy snows often make the simple trip to school a real ordeal.

Then comes spring. Spring is a truly magical time of the year. I can sense spring long before it actually arrives. There's a certain scent in the air, and something is different about the way the sunlight looks. Soon the winter snows are reduced to muddy puddles. The tree branches swell with buds, and the first green shoots of crocus and tulip leaves struggle up out of the ground. Most magical of all, the early morning hours just after dawn are filled with the cries of migrating birds heading back north.

Because my family lives in a small community surrounded by farmland, I get to experience a different kind of spring than many people do. The fields behind our house fill up with wildflowers that season the air with perfume and color. A trip to Jefferson's Pond offers a chance to watch ducks and geese resting on their long

ANALYZING THE PROMPT

Look for the main idea. The first few sentences of the prompt present the subject you will write about. Try restating the subject in your own words.

Understand what's expected of you. What does the prompt ask you to do? Explain something? Persuade someone? State your personal feelings?

ANSWER STRATEGIES

Create an intriguing introduction. The writer arouses the reader's curiosity by leaving out one of the four seasons.

Include specific details. The writer uses specific details about each season to make the description vivid.

Include the kind of information the prompt asks for. Notice how the writer follows the directions in the prompt by explaining what spring is like in her part of the country.

Use sensory details. Details that appeal to the reader's sense of sight, sound, and smell bring the description to life.

Make comparisons. Comparing the blossoming trees to balls of cotton candy helps the reader experience the scene as the writer does.

Write a powerful conclusion. The writer ends the essay by comparing herself to her favorite season.

seasonal journeys. The apple and cherry trees at the McKlintock family orchards explode with blossoms until they look like giant balls of cotton candy.

Mostly, however, I love spring because it is a season of hope. The earth is coming back to life, filled with possibilities. I feel like I am, too.

Writing Test Practice

DIRECTIONS Read the following writing prompt. Using the strategies you've learned in this section, analyze the prompt, plan your response, and then write an essay explaining your position.

Prompt C

You have volunteered to participate in your community's semiannual blood drive. Your task is to write a letter to your community newspaper encouraging everyone in town to consider giving blood.

Think about all the ways your community benefits from having an adequate blood supply. Write a letter that explains what these benefits are. Include specific examples. End your letter by appealing to your fellow citizens' sense of civic pride and duty.

Scoring Rubrics

DIRECTIONS Use the following checklist to see whether you have written a strong persuasive essay. You will have succeeded if you can check nearly all of the items.

The Prompt

☐ My response meets all the requirements stated in the prompt.

☐ I have stated my position clearly and supported it with details.

☐ I have addressed the audience appropriately.

☐ My essay fits the type of writing suggested in the prompt (letter to the editor, article for the school paper, and so on).

Reasons

☐ The reasons I offer really support my position.

☐ My audience will find the reasons convincing.

☐ I have stated my reasons clearly.

☐ I have given at least three reasons.

☐ I have supported my reasons with sufficient facts, examples, quotations, and other details.

☐ I have presented and responded to opposing arguments.

☐ My reasoning is sound. I have avoided faulty logic.

Order and Arrangement

☐ I have included a strong introduction.

☐ I have included a strong conclusion.

☐ The reasons are arranged in a logical order.

Word Choice

☐ The language of my essay is appropriate for my audience.

☐ I have used precise, vivid words and persuasive language.

Fluency

☐ I have used sentences of varying lengths and structures.

☐ I have connected ideas with transitions and other devices.

☐ I have used correct spelling, punctuation, and grammar.

Apuntes

Apuntes

Apuntes

Apuntes

Credits

Illustration

15–16 Nneke Bennett; **20–21** Ruben de Anda; **36–37, 41–42** Rick Powell; **56–57, 61–62** Enrique O. Sánchez; **77–78** Rubén de Anda; **82–83** Fabricio Vanden Broeck; **97–98** Fian Arroyo; **102–103** Rubén de Anda; **119–120** Eduardo Espada; **124–125** Susan M. Blumbaugh

Photography

i, 3, 4, 5 Martha Granger/EDGE Productions; **9** Beryl Goldberg; **10** *top* Patricia A. Eynon, *bottom* Odyssey Productions; **11** Beryl Goldberg; **25** Martha Granger/EDGE Productions; **26** School Division/Houghton Mifflin Company; **31** John Boykin/PhotoEdit; **32** *top left* Martha Granger/EDGE Productions, *top center* Susan Kaye, *top right* J.P. Courau/DDB Stock Photo, *bottom left* Doug Bryant/DDB Stock Photo, *bottom center, bottom right* Martha Granger/EDGE Productions; **42** Robert Frerck/Woodfin Camp; **46** *top* Bob Daemmrich/Stock Boston, *inset* Robert Frerck/Odyssey; **47** *left* Bob Daemmrich, *bottom* Martha Granger/EDGE Productions; **51** *top* Raymond A. Mendez/Animals Animals, *bottom* Jaime Santiago/DDB Stock Photo; **52** *top* Thomas R. Fletcher/Stock Boston, *bottom* School Division/Houghton Mifflin Company; **66** Dave G. Houser; **67** *top* Martha Granger/EDGE Productions, *bottom* Patricia A. Eynon; **68** *top* Martha Granger/EDGE Productions, *center, bottom* Rogers/Monkmeyer Press; **72, 73, 87** Martha Granger/EDGE Productions; **88** *left* "Retrato de Jaime Sabartés" ("Portrait of Jaime Sabartés") (1899-1900), Pablo Picasso. Charcoal and watercolour on paper, 50.5 cm x 33 cm. Giraudon/Art Resource, New York. © 2003 Artists Rights Society, New York / Picasso Museum, Sabartés Collection, Barcelona, Spain, *right* "Maya con una muñeca" ("Maya with Doll") (1938), Pablo Picasso. Oil on canvas, 73 cm x 60 cm. Giraudon/Superstock. © 2003 Artists Rights Society, New York / Picasso Museum, Paris; **92, 107, 108, 109** Martha Granger/EDGE Productions; **113** Jeff Greenberg/PhotoEdit; **114** *top* School Division/Houghton Mifflin Company, *bottom* Eric A. Wessman/Viest Associates, Inc.; **115** Wolfgang Kaehler; **131** "Cumpleaños de Lala y Tudi" ("Lala and Tudi's Birthday Party") (1989), Carmen Lomas Garza. Oil on canvas, 36" x 48". Collection of Paula Maciel Benecke & Norbert Benecke, Aptos, California. Photograph by Wolgang Dietze. © 1989 Carmen Lomas Garza; **169** Lee Foster/Bruce Coleman, Inc.; **179** Timothy Fadek/Corbis; **181** *quinceañera* Martha Granger/EDGE Productions; *Sweet 16 party* Ryan McVay; **183** Dennis MacDonald/PhotoEdit; **185** © 1978 George Ballis/Take Stock; **189** Jacques Jangoux/Getty Images

Understanding Australia

A guide for international students

SALLY A. WHITE

CAMBRIDGE
UNIVERSITY PRESS

PUBLISHED BY THE PRESS SYNDICATE OF THE UNIVERSITY OF CAMBRIDGE
The Pitt Building, Trumpington Street, Cambridge, United Kingdom

CAMBRIDGE UNIVERSITY PRESS
The Edinburgh Building, Cambridge CB2 2RU, UK
40 West 20th Street, New York, NY 10011–4211, USA
477 Williamstown Road, Port Melbourne, VIC 3207, Australia
Ruiz de Alarcón 13, 28014 Madrid, Spain
Dock House, The Waterfront, Cape Town 8001, South Africa

http://www.cambridge.org

Line illustrations by Boris Silvestri. Unless otherwise acknowledged, photographs are by the author. Every effort has been made to trace and acknowledge copyright. The publishers apologise for any accidental infringement and welcome information that would rectify any error or omission in subsequent editions.

First published 2003

Printed in Australia by Hyde Park Press

Typeface Granjon (Adobe) 11/14 pt.   System QuarkXPress®   [MAPG]

A catalogue record for this book is available from the British Library

National Library of Australia Cataloguing in Publication data

White, Sally A.
    Understanding Australia: a guide for international
    students.
    Bibliography.
    Includes index.
    ISBN 0 521 54199 9.
    1. Students, Foreign – Australia – Handbooks, manuals, etc.
    2. Australia – Handbooks, manuals, etc. I. Title.
919.404

ISBN 0 521 54199 9 paperback

contents

acknowledgements

Many people helped with the creation of this book, most of them international students at several Australian universities. To all of them, thank you. My thanks also go to Pius Ang, Enisa Kasar and Sister Virginia Calpotura, Paula Duncan, Liz Wakefield, and Erica Cervini and her professional communication students. Dina Gerolymou, Rico Ngai, Felix Lo and Petra Beschart, in particular, helped me see Australia through their eyes, while Liu Guang, Sarentuoya Bai, Ma Na and Chen Lun taught me much about surviving in their culture. Writing this book would have been more difficult without the perceptive wisdom of my late colleague, Phillipa Bonwick, whose commitment to her international students was unstinting. Last, but certainly not least, Peter Debus; he steadfastly believed in the book, even when my own faith wavered. So this one is dedicated to him.

introduction

Are you thinking of studying in Australia? Or have you already decided to be one of the 165,000 students from around the world who are studying down-under?

The decision to undertake studies overseas is a big one. You will need lots of information about Australia and Australians. This book aims to help you.

The advantage of overseas study is that students get two types of education. They get a formal qualification, as well as the education that comes from living and working in a foreign country, meeting its people, and understanding a little of its history, its society and its customs.

But there is a disadvantage of overseas study. So many things are different about the student's new temporary home. The weather, the food, the physical surroundings, the methods of study, the culture, the daily living habits and the way people speak are not familiar. These things can be confusing, uncomfortable and sometimes even offensive.

The international student is far from the support of family and friends, alone in a strange land. It takes courage and hard work to meet the challenges of study overseas and to get a qualification and a second education. But the experience is worth the effort.

ABOUT THIS BOOK

This book is a basic 'textbook' for students who want more than a formal qualification from their time in Australia. It aims to introduce you to Australia and Australians. Of course, there is no such person as a typical Australian, just as there is no such person as a typical Indian, Zambian, Chinese, German or Indonesian.

Australian society has many different customs and behaviours, based on the different influences that immigrants have brought to the country over the past 200 years and more. So, when you read this book, remember that it can only point out general trends, ideas and habits. You will always find there are exceptions to the rule.

You will find it helpful to start by reading the detailed list of Contents to identify the chapters that interest you most. You can read those parts first. You may even like to read the final part – 'The essentials' – before reading any other section! However, you will benefit most from reading the book the whole way through as soon as you can.

The book will help you to prepare before you come to Australia and will be useful throughout your stay. It will probably be most helpful in the first year. Later, you will be confident enough to add to the book's information by reading newspapers, magazines and other Australian books, watching Australian television programs and movies, listening to radio and, most importantly, talking to Australians.

> **down-under** - a term used by people in the Northern Hemisphere for Australia, New Zealand and neighbouring Pacific island nations. Australians apply it to Australia only.

The book has seven main sections:

► 'The people' tells you about the Australian people and how they live their daily lives.

► 'Customs' tells you about Australian customs and social behaviour.

► 'Communicating' looks at the thing that visitors find most difficult at first – the strange ways Australians use English and communicate with each other.

► 'Campus life' gives a general picture of life on tertiary campuses in Australia. (It does not provide information about each educational institution or their services as this is available on their web sites or from education agents in your home country.)

► 'The systems' outlines Australian institutions and how they work.

► 'Shaping the land' looks at how the land and its history have shaped the way Australians behave today.

► 'The essentials' summarises seven characteristics that make Australians the way they are.

Finally, there's a short reading list and a basic glossary of Australian words and phrases.

The book contains words that you may not know. Where possible, the meaning is explained within the text. Some important word meanings are given in highlighted boxes. Where a word or short phrase is within quotation marks, this means it is a common Australian term which is often used in the Australian media or conversation.

I hope you will enjoy reading the book and learning from it. But, most of all, I hope you will enjoy and learn from a stay with us down-under.

part one:
the people

'I find Australians hard to understand. They don't have a long culture like my country. I had an idea of what Australians were like before I came here. But it wasn't a true idea.'

– a Turkish student, University of Western Sydney, New South Wales

On 1 January 2001, modern Australia celebrated 100 years as a nation. At the time, there was much discussion about the Australian character. What makes Australians the way they are? Are they like the English and Irish who were the main first white settlers? Or are they more like the Americans whose influence is so strong today? Are they lazy or hardworking? Are they radical or conservative? Australians say they support equality, fairness and loyalty to friends. Is this true? Have these qualities disappeared?

There isn't one answer to these questions.

Like most of the world, Australia is changing. Australians find it hard to identify their true nature. It can also be hard for visitors to understand Australia and its people. This section introduces some points about the Australian character.

Who is Australian?

In 1901, 95 per cent of the population of 3.7 million people were born in either Australia or Britain. Today, only about 78 per cent of the 19.5 million Australians are Australian or British-born. About 40 per cent of Australians have at least one parent who was born elsewhere. There are more than 100 ethnic groups in the country.

Australia is a country of immigrants. Scientists believe the ancestors of today's Aboriginals arrived from the north about 50,000 years ago.

In 1788, the British arrived to set up a convict colony on the east coast. Among the arrivals there was a black man from Madagascar, but most people were English, Irish or Scottish.

The gold rushes of the 1850s brought people from all over the world, including Australia's first Chinese migrants. Despite these new settlers, Australia was mainly British in character. From 1901 the country's White Australia Policy meant Asian, African and Middle Eastern immigrants were not welcome.

The big move towards a more diverse Australia began after World War 2 when immigrants from Europe, especially Italians, Greeks and Northern Europeans, arrived. The easing of the White Australia Policy in the late 1960s meant the start of migration from Asia and the Middle East. Many immigrants came from Vietnam and the Philippines and, more recently, from Hong Kong and China.

Academics estimate that Australians speak about 240 languages, including 60 to 100 Aboriginal languages. The languages range from Arabic, German and Hindi to Spanish, Swahili and Vietnamese. But eight out of 10 Australians speak English at home. After English, the various Chinese dialects, Italian and Greek are the most common languages used at home.

AN AGEING POPULATION

The ageing of the population is often discussed. Like many Western countries, Australia has a low fertility rate. It also has one of the highest life expectancy rates in the world. A boy born today can expect to live until he is 77. A girl can expect to live for 82 years.

About 13 out of every 100 Australians are aged 65 or over. Only a fifth of the population are children under the age of 15. Twenty years ago, children made up a quarter of the population.

Cancer and heart disease are the two biggest causes of death. Half of all Australians die from these diseases. So ways to cure cancer and prevent heart disease are topics of importance to Australians and are widely reported by the media.

Australia is a multiracial country.

INDIGENOUS AUSTRALIANS

> **indigenous** – native to a country
> **Indigenous Australians** – all Aboriginal and Torres Strait Islander peoples

Australia has two indigenous peoples: the mainland and Tasmanian Aboriginals and the Torres Strait Islanders who come from the small islands between Australia and Papua New Guinea.

Nobody knows how many Aboriginals lived in Australia when the British first arrived. The estimated population was between 500,000 and one million. Later numbers are unknown because Aboriginals and Torres Strait Islanders were not counted in the national census until the mid-1960s.

> **census** – an official count of a population with details about age, sex, education, etc. The Australian census is held every five years.

Today, 2.2 per cent of the population – or 410,000 people – identify themselves as Indigenous Australians. The population is growing, despite having a much lower life expectancy than that of other Australians. An Indigenous man can expect to live to 56 and a woman to 63.

These Aboriginal people celebrated the opening of the National Museum of Australia in Canberra in 2001 by holding a sunrise ceremony. *National Library of Australia*

Indigenous Australians are very diverse. Some live a traditional lifestyle; many live in the capital cities. Some speak English as a first language; others speak an Aboriginal language or Kriol. Some have the dark skin and brown eyes typical of their race; others are light-skinned with blond or brown hair.

The tragic history of Australian Indigenous peoples' early contact with Europeans (see page 91) means that their role in Australian society has major political significance.

WHERE AUSTRALIANS LIVE

Australian writers and artists of the past created an image of rural life that is still very powerful today. Australians think of themselves as people who live in wide open spaces. This is not really true. Australian cities are small by world standards but Australia is still one of the most urbanised countries in the world. Nearly two-thirds of all Australians live in the eight capital cities. These capitals are growing faster than other places.

Australians sometimes talk about the 'Dead Heart'. They mean the central desert area of Australia where very few people live. But the area of sparse population is even bigger than the Dead Heart. Half of the total area of Australia contains only 0.3 per cent of the population.

Four out of every five Australians live within 50 kilometres of the sea, mainly on the eastern and south-eastern edges and in the south-western corner of the country.

The Australian house

The way Australians design and use their houses shows something about their character. Despite their friendly nature, Australians respect individual privacy. Their homes are places where they can go into a private world. When they are at home, most outdoor activity happens in the back garden, out of sight of strangers in the street. The front verandah or front steps are not a meeting place for friends or neighbours as they are in some other countries.

After World War 2, as ordinary Australians became wealthier, they wanted to own their homes. The dream of home ownership still remains strong for most Australians. Seven out of every 10 people live in homes they own or are buying.

For most of the 20th century, the ideal Australian home was a freestanding house and garden on a 'quarter-acre block'. Eighty per cent of houses are still separate dwellings. In the suburbs, most houses are one or two storeys high. They usually have a low front fence and taller timber fences at the sides and the back.

> **quarter-acre block** – *a piece of land about 0.1 hectares in area. Although Australia changed to the metric system of measurement in the 1970s, people often use the old term when talking about land for housing.*

Like the people, the designs of Australian houses come from many cultures. House builders imported designs from various places. In the early colonial years, the main influence was Georgian and Victorian England. In the 20th century, house builders were inspired by designs from Mexico, Japan, the United States, Holland, Germany and Switzerland. They adapted these designs to local conditions.

INSIDE THE AUSTRALIAN HOME

A typical middle-class 15-year-old family home is probably made of brick veneer (a timber frame faced with brick). The front door is sheltered by a porch or verandah. You usually won't see shoes beside the door because few Australians take off their shoes to go inside.

The house may have a formal sitting room but most activity takes place in the family room, which is used for eating, playing and watching television. This room is often separated from an open kitchen by a bench that is used for food preparation and informal meals. The family room is usually at the back of the house, facing the back garden.

The house probably has three bedrooms. One is the parents' bedroom, which often has a small bathroom next to it, called an ensuite. In most Australian families, each child has a separate bedroom, which is also used for doing school homework.

The main bathroom usually has a shower and a bathtub, although most adult Australians have showers, not baths. The pedestal toilet is often in a small separate room. Toilet paper is flushed down the toilet but sanitary products and babies' disposable napkins are wrapped in paper or plastic and put in the household rubbish bin. Nearly all modern Australian toilets, in homes and offices, are designed to save water. They have a half-flush button on the left.

At the back of the house, you find the laundry. Many families have clothes dryers but they also hang their washing outside on a rotary clothes line.

SYMBOLS OF HOME

The Australian post-war dream of home ownership is symbolised by two items: the Hills rotary clothes hoist and the Victa rotary lawn mower.

Hills Industries Ltd

An Adelaide mechanic, Lance Hill, developed the Hills Hoist in 1945. It was not the first rotary clothes hoist, but Hill included a handle that made it easy to raise the hoist so the clothes could dry quickly in the wind.

During the 1950s, a Sydney man, Mervyn Victor Richardson, designed a lightweight four-wheeled lawnmower which he called the Victa. The cutting blades were fitted to a disc mounted horizontally to the ground.

Both inventions were practical and cheap. They were soon common in Australian backyards.

Until recently, the backyard was often used to grow vegetables. It was also an informal grassed area where children played. These days, it is often an outdoor entertainment area, with a more formal garden and perhaps a barbeque area and a swimming pool. Over the years, the backyard has become smaller as Australians build bigger houses which cover more of the land.

Australians, especially those living in the suburbs and country, need a car because public transport is not very good. The car is kept in an open-sided shed called a carport or in an enclosed garage, which can also be used for storage.

SMALL HOUSEHOLDS

The tall residential blocks seen in many of the world's large cities are much less common in Australia. Only 10 per cent of Australians live in apartments. Another 10 per cent live in small semi-detached homes – often four or six on a quarter-acre block – or terrace houses in the inner areas of the older capital cities.

In recent years, capital cities – especially Sydney, Melbourne and Brisbane – have encouraged medium and high density housing in the central city area. Multi-storey residential blocks in the city are popular with single people or older couples whose children have grown up. They have few families living in them. In design they are much like apartment blocks elsewhere in the world.

Australian families

Advertisements on Australian television often depict families: big noisy Greek or Italian families; newly married couples settling in to their first home; mum, dad, two children and a dog. Which picture shows a typical Australian family? They all do. Like so much else in Australia, family types and values are very diverse. Many migrant families maintain the family arrangements of their native country – at least for some time after coming to Australia.

The statisticians say a family is related people living in the same house. Of course, families are much more than that. But the statisticians' definition is useful to show the way many Australians live.

The Australian family is small. It is usually a 'nuclear family', which consists of one or two generations. Today, four out of 10 Australian families consist of couples and their children. Thirty years ago, couples and children made up six out of 10 families. The average number of children in a family is a little more than two.

Two parents, two children and a dog are one kind of Australian family. *Images On Tap*

The reasons for smaller families and fewer couples with children living at home are many. They include an ageing population, a low birth rate and a high divorce rate.

In general, Australians don't have a tradition of 'extended families' where several generations live together or in adjoining houses. But for important events, the wider Australian family – including grandparents, uncles, aunts, cousins and other relatives – gathers to celebrate.

When children grow up, they leave the family home to start another household. So, many older Australians live in families that contain just themselves and their spouse. This family type is increasing as the population gets older.

MARRIAGE AND DIVORCE RATES

Just over half of all adult Australians are married. About 10 per cent of people are divorced or separated. Changes to divorce laws in 1976 meant a sharp increase in the number of divorces. Now, the rate of divorce has steadied.

The number of divorces means there are more one-parent families. But remarriage after divorce is common. This gives rise to 'blended families' containing parents, step-parents, children and stepchildren.

FAMILY VALUES

There is frequent public debate in Australia about changes to family structure. Some people say family values – which put the needs of the whole family ahead of individual desires – are disappearing. This may be partly true. It is also true that Australian family ties have never been as strong as those in some other cultures.

Visitors – especially people from Asia or the Middle East – are often surprised that Australians seem to have little sense of family obligation. The authority of fathers seems weak. Children often challenge their parents' opinions. They seem to be disobedient. They do not seem to look after their elderly relatives properly. One explanation for this behaviour is the Australian tradition of equality (see pages 7–8).

However, it is a mistake to think that Australians don't think families are important. Many surveys show that people say spending time with family members is the most desirable thing they can do.

A special baptism service in a Roman Catholic Church. *National Library of Australia*

THE FAMILY PET

Australians are pet owners. Nearly half of all households own at least one dog and nearly a third of households have at least one cat. These pets are members of the family.

The Australian practice of allowing dogs inside the house disgusts people who think dogs are unclean.

If you don't want family pets to come near you, tell the owner you are not used to animals or that you are allergic to them.

If you want to buy a pet yourself, remember you have to pay a yearly fee to the local council to register a dog or cat. Pets are often not allowed in rented apartments. Check the web site of the Royal Society for the Prevention of Cruelty to Animals (RSPCA) <www.rspca.org.au> to find out your responsibilities as a pet owner.

What Australians believe

For visitors from countries where religious practice is a daily event, Australians seem irreligious. Nineteenth-century visitors thought this was because so many were convicts who, they said, came from an ungodly class.

RELIGIONS IN AUSTRALIA

Religion and government are separate in Australia, although God is mentioned in the national Constitution and prayers are said in the country's parliaments.

Like their British ancestors, Australians are mainly Christian. But, although nearly seven out of 10 Australians say they are Christian, very few go to church regularly.

The Christian church with the biggest numbers is the Roman Catholic Church. The second largest is the Anglican Church in Australia, which used to be called the Church of England. Other Christians are Protestants of several kinds and followers of the various eastern Orthodox churches.

The 2001 national census found that 2 per cent of people said they were Buddhists, 1.5 per cent said they were Muslims and 0.5 per cent said they were Hindus. Another 0.4 per cent said they were Jews. These religious groups have been in Australia in small numbers for many years.

Significantly, more than a quarter of all Australians did not answer the census question about religion or said they had no religion.

However, religion has played a part in shaping Australian culture. Historically, bad feelings existed between the Roman Catholics, who had a mainly working-class Irish background, and the Anglicans who represented English middle-class values. In politics, the Catholics tended to support the more radical policies of the Australian Labor Party. The Anglicans, and other Protestants, tended to support the conservative parties. But religious differences rarely led to violence.

From the time the British arrived, both Protestant and Catholic religious leaders worried about moral behaviour, especially in sexual matters and art and literature. The Protestants also worried about gambling, alcohol and keeping Sunday as a day of rest.

Until the last few decades of the 20th century, these ideas were upheld in many state laws. These laws outlawed abortion, prevented Sunday trading, restricted the sale of alcohol, censored books, films and theatre and strictly controlled gambling.

Today, most laws have been relaxed. However, there can still be vigorous public debate about the religious and moral aspects of social issues. In recent years, these issues have included stem cell research, cloning, euthanasia and abortion.

In general, Australians distrust people who take extreme positions on any subject. The same is true of religion. There are Australians who are deeply religious. However, the more common attitude towards religion is a detached tolerance. For most Australians, religious behaviour is a private matter that should not be forced on others.

INDIGENOUS BELIEFS

Until recently, Aboriginal religions were rarely mentioned in Australian mainstream society. However, the move towards land rights for Indigenous Australians has put more emphasis on their spiritual beliefs.

Indigenous beliefs are complex and varied. But one common thread occurs everywhere: belief in the Dreaming, or creation story. The details of the Dreaming change from place to place.

The Dreaming is the time when ancestral beings moved through the country creating the natural world and making laws and customs for the people to observe. However, the Dreaming is not only a time in the past. It also exists today and in the future.

> **land rights** – the rights of indigenous people to own their traditional lands or to control how non-indigenous people use those lands

Aboriginals believe the relationship of humans to all other natural things – including animals, birds and land features such as mountains or rivers – was created during the Dreaming. Indigenous people must observe the laws of this relationship and keep the sleeping places of the ancestral spirits from harm. If the spirits are disturbed, the natural order is disturbed. These places are known as 'Dreaming places' or 'sacred sites'.

Each Aboriginal clan has its own special ancestral spirits, which connect the people to the land. The laws are passed to new generations through ceremonies, which include song, dance, mime and art. Some ceremonies are for everyone but often men and women have separate ceremonies, or 'secret business'.

Because the ancestral spirits hold a clan together, the extended family is very important to Indigenous Australians, whether they live on traditional lands or in the cities.

Aboriginal beliefs are passed on through dance, song and art.
National Library of Australia/Frank Hurley

MATESHIP, EGALITARIANISM AND 'A FAIR GO'

In 1983, a ruling of the High Court of Australia gave religion a wide definition. It said that a religion was a collection of beliefs and practices on which a set of values was based. This allowed Indigenous spiritual beliefs to be accepted as a religion. But the ruling did not suggest that mateship was a religion. Many Australians would not agree. If a religion is a set of values, then mateship could perhaps be called an Australian religion.

The ideal of mateship is firmly planted in the Australian mind but it is very hard to define. A mate is more than a close friend; he is someone on whom you can rely completely. One early writer said: 'Your mate is … yourself in another fellow's skin'.

Mateship is also a strict code of conduct among men that stresses equality and friendship. It is a male concept. Women don't have mates; they have friends.

The ideal of mateship probably began in the male-dominated early days of white settlement. The first settlers lived and worked far away from the towns. They depended for companionship and survival on a few fellow workers. But mateship – as the proper way to behave towards a friend – reached its peak among Australian soldiers during the two world wars.

Mates can come from the same social background or from a very different one. But, as mates, they are equal. Equality is an important feature of mateship.

The belief that everybody is equal – or egalitarianism – is also an important part of Australians' self-image. Early white Australia was divided into convicts and free settlers but the country had no aristocratic class as Britain and European countries did. In the hard work of settling the land, the bosses and workers laboured side by side. By the time the Australian states became a nation in 1901, the idea that Australians were all equal was widely believed.

This famous photograph of Sergeant G. R. Ayre helping Private W. O. Johnson in New Guinea during World War 2 captures the spirit of mateship. *Australian War Memorial 127971/Damien Parer*

However, egalitarian beliefs do not mean that Australia is a country without social divisions. People usually group together with others of similar background. The divisions are based mainly on education, jobs and wealth. The important point to remember is that Australians can move from one group to another if they wish.

One result of egalitarianism is 'the tall poppy syndrome'. A 'tall poppy' is someone who excels in something. When that person becomes too famous, rich or powerful, public opinion can turn against them. The tall poppy is cut down. Critics say the tall poppy syndrome results in second-rate performance in many aspects of Australian life.

An idea related to egalitarianism is the belief in 'a fair go'. One meaning of a fair go is reasonable or unbiased action. However, there is a more important meaning. To give people a fair go means to give them the chance to do something. Nothing should stop people from reaching their goals. For instance, everyone should be able to get a good education, a job, a home. Otherwise, they haven't had a fair go. Belief in a fair go was behind a lot of Australian social policy during much of the 20th century.

Social commentators say that mateship, egalitarianism and a fair go no longer reflect reality because the gap between rich and poor Australians is now so wide. This is true; but it does not stop many Australians believing in the ideals.

> **egalitarian** – *asserting the equality of all people, or someone who asserts the equality of people*
> **egalitarianism** – *the belief that all people are equal*

Australians at work

Many international students say Australians are lazy. Some are, of course. Most are not. In fact, one of the enduring Australian figures in Australian literature is that of the 'battler', who works hard in difficult conditions.

About 20 per cent of Australians in the workforce own their own business. The rest are employed in the private or public sectors. Public sector, or government, jobs have decreased in recent years.

TRADE UNIONS AND INDUSTRIAL ORGANISATIONS

Until the late 1980s, most Australian employees belonged to a trade union. Today, only a quarter of workers do. The unions were very important in the Australian political system. Although their influence has become weaker, they still represent nearly two million workers out of a total workforce of around nine million.

The role of the unions is to try to get better wages and working conditions for their members. Minimum wages and conditions are written down in an 'award'. Until recently, most awards applied to all workers in an industry. These were called 'industry awards'. Today, many awards are 'enterprise' agreements and apply to workers employed by a particular employer.

Four out of five employees have their pay set either by an enterprise agreement or an individual contract. In an individual contract, wages and conditions are agreed privately by the worker and the employer.

WORKPLACE HEALTH AND SAFETY

Employers are required by law to provide a safe and healthy workplace. These laws sometimes cause other effects. For example, bans on smoking in restaurants were introduced mainly to protect restaurant workers from the health risks of breathing customers' smoke.

THE WORKFORCE AND WORKING CONDITIONS

The labour market in Australia changed a lot in the late 20th century. Casual and part-time work increased. Today, more than a quarter of all employees are part-time workers. Part-time work is more common among women, who did not enter the paid workforce in big numbers until the 1970s.

Working hours have increased. The standard working week was set at 38 hours in the early 1980s; but many workers now work up to eight hours more a week without extra pay.

SUPERANNUATION

> **pension** – a regular payment in recognition of age, sickness, injury, poverty

Retired workers once got a pension from the government. But since 1986, all workers must put some of their pay into a superannuation fund, which will pay them when they stop work. The employers must also put money aside into each worker's 'super'.

These workplace changes have caused changes elsewhere. For instance, the large amount of money invested in superannuation funds has altered Australian investment markets. Through their super funds, most working Australians now indirectly hold shares in private companies. As a result, there is much public discussion about money and investment.

WORKING STUDENTS

Many tertiary students in Australia work to pay their living and education expenses. They try to get part-time work during the academic year and full-time work during vacations. The competition for suitable jobs is strong. Most students work in shops or restaurants where part-time work is available. Suitable jobs are advertised on campus or in the newspapers.

Your student visa says you cannot work. But you can pay a fee to change this visa once you are in Australia. The new visa restricts how much work you can do: up to 20 hours during term and full-time during vacations. If you are caught working more than the allowed number of hours, your visa is automatically cancelled.

Suitable jobs are advertised on campus noticeboards.

International students – except those enrolled in courses that are shorter than six months – have to pay tax like any other Australian worker. The Australian taxation system is graded, with lower-paid workers paying a smaller percentage of their earnings.

Your employer takes the correct rate of tax out of your wage and sends it to the tax office. When the financial year ends on 30 June, the employer gives you a 'payment summary' which lists your salary and the amount of tax deducted. You send the original summary with your taxation return to the tax office (Australian Taxation Office). The first $6000 you earn is not taxed but you must still put in a taxation return.

Every taxpayer has a Tax File Number (TFN). Your university or college international student centre can help you apply for a TFN. If you don't tell your employer what your TFN is, you will be taxed at the highest rate. The over-payment is returned to you after you put in your tax return. But you can't use the money in the meantime.

Many students are tempted to avoid the system by taking their wages in cash so there is no record of their employment. Avoiding paying tax is illegal. It is also unwise because the worker has no protection against employers who pay low wages or don't provide a safe workplace.

Australians at play

Organised sport – playing it, watching it and arguing about it – is a vital part of Australian culture. But Australians entertain themselves in many other ways. They walk in the bush or head to the nearest beach to surf, swim or fish. They gamble in casinos, on the racetrack and in the local pub or club. They are among the biggest book buyers in the world. They go to movies, plays, opera, dance and musical performances of many kinds. They go to art exhibitions and museums.

> **bush** – any area of uncultivated land with native vegetation
> **the bush** – the countryside in general

A SPORTING LIFE

The English novelist, Anthony Trollope, visited Australia in the middle of the 19th century. He said that sport appeared to be 'a national necessity'. One hundred years later, the Australian social critic Donald Horne wrote: 'Sport to many Australians is life and the rest a shadow'.

Swimming is a very popular sport for both men and women.
Photodisc Australia

Australians take great pride in sporting success. The nation has provided world champions in many sports including boxing, squash,

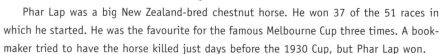

TWO SPORTING HEROES

When Australians list their sporting champions, there are many different names and different sports on each list. But two names are sure to be on everyone's list: Don Bradman and Phar Lap.

Born in New South Wales in 1908, Sir Donald Bradman was Australia's greatest cricketing batsman. He played 52 international, or Test, matches in his international cricketing career from 1928 to 1948. His average score was 99.94 runs.

Known as 'The Don', Bradman was Australian captain 24 times. He first toured to England in 1930 and made 974 runs in that Test series. He was knighted in 1949 and died in 2001.

La Trobe Picture Collection, State Library of Victoria

Phar Lap was a big New Zealand-bred chestnut horse. He won 37 of the 51 races in which he started. He was the favourite for the famous Melbourne Cup three times. A book-maker tried to have the horse killed just days before the 1930 Cup, but Phar Lap won.

In 1932, Phar Lap went to North America where he won a big race in Mexico. Sixteen days later, he was dead. Many people thought he had been poisoned. Recent research suggests he died of a rare horse disease.

tennis, rugby, swimming, motor racing and cycling. At the Sydney Olympics, in 2000, Australians won 58 medals – the highest tally per head of population of any country. The medal tally was mainly the result of 20 years of training top athletes in government-funded institutes of sport.

Half the Australian population regularly attend sporting events. Sports shows on television are the most-watched programs after news and current affairs. The most popular spectator sport is Australian Rules football, followed by horseracing, motor sports and Rugby League.

When playing sport, Australians are more interested in individual activity. About half the adult population takes part in some physical activity, but only a third plays organised sport. Slightly more men than women play or watch sport.

The most popular activities are walking, swimming, aerobics or other fitness programs, golf, tennis, cycling and running. Fishing, surfing and lawn bowls are among the 10 most

AUSTRALIAN RULES FOOTBALL

Sporting Images

When most people in the world talk about football, they mean soccer. In Australia, football often means Australian Rules (Aussie Rules) football. Developed in Melbourne in the middle of the 19th century, the game is very popular in Victoria, South Australia and Western Australia.

Unlike other football codes, it has no off-side rule so players from both sides are spread all over the large oval-shaped field. Players can kick or handle the oval ball. They are not sent off for rough play but can be fined or suspended later. The game's characteristics are its speed and high jumps as players leap to catch the ball (or 'take a mark'). There are 18 players on each side.

Each game is divided into four 25-minute quarters, with extra time for injury. Players score by kicking the ball between four upright posts at the end of the field. A goal, worth six points, is awarded if the ball goes between the two taller middle posts. A point is scored if the ball goes between the middle and outside posts.

Aussie Rules is played from March until the grand final at the Melbourne Cricket Ground on the last Saturday in September. There are 16 teams in the Australian Football League (AFL). Most are in Victoria but Western Australia has two teams, South Australia two and Sydney and Brisbane one each.

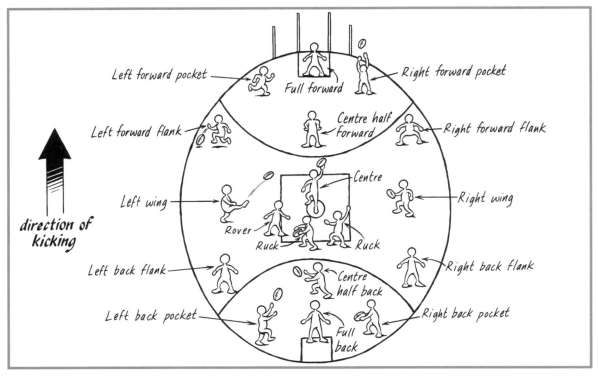

Player positions in Australian Rules football.

popular activities for men. Women list netball, tenpin bowling and martial arts among their favourite activities.

Australian children are more likely than their parents to play organised sport. But their most popular pastimes are watching television and playing electronic or computer games. Lack of physical activity and overweight children are topics of much discussion and concern.

THE BEACH AND THE BUSH

Every summer, between Christmas and the end of January, hundreds of thousands of Australians go to the beach for their holidays. They spend time swimming, walking, fishing, playing games on the beach or just lying around. However, beaches are popular at any time during the year.

Beaches can be dangerous. There are various poisonous creatures in the water and rock pools. It is not wise to touch any sea animals. Many Australian coastal cliffs are soft and can collapse.

Shark attacks – although they receive a lot of media coverage when they happen – are rare. The average death rate from shark attack is less than one a year. In some places, swimmers are protected by shark nets or shark-spotting aircraft. When a shark is seen, a siren sounds and people get out of the water.

Obey all safety signs that warn of danger.

Lifesavers patrol a beach. *Courtesy: Surf Life Saving Australia*

Australian seas differ from those in other parts of the world and newcomers should take special care. Hidden rips, or currents, in the water can carry swimmers out to sea. Sudden big waves can wash people off the rocks.

During the summer, many beaches are patrolled by lifesavers, or life guards. The lifesavers can recognise dangerous water and they place red and yellow flags on the beach to show the safest place to swim. Always swim between the flags. Don't swim on unpatrolled beaches. Never swim alone. Ask the lifesavers for advice about safe swimming. If you get into trouble in the water, don't panic. Raise your arm, float and wait for the lifesavers to swim or row out to help you.

Collecting animals, plants or shells from the beach is discouraged. In some places, such as marine or coastal parks, it is illegal. The states and territories have slightly different regulations so it is sensible to find out about them. Brochures with details of the regulations are usually available at information centres in coastal towns.

Fishing in the sea or inland waters without a licence is forbidden. Even with a licence, there are limits on the size and numbers of fish that people can catch.

The bush and the inland rivers and lakes are also popular leisure destinations. Again, be careful. More Australians drown in inland waters than in the sea. Some are injured because they dive into the water without checking the depth or seeing if there are rocks or dead trees hidden in the water.

Walking in the bush is popular. In most state and national parks, the tracks have good signposts; but it is easy to get lost if you leave the tracks. Even on short walks, carry plenty of drinking water.

Fire can be a hazard in the bush. Never let a campfire burn unless someone is watching it. On days of extreme fire danger when it is hot and windy, don't walk in the bush.

In the bush and on the beach, it is important to leave no rubbish, which can harm native animals and spoil the beauty of the natural surroundings. A government brochure advises: 'If you have carried it in, carry it out'.

PUBS, BARS, CLUBS AND NIGHT-LIFE

Drinking alcohol is an important part of Australian culture. Some critics think it is much too important. People drink at home with friends and family but many people, especially students, drink in hotels, which are usually called pubs.

Pubs can vary from big buildings in the outer suburbs to smaller hotels, often built on street corners in the city. In rural areas, the pub is often the focus of community life.

All pubs serve alcohol and food. Some offer accommodation. Many pubs, except in Western Australia, have poker machines. Others have pool tables or live music.

Large, cheap meals based on traditional Australian cooking are still served in the public bar of some local pubs. These are called 'counter meals'. But these days, many pubs have dining rooms or bistros where the food is more varied and more expensive.

The pub tends to be a male territory, particularly in rural towns. Twenty years ago, pubs used to have a Ladies Lounge, which was a separate room for women. The public bar was reserved for men only. These days, the law does not allow this discrimination against women.

Bars, which are separate from hotels, have become fashionable gathering places in recent years, especially for younger people. They serve drinks and light meals.

Leagues clubs provide food and entertainment. *Courtesy: Brisbane Broncos Leagues Club*

For many older Australians, the club is the local sporting or RSL club. Entry is restricted to members and their guests. These clubs are similar to pubs: they serve food and alcohol and often provide live entertainment. New South Wales and Queensland have a network of clubs called Leagues clubs. Each club is home to a local Rugby League team.

> **RSL** – the Returned & Services League represents men and women who have served in the Australian armed forces

For younger Australians, the club is something different. It is a drinking, dancing and music venue where they meet people of similar tastes. The club scene is very varied. Some people think clubs are places to take drugs and meet casual sexual partners. This opinion is sometimes accurate; often it is not. If you go to a club, make sure you know what sort of club to expect.

Clubs are mainly restricted to the big cities. They go in and out of fashion very quickly. Daily papers in the capital cities list clubs, discos and live music gigs in special entertainment pages, usually published on Thursdays or Fridays. There are also many free street magazines in most capital cities, which review and list music, rave parties and other entertainment for younger people.

GAMBLING

Gambling began in Australia with white settlement. Betting on cards, dice and horseraces was common. During the two world wars, Australian soldiers played a game called two-up. Two coins were put on a flat piece of wood and tossed in the air. The players bet on which way the coins landed. Two-up was banned for many years. It is now played legally in Australia's 13 casinos.

Officials estimate that eight out of every 10 Australians gamble at least once a year. The Melbourne Cup, a horserace held on the first Tuesday in November, is part of the reason for that huge figure. The Cup is known as 'the race that stops a nation'. Having a small bet on the Cup is more a social activity than a real gamble.

Totalisator Agency Boards, or 'the TAB', are

An early advertisement for the Melbourne Cup. *La Trobe Picture Collection, State Library of Victoria*

betting shops where people can bet on the results of many sports. They were set up by state governments to control illegal gambling on horse-racing. These days, the TABs are private companies and their shares are traded on the stock exchange. The TAB shop, with its television screens showing races from around Australia, is a familiar sight across the country.

Lotteries to raise money for charities started early in the 20th century. They were well established by the 1930s. Lotteries are still the most common form of gambling, with about 60 per cent of people buying a ticket either regularly or sometimes.

Poker machines, or 'the pokies', have been legal in some New South Wales clubs for many years. But in the 1990s these gaming machines became widespread in hotels as well.

The increase in gambling machines and casinos worries many people. State governments get a lot of money from taxes on gambling, but some people are concerned about 'problem gamblers' who are addicted to gambling. Other people, and the gambling industry, say gambling is a legitimate recreation for most gamblers.

FILM AND TELEVISION

The first film made in Australia was a documentary of the 1896 Melbourne Cup. Feature films and newsreels were made from the early part of the 20th century. But it was not until the 1970s that Australian film production became firmly established, with the help of federal government money. The state governments also help fund film-making.

Some of the more successful films of the 1970s were historical dramas based on Australian novels. Stories of rural life were common. But later the range of subjects widened to include Aboriginal history, war, migration, crime and life in the cities. There is no typical Australian film, but many contain elements of humour and respect for mateship and egalitarianism.

These days, international film-makers are shooting more films in Australia because it is cheaper than other locations. Big new production studios in the eastern states were built to encourage this trend. Critics worry that making films for the international market will mean that Australian films will lose their national identity. But no one is sure what that identity is.

Australian actors and film-makers have successful careers overseas as well as at home. The directors include Gillian Armstrong, Bruce Beresford, Baz Luhrmann, Phil Noyce, Fred Schepisi and Peter Weir. Recent successful actors include Cate Blanchett, Toni Collette, Russell Crowe, Rachel Griffiths, Heath Ledger, Nicole Kidman and Anthony La Paglia.

Australians are keen movie-goers. Although Australian films are popular, local audiences can see many other kinds of movie: Hollywood blockbusters, British films, martial arts adventures from Hong Kong and non-commercial art films from around the world. However, foreign language films are rarely seen outside the capital cities.

Locally produced television programs are also popular. When television was introduced in 1956, the federal government said some programs had to be Australian-made. Most 'local content' in the early days of television was news broadcasts and low-budget variety shows. The first drama series, the police drama *Homicide*, began in the 1960s.

Police dramas are still common. So, too, are medical dramas, current affairs programs and lifestyle programs about home and garden maintenance, cookery, and animal care. Australian television also produces its own versions of successful overseas quiz shows and 'reality' TV programs.

Foreign language programs are shown on SBS, the multicultural broadcaster.

SOUNDS OF AUSTRALIA

When British free settlers came to Australia, many brought their pianos with them. Playing the piano and singing were the main home entertainments of the 19th century. Amateur musicians and military bands played in concert halls and in the open air. Music-making, especially singing, was enjoyable and cheap.

The musical tradition continued. Australia gave the world a large number of singers, especially of European opera. The most famous is Dame Nellie Melba. Others are Peter Dawson,

The singer Nellie Melba gained international fame early in the 20th century. *La Trobe Picture Collection, State Library of Victoria*

Florence Austral and Joan Sutherland. The national opera company, Opera Australia, was formed in 1970 but several smaller state companies failed because of high costs.

Professional orchestras in each state began during the 1920s, run by the public radio broadcaster, the ABC. Today, the state orchestras and many other amateur and semi-professional orchestras, chamber music groups and contemporary ensembles create a lively classical music scene. About 25 years ago, specialist radio stations were set up to broadcast local and overseas classical concerts and recitals.

Classical music has a small but loyal audience. Government money and increasing amounts of sponsorship from the private sector are needed to keep classical music companies alive. The amount of government money given to the arts and how it should be spent is a topic of endless debate.

Rock and other kinds of popular music have much bigger audiences and little direct government support. When rock'n'roll arrived from the United States and Britain in the 1950s and 1960s, it found an eager audience. The pioneer of Australian rock was Johnny O'Keefe, known as the 'Wild One'.

The Australian popular music industry quickly became part of the global music industry. Many of its bands and individual performers built successful careers overseas. They include the Bee Gees and Olivia Newton-John in the 1960s. Later came Skyhooks, AC/DC, the Little River Band, Midnight Oil, Men at Work, Air Supply, Crowded House, INXS and Kylie Minogue. More recent success stories are silverchair and Savage Garden.

However, it was not until the 1990s that popular music began to develop an Australian accent. For some time, Indigenous musicians used popular music styles from overseas, such as country music and reggae. But in the 1990s they began to blend traditional music, instruments and language with these overseas styles. Names like Yothu Yindi, Coloured Stone, Archie Roach, Ruby Hunter, Jimmy Little, Tiddas and Christine Anu are familiar to Australians interested in popular music.

In 2001 Australian pop musicians were commemorated in a series of stamps. *Courtesy: National Philatelic Collection, Australia Post*

The music that mainstream radio stations play is often dominated by overseas artists. But student radio stations, community stations and the national youth music station, Triple J, play a lot of local music.

Musical performances of all kinds are advertised in the entertainment sections of daily papers. Many classical concerts sell cheaper tickets for students.

ARTISTIC AUSTRALIA

The role of the arts in Australia is confusing. On one hand, Australians are said to be uncultured. They are suspicious of intellectual activity and give little respect to scholars. They value their creative artists less than they value their sports men and women. They complain when taxpayers' money is used to buy works of art that they don't like.

On the other hand, the arts are an accepted part of many Australians' lives. The national arts organisation, the Australia Council, estimates that 85 per cent of Australian adults are involved in cultural activity, as consumers or creators.

One in four people do some form of artistic work, either as a hobby or a profession. The value of the arts sector is growing faster than the economy as a whole.

Most capital cities have permanent theatre companies which stage overseas and local plays. Dance companies, including the Australian Ballet, perform classical and contemporary dance. Australian circus companies are developing their own style of circus. Visual artists sell millions of dollars worth of artworks in commercial galleries each year.

Yet many critics say the Australian arts scene is not healthy. They say the vision that artists portray of Australian society is no longer accurate. In general, Australian creative arts lack the political content common in Europe, Latin America and Asia; they are more concerned with private and individual stories of ordinary people. The themes in Australian art are small-scale and bland, the critics say.

An exhibition opens in a Melbourne commercial art gallery.
Courtesy: Goya Galleries, Melbourne

Australian eating habits

The image of a tall, lean Australian is a familiar one. Unfortunately, it is not true. Australians are growing fatter every year. Health authorities estimate that nearly two-thirds of Australian men and nearly half the women are overweight or obese. Has the Australian diet changed over the years? Is this the reason people are growing fatter? What do Australians eat today?

A SLICE OF HISTORY

Food historian Michael Symons says that the main thing that affected Australian eating habits was that the country had no peasant class. In Europe and Asia, the peasants were subsistence farmers, growing what they needed to survive. They made traditional dishes from the produce they grew. But by the late 18th century, British farming methods had become industrialised to feed people in the growing cities. White settlers brought these industrial methods to Australia.

In the late 19th and early 20th centuries, Australian farmers wanted export markets for their produce. They experimented with ways of preserving food, such as canning, which allowed it to be transported the long distances to European markets. An Australian Scot, James Harrison, invented a way of refrigerating ships to export meat.

Symons says Australians didn't need to develop their own cooking styles. They cooked meals based on English recipes. Roasted meat, potatoes and bread were staple foods. Food was bland and not spicy. Chinese goldminers established market gardens during the 1850s; but meals based mainly on rice and vegetables were not common.

Then, in the 1960s, something happened to Australian eating habits. Australians began to eat Greek, Italian, French and other European dishes. Middle Eastern and Asian foods gradually appeared on menus.

Most people say post-war immigration led to these diverse cooking styles. Symons disagrees. He says the rise of Chinese restaurants occurred in Australia in the 1950s when Chinese immigration was banned. The sudden popularity of Thai food during the 1980s happened without the arrival of lots of Thai immigrants.

However, migrant families cooked traditional foods at home. This kept the traditions alive and created a demand for traditional ingredients. So, when Australians began to dine out more often in the 1970s, the different cooking methods of many different cultures moved from homes to restaurants. Another factor was that Australians began to travel more and were introduced to the foods of other countries.

DRINKING HABITS

Australians spend more of their household income on alcoholic drinks than on non-alcoholic ones. Beer, served cold, was the most popular alcoholic drink but now wine is equally common. Beer is probably one reason why so many Australian men are too fat; a fat stomach in men is often called a 'beer gut'.

Coffee is more popular than it was, but many people drink tea. Tea is usually served in the English style, with added milk and sugar. Green teas and herbal teas are becoming increasingly popular among younger Australians. Tea and coffee are served with food at breakfast but after food at other meals.

Tap water is safe to drink but in some places it doesn't taste nice. So, more and more Australians buy bottled water. Students often carry small bottles of water with them to class. Young Australians also drink international brand soft drinks and bottled fruit juices.

Visitors are surprised by the amount of milk that adult Australians drink. Flavoured milk in cardboard containers is sold everywhere.

MEAT, MEAT AND MORE MEAT

In the early colonial days, the government gave rations of salted beef or pork, flour, sugar and tea to the convicts and soldiers. The importance of meat in the Australian diet continued; after

Australians like eating out. *Photo: Courtesy of Nick's Bar & Grill; Tourism New South Wales*

World War 2, an immigration slogan promised migrants 'meat three times a day'.

Today, Australians eat a little less meat. Beef is the most popular type of meat. Thirty years ago, chicken was only served on special occasions. Now Australians eat almost as much chicken as beef. Pork and lamb are also eaten.

Australians prefer prime cuts of meat with a lot of muscle, a little fat and not much bone. They make pet food from many of the parts of an animal – such as hearts, heads and innards – that are delicacies in other countries.

THREE MEALS A DAY

Australian meals are as varied as the Australian population. Migrant families often eat as they did in their home countries. But the following inform-ation is true about many urban Australians.

Many people start the day without eating breakfast. They might just drink a cup of coffee. Those who eat breakfast don't usually eat much. During the week, breakfast might be fruit juice, a bowl of cereal with milk, or toasted bread spread with jam, honey or Vegemite (see page 19) and a cup of tea or coffee. At weekends and on holiday, people sometimes add eggs, bacon, grilled tomatoes or tinned beans. Breakfast is generally eaten at home, although these days more cafes and fast food outlets sell breakfast.

Lunch is usually eaten between midday and 2 p.m. Lunch is a quick meal. Sandwiches or bread rolls with fillings of cooked meat, salad vegetables, cheese or eggs are typical lunch foods. So too are meat pies and pastries, hamburgers, potato chips and other fried foods.

The main meal of the day is dinner, which is often called 'tea'. If someone invites you to their home for tea, you get much more than a cup of tea. Tea is normally eaten between 6 p.m. and 8 p.m.

If the tea is home-cooked, it is likely to be the traditional piece of meat with potatoes and one or two other vegetables, served in individual portions. The sharing of communal dishes isn't usual at family meals. The meal ends with a sweet dessert or cooked fruit. Soup is eaten at the start of the meal.

Few Australians prepare all their meals from raw ingredients. One reason is that many women

AUSTRALIAN DELICACIES

Here are some dishes that Australians call their own:

Anzacs: biscuits made of oats, dried coconut and a sweet syrup called golden syrup.

Damper: a mixture of flour and water cooked on the coals of a campfire. Although it is not eaten often today, damper was the traditional bread of the early settlers.

Lamington: a small square of plain sponge cake, dipped in chocolate and rolled in dried coconut.

Meat pie: a small pastry case filled with finely chopped meat and gravy, it is a traditional snack at sports events.

Minties™ and Jaffas™: two popular Australian sweets, or 'lollies'. Minties are chewy and mint-flavoured. Jaffas are chocolate balls inside a thin, orange sugar coating.

Pavlova, (or 'pav'): a dessert, named after the Russian ballerina, Anna Pavlova. A meringue base – with a crisp outside and a soft inside – is covered with fresh fruit and whipped cream.

Vegemite™: a thick dark paste made from the yeast left over after brewing beer. It is spread on toast or in sandwiches. Many non-Australians agree with the French student who said 'Vegemite tastes disgusting'.

work and have less time to cook. Another reason is the wide availability of pre-cooked, frozen meals prepared by the food industry, or fresh food, partly prepared by shopkeepers.

Australians spend more than a quarter of their household budget on dining out or eating 'takeaway' food, which is commercially cooked. People collect the meal from the takeaway shop or have it delivered. Popular takeaways are pizzas, fish and chips, fried or roast chicken and Asian dishes.

Greater use of fast foods, which are often high in fat and sugar, is probably one reason why today's Australians are fatter than their parents and grandparents.

SHOPPING FOR FOOD

The reliance on processed food means that urban Australians do a lot of their food shopping in supermarkets. A supermarket is usually the hub of any shopping centre.

Shopping hours vary from state to state.

However, supermarket hours are being increased and 24-hour 'convenience stores' are appearing in the bigger cities.

In much of Asia, the Middle East and some parts of Europe, markets made up of small stalls that sell raw and cooked food are common. These markets are rare in Australia. But there are specialist food shops, such as butchers and greengrocers, in most shopping centres.

The Australian climate allows people to buy a variety of fresh fruit and vegetables throughout the year. Warm areas in the north provide tropical fruits and other vegetables to markets in the south during cooler winter months. Southern areas grow cool weather crops like apples, cherries, potatoes and cabbages.

Migration has also contributed to variety in ingredients. Middle Eastern and Asian ingredients are now available in bigger cities. The range of vegetables and fruits has grown. Halal food can be found in areas with large Muslim populations.

part two:
customs

APL/Retina Lifestyle

'What I want to know is Australian behaviour. What are Australian celebrations? What is proper behaviour when I am in someone's home?'

– email from a Chinese student before her arrival

Thoughtful travellers worry about making mistakes when they visit another country. But making mistakes is not very important in Australia because Australians are usually tolerant. Their attitude is casual and relaxed, so there are few formal rules for newcomers to learn. However, some behaviour and customs are useful to know.

At the table

Manners at the table differ a lot from culture to culture. For example, slurping when you eat is polite in some countries, but not in Australia. Burping is not polite, either.

Chewing food with your mouth open or talking when chewing is bad manners. Spitting out food on to your plate or the table is not polite. If you can't eat something in your mouth, take it out with your fingers and put it on the side of your plate.

The custom about refusing food is easy to remember. A direct response is best. If you are hungry, accept the offer of food immediately. The practice of refusing at first and then accepting, which is polite in some cultures, does not apply in Australia.

No one will be offended if you refuse food. The polite way is to say: 'No thank you, I have had plenty' or 'It looks good but I won't have any, thank you'. If there are foods you cannot eat – for religious or health reasons – say: 'Thank you, but I can't eat that'. When someone invites you to their home for a meal, it is polite to tell them in advance about foods that you cannot eat.

Australians usually serve meals in individual portions on separate plates. Sometimes, though, food is served in common dishes. These dishes are passed around the table and people take the amount they want. At barbeques or informal parties, the dishes are put on a table. People put their food on a plate and move away from the table to eat, often standing up!

Leaving a little food on your plate is not considered rude, but eating only one or two mouthfuls is not polite. Move any uneaten food to the side of the plate.

Most food is eaten with a knife and fork or spoon. These days it is acceptable to eat meat off small bones, such as chicken wings, in your fingers. Put the bones on the side of the plate, never on the table. Other foods eaten in the fingers include asparagus, sandwiches, bread rolls, pizza, fried chicken pieces, chips and corn on the cob.

It is customary to wait until everyone is seated at the table before starting to eat.

TABLE SETTINGS

The Australian table looks complicated to people used to chopsticks or a simple fork and spoon. It isn't really. Cutlery – knives, forks and spoons of different sizes – is laid out on each side of the space where a person's main plate of food is put. You use the outside pieces for the first course of food and move towards the middle as the next course arrives.

A small plate on the left is used for bread rolls or slices of bread. These are broken into smaller pieces with the fingers. If you want butter, put it on each piece separately. Glasses are put on the right of the plate. Paper or cloth napkins are usually provided. You put them on your lap and use them to wipe your mouth when necessary.

DINING OUT

The range of cafes and restaurants in Australia is wide. There are few small street stalls like those in Asia and the Middle East. Some eating places are very formal; others are casual.

In formal restaurants, you stand inside the door until a waiter shows you to a table. If you are a guest, your host will tell you where to sit. In

How an Australian table is set for a meal.

more informal cafes and pubs, you can go straight to a vacant table.

Sharing a table with strangers, especially in busy cafes, is not unusual. This is particularly true at lunchtime or if you are eating by yourself. However, it is unusual to share a table with a stranger if another table is vacant. It is also rare for a man to share a table with a woman. Men share with men and women share with women. If you see a vacant seat at a table, you ask: 'May I share this table?' The other person will often say yes. Be prepared to make conversation if the other person wants to talk to you.

You attract the attention of a waiter by beckoning with your hand. If the waiter is passing close by, you attract attention by saying 'Excuse me'. It is not usual to call out to the waiter.

PAYING THE BILL

An Australian custom that seems very odd to people from some cultures is the practice of 'splitting the bill'. If you go out for a meal with friends, each person pays a share of the bill. This is sometimes known as 'going Dutch'. If someone invites you to a meal in a cafe or restaurant, expect to pay your share unless the person makes it clear you are going as their guest. Some cafes write out separate bills for each customer; most do not.

Splitting the bill is less common among courting couples. The man usually pays, particularly on the first few dates. Later in the relationship, the couple may decide to share the cost.

In some cafes and pubs – especially those with outdoor dining areas – you pay before you get your meal. You order the meal, pay at the counter and then sit down. When the meal is ready, the waiter brings it to you.

In other places, you ask the waiter to bring the bill. In formal restaurants, you pay at the table, not at the cash register. In cafes, you sometimes pay at the register.

TIPPING

Tipping is not standard practice, except in expensive restaurants where people can pay an extra 10 per cent if they wish. Many cafes have a jar for small tips near the cash register.

The good guest

Your first visit to an Australian home is sure to make you anxious. Don't worry. Your host invited you as a friend and will not criticise your behaviour.

PARTIES AND MEALS

When you are invited to a party at someone's house, you can take a bottle of wine or some cans of beer if you drink alcohol. But it is not essential.

If the invitation to a party says it is BYO or BYOG, you must provide any alcohol you want to drink. BYO (G) stands for 'Bring Your Own (Grog)'. If you don't drink alcohol, you can take a bottle of soft drink but it isn't necessary.

A message on some party invitations is 'Bring a plate'. This doesn't mean you take an empty plate. You take a plate of food to share with others. The food can be homemade or bought from a food shop. It can be savoury or sweet.

Friends enjoy a dinner party. *Images on Tap*

Some invitations include you and a friend. If you are not sure if the invitation includes someone else, ask your host if it is all right to bring a friend.

If you are invited to a meal, rather than a party, in someone's home, you can take a small gift of flowers or chocolates. However, the giving of gifts to your host is less widespread in Australia than in some cultures.

It is polite to offer to help with the washing-up after a family meal. This applies equally to men and women. The host will probably say no, but will be pleased that you offered.

Australian hosts have one unusual habit. If it is your first visit, they often show you through the whole house. They are proud of their homes so it is polite to say something nice about the house.

There are not many rules about when you should end your visit. But it is impolite to leave immediately after the end of a meal. At parties, watch when others leave. Try not to be the first or the last to leave.

Always thank your host when you say goodbye. You can also send a short thank-you note or make a phone call the day after the party. This custom pleases older people but is not followed much by young people.

The one thing that everyone agrees is very rude is accepting an invitation to a party or a meal in someone's home and then not going.

AN OVERNIGHT STAY
The key to a happy stay in an Australian home is to ask if you are not sure about anything. For instance, ask what time the family normally goes to bed. You go to bed about 15 to 30 minutes earlier to give them some private time.

Before you go to bed, ask what time the family has breakfast. Stay in your room until that time. If you need another blanket, ask for it. Ask permission if you want to use the phone and keep the phone calls short.

Keep your guest room tidy and leave the door open when you are not in the room. Remember that a closed door in a house usually means someone is inside. Always knock on the door and wait to be invited before walking into a room.

Don't stay in the bathroom for longer than 15 or 20 minutes. Make sure it is clean and dry when you leave. You can use the bathmat or your towel to mop up any spilt water.

It is important to write a thank-you note or make a phone call after your stay.

Behaviour in public places

Australians are generally considerate about the needs of strangers when they are in public places. Some behaviour – such as queuing – aims to make sure everyone is treated fairly and equally.

SHOPPING
Bargaining is rare in most Australian shops and there is no tradition of giving lower prices to the first customer of the day.

However, you can bargain when you buy cars, furniture or electrical goods. The same thing applies when buying clothing. For example, if you buy two pairs of shoes instead of one pair, you can ask for a better price. In cities that have general markets – such as Sydney and Melbourne – asking for a better price is acceptable. However, the complex bargaining customs of Asia and the Middle East don't exist.

The rules about credit card purchases have changed. The law now allows sellers to charge a lower price for cash because they have to pay fees to the credit card companies. Many shopkeepers don't do this but it is sensible to ask if there is a discount for cash.

THE QUEUE
Australians are surprisingly docile in crowded places. They queue patiently to buy things such as tickets at the cinema or to get service in a shop or bank. When buying tickets to very popular sporting events or entertainments, they sometimes sleep overnight in the street to keep their place in the queue.

Queues are organised in different ways. Banks and airports have areas bounded by ropes so that customers form a single long queue. Even when the area is not roped off, customers usually form a line by themselves.

In some fast food outlets and supermarkets, customers take a numbered ticket and then stand

A queue at an automatic teller machine.

back from the counter. When their number is called, they move forward to be served. In other places, you may not see a queue but people behave as if there is one. This invisible queue means that when the shop attendant asks 'Who's next?', it is bad manners to be served if someone else has waited longer than you.

When getting money from an automatic teller machine, or 'ATM', people also form a queue. The person at the start of the queue stands at least two metres away from the customer who is at the ATM. This gives the customer some privacy.

AT THE THEATRE

Australians think people are rude if they talk during a film or a live performance because it can spoil other people's enjoyment. They don't mind people eating at the theatre; but they don't like people making a noise opening sweet wrappers or eating noisy food such as potato crisps (see also 'Mobile phone manners' on page 25).

Most people disapprove of others who arrive after any live performance has started. This includes theatre, concerts, operas and dance performances. Some companies do not allow latecomers to go to their seats until there is a break in the performance. You might not be allowed in until the interval; so it is wise to get to the show on time.

A SENSE OF TIME

Australians are a relaxed people. But they are not relaxed about time. They think punctuality is good, especially on formal occasions. When you receive an invitation, you will be told what time to arrive. If you are unsure, ask. Try to arrive on time or not more than five or 10 minutes late. It is not polite to arrive early.

Being on time also applies to meetings, classes, concerts and all appointments.

PUBLIC TRANSPORT

In general, Australians do not push and shove when getting on and off buses or trains. They stand back to allow people to get off the vehicle

---

SPEAKING IN YOUR MOTHER TONGUE

Sometimes it is a relief to be able to speak your own language. It gives your brain a rest. But there are times when it is not appropriate. In your English language classes, your teacher tells you the rules, which makes life easy. Outside the classroom, you must use common sense.

If you are in a mixed group where some people cannot speak your language, it is polite to use the common language, English. If you have to use your language – for instance, because a friend from your country doesn't understand something – tell the others in the group what you are talking about. You don't have to translate the whole conversation but give a summary. It is particularly rude to talk in your mother tongue at the table when dining.

When talking in your mother tongue to friends in public places, speak quietly.

---

before getting on it themselves.

Public transport rules don't allow people to put their feet on the seats. It is not illegal to put your bag on the seat beside you; but it is inconsiderate if the vehicle is crowded and other passengers are standing up.

Usually, a few seats near the door are reserved for elderly people or people with disabilities. You can sit in these seats if no older people or disabled passengers need a seat.

In the past, young people always gave their seats to older people and men gave their seats to women. This does not happen very often today. However, it is kind to give your seat to pregnant women, parents with small children and older people.

ROAD RULES

Behaviour on Australian roads is strictly regulated for safety reasons. The rules vary slightly from state to state. Wearing seatbelts in cars is compulsory and throwing rubbish, including cigarette butts, out of a vehicle is banned. Rules also stop people using their mobile phones while driving.

By law, bicycle (bike) riders must wear safety helmets. They must also use lights when riding at night. They are not allowed to have a second person on the bicycle, unless it is a child in a proper child's seat and the child is wearing a safety helmet.

NASTY HABITS

Some international students find certain Australian habits disgusting. One is the way Australians blow their noses into a cloth or paper handkerchief. But, in Australia, sniffing or blowing one's nose directly onto the ground is considered bad manners. Spitting and picking one's nose with a finger are also impolite.

MOBILE PHONE MANNERS

In 2003, telecommunications companies in Australia started a campaign to improve Australians' mobile phone manners. The campaign followed a survey which showed that many Australians thought bad manners were increasing.

Phones with loud ring tones offend many people. They don't like people talking too loudly on their mobiles.

Interrupting a conversation with someone to answer your phone is not polite. So, too, is using your phone during formal occasions such as weddings.

Many restaurants and cinemas ask customers to turn off their phones. Other places where it is rude to use your phone are theatres, classrooms and places of worship.

Personal celebrations

Like people everywhere, Australians celebrate the important milestones in their lives.

> **milestone** – an event that marks a significant point in a person's life or career

But they stress different milestones from other cultures. For instance, a child's first birth-day is very important in some Asian countries. It is less important in Australia. The ways that people celebrate weddings and funerals are very varied; many immigrant families mix the traditions of their home country with some Australian customs.

BIRTH OF A CHILD

The birth of a new child is a happy occasion. It is usually announced in the birth notices of the main local newspaper.

It is customary to send a card to the mother, congratulating her on the birth. Most Australian births happen in hospitals. Close friends send flowers to the hospital for the mother and, sometimes, a small gift for the child. Mothers and babies go home in a few days. New mothers are seen in public immediately, unlike in some countries.

While immigrant families may follow their own customs, there are no special Australian ceremonies to welcome the baby.

The birth of a baby is announced in daily newspapers. *Geelong Advertiser*

BIRTHDAYS

The anniversary of a person's birth is important in Australia, especially during childhood. This reflects the importance of the individual in Australia. A birthday is an individual's own special day. However, some birthdays are more significant than others.

By law, an Australian becomes an adult at the age of 18. They can vote, buy alcohol, sign binding legal contracts and marry without their parents' permission; so their 18th birthday is very important. It marks the boundary between childhood and adulthood. Australians also celebrate their 21st birthdays as especially important. That is because, in the past, 21 was the age when a person 'got the key to the door', or became an adult.

After a person's 21st birthday, the next significant birthday is the 50th. The 70th, 80th and 90th birthdays are all important. When people celebrate their 100th birthday, they receive special letters from the Queen and political leaders.

The important birthdays are usually occasions for big parties attended by members of the extended family and friends. The parties can be formal or informal. Often – but not always – a senior family member gives a speech and proposes a toast.

> **propose a toast** – to call on others to drink to a thing or organisation or to the health of a person

Parties on less important birthdays are mostly informal. They are usually attended by friends and/or the immediate family only.

A birthday cake decorated with small lighted candles, one for each year, is the only traditional birthday food. The birthday person blows out the candles and the guests sing 'Happy Birthday' and cheer three times.

Written invitations are usually sent if the birthday is an important one. If the style of the invitation is formal, you reply in writing. If it is casual, you can phone to say whether you accept or not. Always reply to an invitation which has the letters 'RSVP' on it. This means 'please reply'.

Guests are expected to bring gifts. Gifts do not need to be expensive but should show thought about the individual's interests. For example, a cookery book or a pot of herbs is suitable for someone who likes cooking.

GIVING GIFTS

In most cultures, people don't open gifts in front of the person who gave them. In Australia, gifts aren't opened on some occasions, such as weddings and birthday parties. But if you give someone a gift when visiting their home, he or she usually opens it straightaway.

ENGAGEMENTS

Engagement parties are normally casual occasions. The engagement is usually announced in the newspaper by both sets of parents or by the couple. It is nearly always celebrated with a party of friends and family. There are no set rituals, except the man gives his fiancée an engagement ring privately before the party. Guests are expected to admire the ring. They also bring a gift, usually something small for the couple's future household.

The length of engagements varies. It is often affected by the couple's ability to save money. The dream of owning a house means a lot of couples do not marry until they have a deposit for a house. Some couples are engaged for a few months; others are engaged for one or two years or longer.

WEDDINGS

Wedding customs have changed a lot in the last 30 years. In general, weddings are much less formal than they were. These days, nearly three-quarters of all couples live together before marriage, so the significance of the wedding day has changed.

Today, half of all weddings are secular. They are performed by a person known as a civil celebrant. The wedding ceremony can be held anywhere. The couple often choose a place that has personal significance for them. For example, if a couple are keen surfers, they might marry on a beach. And they might wear surfers' wetsuits! Many couples create their own vows. The couple have to sign the marriage register in front of witnesses for the marriage to be legal.

Even traditional-style weddings are more informal these days.
FINE ART video & photography

register – *a book used to list names, events and so on as a record*

The celebrations after a civil ceremony might be a casual party at home or a formal dinner at a restaurant.

In the past, couples were nearly always married in a church by a minister or priest. Many still are. The ceremony is mainly a religious event but the couple also sign the marriage register at the church. The religious ceremony is followed by a formal wedding reception.

The religious ceremonies and customs at wedding celebrations in Australia can vary greatly because of its big immigrant population. However, at an old-style Australian wedding reception, there are few rituals. Speeches are made, toasts to the couple's good health drunk, a wedding cake cut. If there is dancing, the bridal couple begin the dancing. When the couple leave, the bride throws her bouquet to the unmarried female guests. It is rude to leave the reception before the bridal couple leaves.

A popular practice is the gift register or list. The couple chooses suitable gifts at a big store. The choice is written in a register. The guests go to the same store and look at the register so they can buy something they know the couple wants. But guests do not have to use the register.

Wedding gifts never include money. Gifts should be delivered to the bride's house before the wedding; but these days, guests often take the gifts to the reception.

Guests always receive a written invitation to a wedding. It is polite to reply promptly. It is also polite to send a thank-you note to the people who issued the invitation. Another nice thing to do is to give the couple a copy of any photographs you take at the wedding.

CORRECT DRESS

Australians are normally casual dressers but an invitation may sometimes say 'Black tie' or 'Lounge suit'. Black tie means men wear a dinner suit with a bow tie and women wear long dresses. Lounge suit means men wear a suit and tie and women wear short or long dresses. Traditional dress from other countries is suitable at all formal occasions.

There are no strict rules about the colour of dress. Australians don't attach meanings to colours. However, mourners at funerals wear dark colours.

There are also no rules about covering parts of the body. Australian women can uncover their shoulders or wear short skirts. But they normally dress more modestly if they are in a church.

Baseball caps are worn everywhere but hats are not worn indoors, except in church.

WEDDING ANNIVERSARIES

Anniversaries of a couple's wedding are usually celebrated privately. But two anniversaries are often the excuse for a party with family and friends. These are the 25th or silver anniversary and the 50th or golden anniversary.

HOUSEWARMINGS

A housewarming party is sometimes held when someone moves into a new house. These parties are no different from any other type of party except that guests usually bring a small gift for use in the house.

FUNERALS

Because Australia is a multi-faith society, funerals usually follow the rituals of the dead person's religion. But more and more funerals are conducted by civil officials.

Most Christian and secular funerals happen between three and five days after the death. A person can be buried or cremated. Death and funeral notices are published in the newspaper. Any friend can attend a funeral without an invitation, unless the ceremony is private. The funeral notice says if the funeral is private.

People can send flowers to the funeral as a mark of respect, even if they do not go in person. Sometimes, the funeral notice asks that no flowers be sent but that money is given to a charity or hospital. Money is never given directly to the family of the dead person.

Some funeral ceremonies are conducted at a church and the family then go to the cemetery or crematorium for the burial or cremation. Other funerals are held in special chapels at the undertaker's premises or the cemetery or crematorium. Correct behaviour is influenced by the mood of the service, which can vary a lot.

After the funeral ceremony, people are often invited to go to the family home for refreshments but they do not have to do this.

Public celebrations

Australians celebrate many festivals brought to the country by its immigrants. Chinese New Year and Tet celebrations are common, particularly in cities with big Chinese and Vietnamese populations. But the main holidays are New Year, Australia Day, Anzac Day and the Christian celebrations of Easter and Christmas.

NEW YEAR

For most Australians, the New Year is a time for parties, rather than a celebration of the passing of the old year. The traditions of cleaning the house and repaying debts that occur in some other cultures don't apply. There are no special foods for the New Year and few common rituals.

However, many Australians go to a New Year's Eve party or attend public entertainments and firework displays. At midnight they sing the Scottish song , 'Auld Lang Syne', drink a toast to the New Year, dance and make a lot of noise. The next day is a public holiday when many people sleep late.

A flag-raising ceremony on Australia Day 1997. *National Library of Australia*

AUSTRALIA DAY

Australia Day is 26 January. It marks the date when Captain Arthur Phillip and the First Fleet landed at Sydney Cove in 1788. It has been celebrated under different names for more than 175 years. In 1946, the various state governments decided to observe one national day called Australia Day.

Around the country there are flag-raising ceremonies and it is a popular day for new migrants to become Australians in citizenship ceremonies. Celebrations are usually held outdoors. They include various sporting events, historical re-enactments and other community entertainments.

However, Australia Day is controversial. It commemorates the arrival of white settlers, which Indigenous Australians say was an invasion of their land. Much of Aboriginal Australia marks Australia Day as a day of mourning. At the same time, Indigenous people celebrate their survival and therefore some call it 'Survival Day'.

EASTER

The celebration of Easter, which commemorates the death and resurrection of Jesus Christ, is an important celebration, even though many Australians are not Christian.

It is a mixture of religious observance and commercial activity. For example, people used to eat traditional hot cross buns only on Good Friday. These days, shops start selling the buns many weeks before Easter. Australians eat more chocolate Easter eggs per person than any other people in the world. Eggs are sold for several months before the holiday.

Practising Christians go to church on Good Friday and Easter Sunday, but for many Australians, Easter is simply a chance to have a four-day holiday.

The Orthodox churches – such as the Greek Orthodox Church and the Russian Orthodox Church – celebrate Easter at a different time.

ANZAC DAY

The most solemn Australian commemoration is Anzac Day. On 25 April 1915, during World War 1, members of the Australian and New Zealand Army Corps landed on the Gallipoli Peninsula in Turkey. When troops withdrew eight months later, 8700 Australian soldiers were dead and nearly 16,500 had been wounded.

> **Anzac** – *a member of the Australian and New Zealand Army Corps during World War 1*

The campaign was unsuccessful but it established the Anzac tradition, which regards courage, endurance and mateship as essential Australian characteristics. Many say that Australia became a real nation on the Gallipoli Peninsula.

Anzac Day begins with a gathering of former soldiers at dawn in many cities and towns throughout the country. This is the Dawn Service or Dawn Stand-To. Later in the day, war veterans march through the streets of the capital cities, watched by thousands of people. Over the past 15 years, Anzac Day has become an increasingly important national event. It produces more open patriotism in Australians than any other occasion, except, perhaps, an international sporting triumph.

The Anzac Day parade in Melbourne, 1996. *National Library of Australia*

CHRISTMAS

Like Easter, Christmas on 25 December is a mixture of religious festivity and secular activity. Practising Christians go to church on Christmas Eve and Christmas Day, but many Australians see Christmas mainly as a time for families to get together.

For several weeks before Christmas, people go to parties with their friends and work colleagues. Shops and city streets are decorated and advertisements urge people to buy presents for friends and family. Radio stations play traditional Christmas music and children sing carols.

Celebration of Christmas keeps alive many of the British traditions of earlier times. However, its rituals have lost their religious significance for many people. Most families decorate a tree for the house, hang a wreath on the front door or hang coloured lights in the house and garden. They put presents under the Christmas tree and hand them out to the family on Christmas Eve or, more often, on Christmas Day.

Some people still eat the traditional English food of roast turkey, hot ham, roast vegetables and rich puddings made from dried fruits. This food suits England's cold winter climate but not the hot weather of Australia in December. So, in recent years, more people have adapted their Christmas food to suit the weather. They eat cold meats, seafood, salads and iced desserts.

The day after Christmas – Boxing Day – is the traditional day to have a barbeque with family and friends.

Building relationships

Making friends and building personal relationships affect all young people. However, cultural and language difficulties can cause problems. These problems arise for young Australians from migrant backgrounds as well as for international students.

One aspect of Australian society that is hard for some visitors to understand is the relationship between men and women. In general, most Australians think that men and women are equal partners in a relationship. Few people think that women should always give way to men's wishes.

MAKING FRIENDS

Australians believe they are an open, friendly people; but some international students say that Australian students are not easy to make friends with. 'We are always the ones who have to start the conversations,' one Malaysian student said.

> **contradiction** – a statement, action or behaviour that is the opposite of another statement, action or behaviour

One explanation for this contradiction is that Australians are perhaps less confident than they think they are. They feel more secure with people and cultural attitudes they understand. Their behaviour is the same as that of the international students who choose friends from their home country because they feel more at ease with them.

International students say that they are more successful in making Australian friends on campus if they separate themselves a little from their fellow nationals. But none say this method is easy.

Making friends across cultures is always a slow process. But remember that in first year at university or college, everyone has to make new friendships. You are more likely to make Australian friends if you make the effort to start the conversations early in the first semester.

DATING AND COURTSHIP

Dating behaviour in Australia depends a lot on people's background. Young Australians from migrant families often argue with their parents who want them to obey the rules of the home country.

The main difference between dating in Australia and in many other places is that a date in Australia is not necessarily a part of courtship. People go on dates as a social activity rather than as a prelude to marriage.

Australians begin dating as young as 11 or 12. These early dates are nearly always group dates, involving several young people. Movies, concerts, discos, sports events and parties at friends' houses are all common activities. Later, the dates are more likely to involve just one couple who are romantically attached.

Usually, men ask women for a date, although, in recent years, more young women make the first move. There are no set dating customs. But most Australians are probably more comfortable with a casual, rather than an intense, approach.

Like so much else in Australia, courtship and marriage are very much a matter of individual choice. Arranged marriages occur only in some immigrant families.

Australian couples usually date for several years and many have a sexual relationship for a time before deciding to marry. Young men sometimes follow the tradition of asking their girlfriend's father for permission to marry. However, parental permission is not necessary if the female is an adult.

SEXUAL RELATIONSHIPS

Sex is not a taboo subject in Australia. Topics such as homosexuality, safe sex and sexual practices are discussed. However, a recent survey found that young Australians are ignorant about sexually transmitted diseases.

There is an apparent tolerance of different expressions of sexuality. For example, homosexual relationships between adults are no longer illegal. But many Australians are still shy about talking about sexual matters.

Surveys suggest that many young Australians have their first sexual encounter at about 16, several years earlier than their parents' generation. Most of them use contraceptives.

On the surface, behaviour on tertiary campuses doesn't support the idea that Australians are shy. There seems to be a lot of open talk about sex. But students are often more moderate in their individual sexual lives than it appears.

Public displays of affection are common.

part three:
communicating

Image supplied courtesy of Tourism Queensland

'When I first arrived, I couldn't understand a word. My English was not bad but the Australians sounded strange. And they used lots of words that weren't in my dictionary.'

– a Singaporean student, Curtin University, Western Australia

Visitors to Australia joke that Australian airline pilots have a very unfriendly welcome: 'Welcome to Australia to die'. The pilots are really saying 'Welcome to Australia today'. A typical Australian accent changes the sounds in words like *bay* and *male* to *buy* and *mile*.

Features of Australian English

Understanding the Australian accent is one of the first problems facing international students.

Most of you have used British or American English-language textbooks and have listened to British or American speakers on tapes or in movies when you were learning English. Australian English can sound like a completely different language.

Australians use familiar English words in unusual ways. They also use words that are not found in British or American dictionaries. They make use of strange idioms. They have a habit of using some words as both an insult and a term of affection. They sometimes express themselves in ways which sound rude and impolite. Their non-verbal communication – their smiles, gestures and body position during conversation – is often unlike that of other cultures.

This section outlines some of the more important features of Australian communication. It does not deal with the formal written language you will use in university and college work because there are many textbooks to help improve your written English. It looks at the informal language that you will hear every day.

How Australian English grew

Both British and American English vary from place to place. In Australia, however, regional variations in accent are few and not very noticeable. Regional word differences are small. Some variations in accent occur between the different classes in society and between city and country speakers, but slang and idioms are used by everyone. So, like much else in Australia, modern speech is basically uniform and egalitarian.

THE FIRST 150 YEARS

The first European Australians born in the colonies, not the immigrants, developed Australian English. For the first 150 years of European settlement, Australian English grew from the English spoken by working-class people, mainly from London and the Midlands of England or from Ireland. Some Aboriginal words – especially the names of the country's unusual plants, animals and natural features – were added. Other additions were words and phrases that came with goldminers from America and Asia or were brought back by soldiers who served in Europe and the Middle East during World War 1 (1914–1918).

By the start of World War 2 in 1939, Australian English was distinctive. It had been protected from change by Australia's distance from other English-speaking countries.

POST-WAR CHANGES

Although large numbers of non-English-speaking immigrants arrived after World War 2, their impact on Australian English was small. New foreign words – often food words such as *cappuccino*, *paella*, *smorgasbord* and *salami* – entered the vocabulary but English remained dominant. But because of post-war migration, one in four Australians today comes from a non-English-speaking background and nearly one in five speaks a language other than English at home.

The introduction of television in the mid-1950s and increased overseas travel by ordinary Australians had a big impact. These things helped people accept American English more easily. For example, Australians now use either the British *flat*, *film*, *lift* or the American *apartment*, *movie*, *elevator* and so on. Some older Australians do not like the trend of using American words. The vocabulary of a student who has learned English from an American teacher will be understood in Australia; so, too, will someone who has learned British English.

The Australian accent

For 200 years, visitors have criticised the distinctive Australian accent. They say it is a flat, lazy, nasal whine. It is true that Australian speech lacks the strong rises and falls of European languages such as French or Italian or the tonal languages of Asia. It is also true that Australians do not move their lips much when speaking. One 19th-century critic said this habit stopped flies from flying into the speaker's mouth!

LAZY LIPS AND TONGUES

Australians often run words together and leave out or change consonants, especially in the middle of words. In the 1960s, a popular book made fun of this characteristic. Its title, *Let Stalk Strine*, translates as 'Let's talk Australian'. *Strine* is now a colloquial word that means Australian English.

Common examples of lazy sounds are *Estraya* (Australia), *Estrayen* (Australian), *Sinny* (Sydney), *Cambra* (Canberra), *efta* (have to), *evva* (have a), *giz* (give us), *gunna* (going to), *imfemation* (information), *imput* (input), *laze en gem* (ladies and gentlemen), *semmitch* (sandwich) and the famous Australian greeting *g'day* (good day).

THE RISING TONE

Another confusing feature of the Australian accent is an unusual use of the rising tone.

Australian English is the subject of many books.

Students learn that a rising tone at the end of an English sentence signals a question, needing a 'yes' or 'no' answer. Australians use the rising tone for 'yes/no' questions but they also use it in, or at the end of, statements. Here is an example from a schoolgirl:

> My friend and I were in my dad's *study* ↑, and she touched some *books* ↑. They fell off the *shelf* ↑ .

In this example, the rising tone indicates that the speaker wants a sign – like 'mm-hmm' or a nod or smile – to show that the listener understands. It does not require any answer. You will probably hear the typical Australian rising tone when a female fellow student is explaining something in class. This is because it is used much more often by younger people, and by women.

It takes time to adjust to the Australian accent. Some international students say that, at first, Australian speech sounds like a fast mumble. Don't worry. Just ask someone to repeat themselves slowly if you don't understand. Most Australians are tolerant of language misunderstandings and different speech patterns. This is because so many Australians don't speak with an Australian accent but with the accent of their first language: Italian, Vietnamese, Arabic, Greek, Cantonese and so on.

Using Australian words

English got much of its rich vocabulary by borrowing words from other languages. Australian English is the same. Many languages and dialects have contributed to Australian English. Among them are Cantonese, Hokkien, Spanish, Portuguese, the various dialects of Great Britain, German, various Aboriginal languages and American English. Even common English words were adapted to local conditions and now have an extra meaning. A good example is *bush*: in Britain, a bush is a small, woody shrub. But when Australians say *bush*, they usually mean any land with native vegetation.

The vocabulary used by many Australians differs from the English in language textbooks. Some patterns of conversation are also different: for example, Australians don't ask personal questions when talking to strangers.

Australian informality extends to the language. People from all social groups use slang words and idiomatic phrases all the time. Informal language is also found in the written Australian English of newspapers, magazines, advertising and popular books.

This book introduces some common patterns of Australian word usage. At the back of the book is a short list of Australian words or sayings you may see or hear. But it doesn't list everything. Only an Australian dictionary and a dictionary of Australian slang can do that.

> ### SURVIVAL TIP
> *Do not rely on the dictionary you used during your school days at home. Buy a good concise Australian dictionary. The standard is* The Macquarie Dictionary. *There is also a* Macquarie Learners Dictionary, *especially designed for non-native English speakers.*

SHORTENED WORDS

First, let's look at a group of words that you will not find in the dictionary. Australians are a bit lazy when forming some words. They like to shorten a long word to one or two syllables and then add a vowel sound on the end. In this way, an *Australian* becomes an *Aussie*, *breakfast* becomes *brekkie*, *vegetables* are *vegies*, *football* is *footy* and *university* is *uni*.

Other common examples are: *aggro* (aggression or aggressive); *arvo* (afternoon); *barbie* (barbeque); *bickie* (biscuit); *blowie* (blowfly); *Brissie* (Brisbane); *chockie* (chocolate); *Chrissie* (Christmas); *cocky* (cockatoo); *deli* (delicatessen); *demo* (demonstration); *garbo* (garbage or rubbish collector); *hankie* or *hanky* (handkerchief); *hubby* (husband); *mushie* (mushroom); *muso* (musician); *mossie* or *mozzie* (mosquito); *nana* (banana); *nightie* (nightdress); *oldies* (old people, parents); *pokies* (poker machines or coin-operated gambling machines); *possie* (position); *postie* (postman or mail delivery person); *pressie* (present or gift); *rego* (car registration); *rellies* (relatives); *sickie* (sick day or a day taken off work while pretending to be ill); *speedo* (speedometer); *sunnies* (sunglasses); *Tassie* (Tasmania); *tellie* or *telly* (television); *tinnie* (tin of beer); *trannie* (transistor radio); *undies* (underpants) and *vego* (a vegetarian).

The habit of putting a vowel on the end of a syllable extends to Australian nicknames, particularly those of men. A man whose given name is *Thomas* or whose family name is *Thompson* is likely to be called *Thommo*; *David* is often *Davo*; a man whose family name is *Richardson* becomes *Richo* and *John* is *Johnno*. Men whose family name begins with *Mac* (as in *McDonald*) are often called *Macca*.

MAKING WORDS STRONGER

Another feature of Australian language is the number of words used to strengthen the meaning of another word. Standard English uses *very* for this purpose. Australians use *very* in written work but they are more likely to use a different word when speaking. *Real* and *really* are favourites. A boy might say 'John is a real friend to me'. This does not mean the boy's other friends are false; it means John's friendship is particularly strong. If a boss calls an employee *a real worker*, she is saying the employee works very hard.

Real can also be used to strengthen criticism as in 'He's a real pain in the neck', which means he is a very boring or annoying person. *Really* is used to strengthen verbs and adjectives. 'He really likes that car' means he likes it very much.

Awful and *awfully* are used in a similar way. 'That's an awful lot of work' is a great deal of work. 'I am awfully hot' means I am very hot. In conversation, younger Australians sometimes use *heaps*. An example is 'I like Indonesian food heaps'. This doesn't mean I like Indonesian food served in a pile; it means I like Indonesian food very much.

Good words, bad words

One of the first things that many international students want to know about Australia is how to be polite. They know that proper behaviour varies from society to society and they do not want to offend by using inappropriate actions or words. Knowing how to say the right thing at the right time is important. So, too, is knowing how to avoid saying the wrong thing.

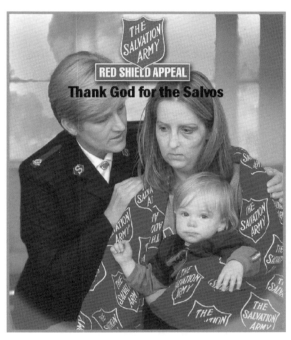

The Christian group, the Salvation Army, uses its Australian nickname, the Salvos, in campaigns to raise money for its welfare work. *Courtesy: The Salvation Army*

When international students arrive in Australia, they are often surprised by the informality of Australian speech. Children speak casually to their parents; students speak casually to their teachers. The patterns of respect that students are familiar with at home don't seem to apply. Sometimes it seems there are no rules of good manners in Australian speech. There are, but they are indirect and hard to observe.

It is not only the casual style of speech that is different, but when people speak and what they speak about. For example, a student brought up in a traditional Chinese family in Malaysia will find that eating an evening meal with an Australian family is a strange experience. Everyone at the table will talk equally and little respect will be shown to older people. At university, lecturers will say hello to students and not wait to be greeted first by the student as might happen in Malaysia or Indonesia.

This informality makes things hard for international students. As one student from Japan said, 'I do not know when I am polite in Australia, [and] when I am not'.

SWEARWORDS AND OBSCENITIES

Australians have had a reputation for rough speech since European settlement. They probably don't swear more than people in other Western English-speaking countries. But visitors say that many Australians swear a lot and use casual blasphemies. Certainly, conversations on campus between students often contain words like *bugger*, *wanker*, *shit* and *fuck* or exclamations of *God* and *Jesus*. Such language is never appropriate when talking in public places or to older people, teachers or other staff, although you will hear it.

In recent years, rude words have begun to appear in the media although sometimes they are not written in full. Dashes or asterisks are used in place of some letters, like this: *f**k*, instead of *fuck*. On radio and television, the words are covered with a bleep sound or the audience is warned by an announcement at the start of the program.

It is sometimes difficult to know if, and when, a word is acceptable. Some words that were once rude are now commonly used. For example, *bloody* was once called 'the Great Australian Adjective' and never used in polite speech. But, in the 1990s, in an advertising campaign to discourage drink-driving, a government organ-isation used the slogan: 'If you drink, then drive, you're a bloody idiot'. These days *bloody* is often used informally to mean *very*, as in 'It is bloody cold this morning'. Young people will also use *fucking* in the same way, but this is offensive to a lot of people.

CHANGED MEANINGS

Some words in Australian conversation can mean the exact opposite of what the dictionary says they mean. The habit of turning meanings upside down is important to the Australian sense of humour (see page 42). It also provides nicknames: for instance, a short person may be called Lofty and a red-haired man may be Blue. The habit is particularly true of swearwords and other offensive phrases.

Shorty   Slim   Lofty   Happy

These nicknames show the Australian habit of reversing the meaning of words.

For Australians, it is not the actual word, but the way a word is said and the context that cause offence. The common words *bastard* and *bugger* are examples. One 19th-century writer wrote that *bastard* can be used in two completely different ways: 'If we wish to express our contempt for a man, we say "He's a proper bastard", meaning, he is vile. If we wish to praise him, we say: "He's a good bastard", meaning that he is a good fellow.'

The word can also be a term of affection in a sentence like 'He's a nice old bastard' or used to express affectionate irritation as in 'Don't be a silly bastard'. *Bugger* can be used instead of *bastard* in the above examples.

Both *bastard* and *bugger* are usually used – in both negative and positive ways – about men. Men use them about other men, but not about women. Women use them about men but rarely about women. Among females, especially younger ones, the word they use about each other, in both negative and positive ways, is *bitch*.

Words that are not offensive can also be used in many ways. An example is the word *mate*. This can be used positively as in 'He is my best mate'. It can be used as a neutral word: 'How are you, mate?' or 'I don't know, mate'. It can be threatening as in 'I don't like your attitude, mate'. The word *sport*, which is another general term of address, can be used in the same ways. Both *mate* and *sport* are usually applied only to men.

RACIST INSULTS

Racist comments that encourage violence or hatred are illegal under Australian anti-discrimination laws. But you will still hear and read them.

Australians can use racist words either negatively or positively. *Pom* and *Pommy* are old terms for English people. These words were negative but now can be used positively. Some negative terms have been given positive meaning by the people they refer to. *Wog*, which is used for Italians, Greeks and Arabic-speaking people, is an example. These ethnic groups sometimes now refer to themselves humorously as *wogs*. This has taken much of the offence out of the term.

Writer/actor/comedian/producer Nick Giannopoulos helped to make the word *wog* acceptable in the 1980s stage show *Wogs Out of Work*. The show was followed by a television series and films. *Courtesy: Go Productions*

The once offensive *Black*, meaning an Australian Aboriginal, is now mostly used in a neutral way. The word *Abo* is negative if used by a non-Aboriginal and positive if used by Aboriginal speakers. *Blackfella* and *whitefella* used by Aboriginals are not offensive.

The word *ethnic* used as a noun about a person is insulting, as in 'She's an ethnic'. But, as an adjective, *ethnic* is the preferred way to describe immigrant cultures.

Kanaka, used about people from the South Pacific, is a neutral term. Neutral words for non-Australians that can be used freely include *Brit* (a person from Britain), *Kiwi* (New Zealander) and *Windies* (West Indians).

DEALING WITH RACIST INSULTS

Sadly, international students may be the target of racist insults. Most are comments in the street. Students who have suffered from such insults say the best thing is to ignore them. Responding with aggression or fear may only make things worse.

Sometimes your fellow students may call you a *slope* (an Asian), *nog* or *noggy* (any dark-skinned person), *wog* or a similar insulting term. Often, they are testing your reaction to their group behaviour. Australian men often exchange casual insults with their friends. They test any new person, including international students, to see if they can fit into the group.

Listen and watch carefully. If a person smiles, looks relaxed and doesn't speak loudly or angrily, the chances are the words are not meant as a true insult. A smile in return is the best response.

A third type of insult can occur if you are driving a car. Most road insults are harmless. If your driving causes another driver to swear at you or yell 'Why don't you go home, you wog', don't feel that you are being singled out because of your race. A female driver would be abused as a 'bloody woman driver' and an elderly man might be called a 'stupid old bastard'.

As with insults in the street, the best way to deal with abuse on the road is to ignore it. Don't speed up in an attempt to get away. However, make sure the windows of the car are closed and all doors locked. This precaution is probably unnecessary, but it will make you feel less anxious.

WORDS TO AVOID

It is hard for international students to tell whether commonly used words are offensive or not. As a rule, it is better not to use any offensive words, but sometimes that is impossible – especially if you are trying to speak like an Aussie.

The following words may be used without causing much offence, but use them rarely and not to strangers: *bloody*, *bullshit* (or its short form, *bull*), *bugger*, *crap*, *dickhead* (a fool), *piss* and *shit*.

The next category contains the confusing words. In some usages and in some company, they are highly offensive; in others, they are either inoffensive or positive. To be on the safe side, don't use them. They include *arse* (and phrases including it), *balls*, *bastard*, *bitch*, *dago*, *fuck* (and phrases containing it), *Pom*, *wank*, *wanker* and *wog*. The insulting terms for Australians are *Skip* and *Skippy*.

Never use the following words as they are always offensive: *Abo*, *boong* (Aboriginal person; dark-skinned person); *ching-chong*, *Chink* (all Chinese); *coon* (dark-skinned person); *grease-ball* (Greek); *kike* (a Jew); *nigger* (a dark-skinned person); *Nip* (Japanese); *slant*, *slant-eye*, *slope*, *slope-head* (all Asian).

There are many negative words describing male and female homosexuals. To avoid problems, use only *gay* and *lesbian*.

APPROVAL, COMPLIMENTS AND GRATITUDE

Despite the country's big non-English migrant population, Australians tend to share the British reluctance to express emotion openly, even when paying compliments or saying thank you. Extravagant or sentimental language, except between lovers, is seen as suspicious and possibly insincere.

Perhaps the most common phrase used to show approval of someone's action or behaviour is the informal *good on you*, often pronounced *ged onya*. Younger Australians might say *good one* or *great* or *super*, while an older Australian might say an action or person is *bonzer*.

Personal compliments are restrained. A smart dress or a new hairstyle might yield a brief 'Nice dress' or 'Your hair looks good'. The appropriate reply to a compliment is a simple *thanks*. A compliment paid by a member of the opposite sex is not always a sexual advance, although sometimes it is.

In some cultures, if you admire something that a person owns, the person will give it to you. Australians do not do this. They are embarrassed if it happens.

Australians like to be thanked for simple actions and service. For instance, it is normal (but not essential) to thank shop assistants, bank tellers and similar service staff. *Thanks* or *thank you* is usually sufficient. If you are very grateful, you can add *a lot* or *very much* to *thanks*. A casual word for thank you is *ta*.

Names and forms of address

From your English studies, you will know that native English speakers have two main names: the given name which comes first and the family name which comes last.

The family name is usually the father's. The given name is sometimes called the first name. Australians often use the old phrase 'Christian name'. They do not mean to be offensive to non-Christians; they are speaking without thought and out of habit. Some people have a second, or even a third, given name. These are known as middle names.

As well as their formal full names, many Australians are known by a short version of their given name – for example, *Liz* or *Beth* for Elizabeth, *Rob* or *Bob* for Robert – or by a nickname given by friends or family. It is polite to use only the name or nickname that people use themselves. For instance, if someone says 'My name is Robert McDonald but people call me Bob or Macca', you can safely call him Bob or Macca. If you are not sure, ask which name the person prefers.

Australians' dislike of formality and their egalitarianism means that the way they address people can seem disrespectful to some visitors. But Indians and Thais may feel at home with the Australian habit of extensive use of each other's given names, rather than family names or professional titles.

Many Australians feel uncomfortable calling fellow workers or neighbours by their family name and title. However, if the person being spoken to is much older and has higher status than the speaker, the formality of the family name with title is mostly used.

TITLES

The titles used in Australia have changed a little in the last 20 years. The short form of *Mister*, *Mr*, is used for adult men. *Mrs* (pronounced *missus*) is used for married women and widows. *Miss* is for unmarried women of any age or for married women who keep their maiden (single) name at work. However, a number of Australian women prefer to be called *Ms* (pronounced *miz*), which doesn't show if they are married or single. Official letters are usually addressed to Mr or Ms.

The words *Sir* and *Madam* to address a stranger are not used much, although you sometimes hear customers in shops or restaurants addressed this way. *Miss*, to address a young female, is rarely used.

In some European countries, a person's profession is used in front of the family name. This rarely happens in Australia. The exceptions include *Professor* and *Doctor* (shortened to *Dr*). A person is addressed as *Doctor* if they have a doctoral degree in any field of study or if they are a medical practitioner. In some states, dentists or veterinarians are also called *Doctor*. Religious leaders are addressed as *Father*, *Brother*, *Sister*, *Rabbi* and so on, depending on the tradition of each religion.

The practice in some countries of addressing a person by their profession or work – the Mandarin *laoshi* for teacher or the Italian *maestro* for a music conductor, for example – is not followed in Australia.

ADDRESSING TEACHERS

Some international students are shocked to hear Australian students calling tutors and lecturers by their given names. Senior academics often prefer to be addressed more formally but there is no strict rule. Staff members will probably tell you their preference.

The higher the position of an academic is, the more likely he or she will be called by their title alone when talking directly to them: *Chancellor*, *Vice-Chancellor*, *Dean*, *Master* (of a residential college) and *Professor* are all examples. Associate professors are also called *Professor*.

NAMES IN THE FAMILY

English-speaking societies lack the detailed kinship terms found in many cultures. The precise words that describe family relationships found in languages such as Mandarin or Khmer are missing. Grandmothers are just grandmothers and you cannot tell whether it is the father's mother or the mother's mother unless you ask. Cousins are just cousins. Sometimes extra words –

such as *paternal* or *maternal* and *blood* and *by marriage* – are used to explain the relationship. Brothers and sisters are distinguished by the addition of *older*, *younger*, *oldest* or *youngest*.

Australians choose from many family titles for their parents and grandparents. Fathers are most often *Dad* and mothers are *Mum*. Young children use *Daddy* or *Dadda* and *Mummy* or *Mama*. But you will also hear parents referred to as *the oldies*, *Father*, *Mother*, *Ma*, *Pa* or even by their given names. Grandfathers are *Grandad*, *Gramps*, *Pop* or *Grandpa*, while grandmothers are *Gran*, *Grandma*, *Nanna* or *Granny*.

Greetings and farewells

The most common greetings in Australia are *hello* and *hi* which are used even in quite formal situations. The famous *g'day* can still be heard in rural areas but is less common in the cities. You will hear *good morning*, *good afternoon* and *good evening*, but usually only in formal settings. The correct reply is to repeat the greeting.

Other greetings are *How are you*, *How are you keeping*, *How are you going*, *How's things* and *What do you know*. None requires a full or truthful answer. When talking to strangers or acquaintances, Australians do not like to seem inquisitive about personal matters. When they say *How are you*, they are not really asking for details. They expect you to answer *fine* or *good*, even if you don't feel that way.

It is not wrong to tell the person that you feel ill or unhappy; but such an answer means they must ask more questions, which is not the purpose of their greeting. Among close friends, of course, a detailed and truthful answer is more common.

The reverse is the case if an Australian asks *Have you eaten?*, a common greeting in parts of Asia. The Australian is asking a question and expects a truthful reply so that they can offer food if you haven't eaten.

People often greet one another at almost the same time with *How are you*, spoken with a falling tone. They also reply together: *Fine, thanks*. But if a person says *How are you* before you have the chance to speak, the proper reply is *Good, thanks. How are you*.

Night-night is a common Australian term to say goodnight to children.

The usual formal phrase for farewell is *goodbye* at any time of the night or day. *Good-night* is used after about 8 p.m. or when you are going to bed and talking to the people who live in the same house. *Nightie-night* or *night-night* is sometimes used when saying goodnight to children.

Informal farewells are *bye*, *see you*, *catch you later* and, particularly among younger people, the Italian *ciao*.

Talking to Australians

A student from Hong Kong once said it took him nearly four years to understand casual conversation in Australia. He used to wonder why Australians always talked about the weather or, especially if they were men, about sport. Once he began to support an Australian Rules football team, he found it much easier to have conversations with Australians.

Every culture develops its own patterns of conversation. Australia shares some patterns with other English-speaking countries but also has its own features.

One of the first things some international students notice is that Australian conversations are all talk and no silence. The pauses for thought that are common and polite in some societies don't exist. It is not rude to overlap your sentences with another speaker's, except if you change the topic of conversation.

There are no rules about who starts a conversation. It is not necessary to be introduced formally to a person before speaking to them.

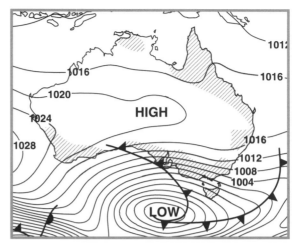

The weather is a common topic of conversation. *Courtesy: Bureau of Meteorology*

ASKING FOR HELP

Australians pride themselves on being open, friendly and direct. In some ways they are; in other ways they are not. They often speak to, and exchange greetings with, strangers, although this happens less these days than in the past. They are willing to give practical advice on everyday matters, such as how to find the nearest post office. They rarely, however, offer advice unless asked. If you need practical help, don't hesitate to ask. It will be freely given.

Australians are unwilling to make decisions for others, because they do not like to seem bossy. For example, if you ask an Australian for advice about which dictionary to buy, the person is likely to list the alternatives but leave the final choice to you.

TOPICS OF CONVERSATION

Australians balance their openness with a strong sense of privacy. They rarely ask personal questions of strangers or casual acquaintances. They do not ask someone's age or marital status or about their finances and political or religious beliefs. They prefer to let the other person offer that information.

In common with people in many other countries, Australians prefer agreement to disagreement. So, casual conversations tend to be about a neutral shared experience: the weather, sport, children, the garden, food, jobs. For example, a standard question to someone to whom one has just been introduced is *What do you do?* This means what is your profession or trade. Explaining one's job is seen as a suitable and impersonal topic to discuss.

The exception to the rule is in the classroom, where as you will read in Part four, 'Campus life', debate and disagreement about ideas is encouraged.

MAKING REQUESTS

Because Australians dislike authoritarian behaviour, they ask for things in an indirect way. Instead of saying 'Put the book on the table', an Australian might say: 'Would you put the book on the table?'. The order may be further softened by adding *please* or a phrase such as *would you mind*. 'Would you mind putting the book on the table, please?' But in situations where the speaker is in a position of authority – as when a lecturer gives instructions about an assignment – the order is expressed more directly.

When shopping, an Australian is unlikely to say: 'I want two dozen eggs'. She says: 'I would like two dozen eggs, thanks' or 'May I have two dozen eggs please?'. You can use either *please* or *thanks* to make a request more polite.

Australian parents teach their children at an early age to add *please* or *thanks* when asking for something and always to say *thank you* when the request is granted. So you will find that Australian English contains many *please* and *thank you*s.

SAYING 'NO'

Although Australians make requests indirectly, they are more direct about expressing their preferences than people from some cultures. Saying 'no' to a suggestion is not impolite. However, a negative is usually softened with an apology and a reason. For example, if you ask a fellow student 'May I borrow your lecture notes, please?', he may say 'Sorry, no. I'll need them this weekend'. He would be thought rude if he just said 'No, you can't'.

MAKING APOLOGIES

Australians' directness is obvious when they apologise. For example, if they break a vase in someone's home, they say: 'I'm very sorry. I tripped and broke your blue vase'. They don't give long explanations. Sometimes they won't give any explanation at all.

They don't think this direct approach is impolite. The rule to remember is: keep an apology short and simple.

The Australian sense of humour

Australians pride themselves on their sense of humour but it takes time for newcomers to get used to it. Like much of the Australian character, the national sense of humour is irreverent. Anyone and anything – however important – can be a target of humour.

Like many other peoples, Australians like slapstick and stand-up comedians on stage or television. Their everyday humour, however, is based on understatement and irony.

> **contradiction** – a statement, action or behaviour that is the opposite of another statement, action or behaviour

What makes it hard for visitors is that Australians don't show on their faces that they are making a joke. Even native English speakers find this hard. One woman from New Zealand said: 'After five years in Australia, I still don't always know when my Australian friends are making jokes. They say something that makes me cross and I think they are being serious. It is only when they laugh at my reaction that I realise they're joking'.

Communicating without words

Research suggests that talking makes up less than 10 per cent of human communication. We communicate by gesture, eye contact, speed of speech and in many other ways. This non-verbal communication is as different between cultures as languages are. It needs to be learned, just like vocabulary and grammar.

Australians use their bodies in ways that are offensive in some cultures. If an Australian does something that you find offensive, remember they are not trying to insult you. They are acting normally and may not know enough about your culture to realise that they may be being rude.

Here are some general points about non-verbal communication in Australia.

UP CLOSE AND PERSONAL

Australians share ideas of polite space with other Westerners. The social distance, between strangers or acquaintances who are talking, is between an arm's length and three metres. If you stand closer to people than an arm's length, they will think you are crowding them. Closer personal space is reserved for friends and family.

Talking to someone who is further than three metres away is not polite. The conversations at a distance that occur in China, for example, seem very rude to most Australians.

Sometimes, in a crowd, you cannot avoid moving into someone else's space. But if you bump into someone or accidentally touch a stranger, say *sorry*. Continuing on is not polite.

In some countries, there are rules about passing in front of people. In Australia, there are not. But in cinemas or in lecture theatres, if you have to pass people to get to your seat, it is more polite to face them and walk sideways if possible. You should say *excuse me* or *sorry* as you go past.

RULES ABOUT TOUCHING

Even though Australians like to keep their distance from strangers, they are more likely to touch each other than people from some cultures. However, there are unwritten rules about touching. These vary between the ethnic groups that make up Australian society. The rules outlined here apply to the dominant British-based culture.

In formal situations, a man usually shakes hands when first meeting another man. Handshakes at other times are not necessary, although men will often shake hands in business situations or to express sympathy to relatives at funerals. A brief, firm handshake is preferred to a gentle one. Handshakes are very rare among students.

Friends sometimes touch the upper arm when they shake hands.
Image © copyright 2000 imageaddict.com

In greeting or during conversation, Australian male friends often slap each other on the upper arm or back. Occasionally, a man might put one arm around his friend's shoulders.

Heterosexual Australian men do not hold hands as this is regarded as a sign of homosexuality. Unlike southern Europeans and others, they do not hug or kiss each other, even if they are a father and adult son. The exception is when a player does something well on the sports field or a sporting team wins.

Most Australian women do not shake hands when being introduced to another woman. On meeting or saying goodbye to friends, they might hug briefly, kiss each other on the cheek or touch cheek to cheek; they might not. Young women or teenage girls occasionally hold hands but they are more likely to walk arm in arm with girlfriends. When sitting, they sometimes put their arms around their girlfriend's neck.

In professional and formal situations, handshakes between males and females are more usual now than they were. If in doubt, wait until the person to whom you are being introduced offers a hand. Then you can respond.

If you come from a culture where touching the opposite sex in public is not acceptable, you can easily stop people shaking your hand without offending them. Put your own hands by your sides and dip your head forward briefly at the same time as you say *hello*.

Although touching between the sexes in public is now more common in places like China, Singapore and Korea, students from these and other countries might be shocked to see how much touching occurs among young Australian men and women in public. Some Australians feel uncomfortable about this behaviour. If it offends you, do as they do: ignore it.

THE HEAD, HANDS AND FEET

Australians have no taboos about touching the head or shoulders. They frequently touch children's heads as a sign of affection.

Australians nod their heads up and down to show agreement and shake them from side to side to show disagreement. They may tip their heads to one side slightly to show they are listening closely. But if they frown a little or push out their lips when they tip their heads, it tells you they are puzzled or cannot understand.

Staring at strangers is impolite. However, looking directly at someone and maintaining some eye contact when talking to them is thought to show openness and honesty. Western women, unlike their sisters in Asia or the Middle East, use more eye contact than Western men. They rarely drop their gaze in submission but may do so if they are embarrassed.

In Australia, smiling does not show

Smiles show happiness and good humour.

embarrassment or distress. A smile is almost always an expression of happiness or good humour. So, too, are laughing and giggling. A smile can also show approval.

Crying can be a response to pain, distress, frustration, pity, anger or extreme happiness. Until recently, it was almost always a female response. An Australian saying, 'Balmain boys don't cry', sums up the traditional view that crying was unmanly. However, recent instances of crying in public by male politicians and sportsmen have lessened the shame of men crying.

Movements of the shoulders, arms and hands also communicate. A shrug of the shoulders in response to a question indicates the person doesn't know the answer. It rarely suggests that the person doesn't care about the conversation.

Australians don't share some cultures' dislike of pointing at objects. They use the forefinger to point at things, and even people, and to show direction.

Several uses of the finger, however, are less acceptable. A forefinger pointed directly at a person's face is aggressive. A raised forefinger wagged from side to side shows displeasure and is often used to scold children. 'To give someone the finger' refers to the rude gesture made when a person jerks an extended middle finger (or extended middle and forefinger) into the air with the palm facing upwards. But if someone raises extended middle and forefinger in a V-sign above the shoulder with palm facing outwards, that is a sign of approval!

In some cultures, the use of the left hand is restricted. In Australia, few people worry about which hand is used. Australians hand objects to each other with either hand and will eat with their left hand.

Australian men often put their hands in their pockets. This merely demonstrates they are confident and relaxed. It is not disrespectful as it is in some countries.

Some international students are confused by the way Australians use their hands to ask people to move closer or further away. To send someone away, they stretch the arm, palm downward and move the fingers back and forth. To beckon a person forward, they stretch the arm, palm upward, and move the arm back and forth from the elbow or the wrist.

The relaxed Australian attitude to the head also applies to the feet. Australians don't worry about the position of their feet and legs. Crossing one's legs is not considered rude, nor is pointing one's foot at another person. However, it is bad manners to put one's feet on chairs, desks or tables.

part four:
campus life

'In Australia, students are more independent and have to do their own research, using the library to find their learning materials.'

– a Vietnamese student, Holmesglen TAFE, Victoria

As an international student you know that you will find Australian society strange. Most international students know that they will probably suffer culture shock. But few people warn you that culture shock can be most intense in the classroom.

Culture shock in the classroom

The difference between study in Australia and study in your home country can be huge. Every country's education system is based on its culture. Teachers and students in a single culture know what to expect from each other. Mix the cultures and things can become confused and stressful.

Australian society values individualism and equality. These qualities are also valued in the education system. You will often hear the phrases *independent learning* and *self-directed learning*. What do they mean? How will they affect you?

In Australia, students receive much less individual attention from lecturers and tutors than in some other countries. This is not because the teachers don't care about their students. They do, but they want students to think for themselves. They expect students to be self-disciplined and self-reliant. If you do not ask for help, teachers assume you don't need it.

Your teachers might tell you to do a task you have never done before. But they will not tell you how to do it. How can you do the task properly? Don't go away and do what you think is wanted.

You may be wrong. Work out what you need to know and then ask for help. Librarians, other students, and study skills advisers can all help. Your teacher, too, will explain if you ask. It is only by searching for answers that you will find them.

The aim of education in Australia is to build each individual's ability to collect information and analyse it. Instead of learning things by rote, you are expected to question all information and ideas. That way, you learn to understand the complexity of your discipline. You are encouraged to develop your own ideas, based on evidence, and to present those ideas in a logical way. Under this system, there is no one correct answer to any question. This especially applies to humanities and social sciences subjects.

learn by rote – to learn something so that it can be repeated automatically without the student having to think about the meaning

Much of your time at an Australian university or college is spent in individual research in libraries or laboratories. But you are also expected to work in teams with your fellow students on tasks and projects.

You are also expected to discuss and debate issues with other students and your teachers. The emphasis on debate – in which you listen to and analyse someone else's ideas and defend your own ideas – can be uncomfortable for students from cultures where disagreement is discouraged. People who were raised to believe that silence is a virtue find it hard to understand. But asking questions is the key to successful study in Australia.

CLASSROOM ETIQUETTE

The relationship between teacher and student is more equal in Australia than in many countries.

Students show less respect. But don't believe what you first see. To the newcomer, the relationship might look equal but some student behaviour is still unacceptable. Although you are encouraged to discuss ideas and information in some sorts of classes, talking to friends during lectures is rude. Arriving late disrupts a class. Letting your mobile phone ring during class is not polite.

On Australian campuses, male and female academic staff members have the same authority. You are expected to give men and women equal respect, even if this doesn't happen in your country.

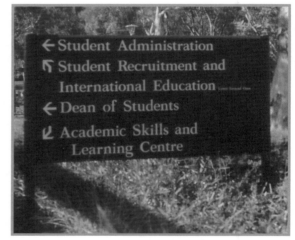

A campus signpost at the Australian National University.

Campus staff

Finding your way around university or college is hard for all new students. Finding the right building or lecture theatre is difficult because Australian universities are large. Some have several campuses. Many institutions close to the city centres have buildings spread over several city blocks.

It is also hard to find which member of staff is responsible for giving course advice or changing a subject enrolment. One Singaporean student said the hardest thing about the first months at university was learning how the administrative systems worked.

ORGANISATION OF EDUCATIONAL INSTITUTIONS

Australian universities are organised in four levels. At the top is the office of the vice-

FIGURE 1 *A typical example of university organisation.*

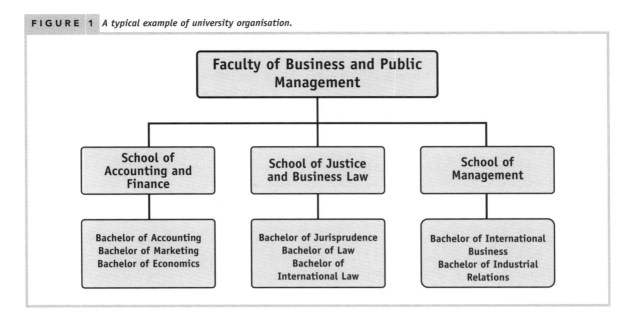

chancellor or president which is responsible for making policy and running the whole institution. Below that are the faculties or divisions. Each faculty has several departments or schools, according to their academic area. Within each department are a range of courses (see figure 1). TAFE colleges, private colleges and institutes have slightly different structures.

The dean of each faculty is in charge of academic and administrative matters. The faculty administrative staff help with enrolments, course changes and other paperwork. If you need advice in choosing subjects, they can help. Academic staff also help with subject choice.

ACADEMIC STAFF

The head of a department is a professor. Course coordinators – who are usually senior lecturers or associate professors – run a specific course. The senior lecturers and lecturers give lectures and sometimes take tutorials. They also do research and supervise postgraduate research. Under-graduates have most contact with their tutors. Tutors usually mark students' work. Your tutor is the first person you should go to if you have questions about the subject or your course. Postgraduate students go first to their supervisor.

OFFICE HOURS

Administrative staff usually work from 8 a.m. or 9 a.m. to 5 p.m. They are available to help students during these hours. But avoid lunch-times from midday to 2 p.m., which can be busy.

Academic staff have flexible hours but they must set aside regular times for students to discuss academic matters. These 'office hours' are usually put on the person's door. It is better to make an appointment, but it is not necessary.

Always think in advance about what you want to say or what you want to ask. Write it down so you don't forget anything.

If your question is simple, you can sometimes ask it after a lecture or tutorial. But remember that the lecturer may have to go to another class and won't have time to answer.

Some academics encourage a lot of student contact. They even give their home telephone numbers to students. Others don't. They usually tell you what they like at the start of the semester. Respect their preference.

Email is a good way of contacting your tutor or lecturer. Again, some academics prefer email contact while others don't. When you send an email, keep it short, direct and polite.

The academic year

The normal academic year has two semesters. The first semester starts in late February or early March and the second ends in late October or November. Each semester is usually 12 teaching weeks long, with one week without classes in the middle. At the end of each semester is a study week, called swotvac, and then two or three weeks of exams. Between semesters is a four- to six-week break. There is a three-month summer holiday between years. Some – but not all – universities run courses during this long break, which allows students to get their degrees faster or repeat subjects they have failed.

A few universities let international students start their studies in the middle of the year. However, this is not common and does not apply to all courses.

An orientation week, often called O-week, is held for all new students before teaching begins at the start of each year. Many universities also have special orientation programs for international students.

O-week is full of activities designed to help students become familiar with the social and serious sides of university life. *Nich Farrelly*

The academic week

Your working week depends on your course of study. English language courses and many vocational courses usually involve a lot of class hours. But humanities courses have fewer class hours and a big load of independent study. A Japanese student said that she found a big change between her intensive English course and mainstream study: 'In the mainstream course, I spent much more time studying at home'.

You may have up to three to four classes a day. Students in humanities courses should do

two hours of independent work for each hour of class time. But in science-based and vocational courses, longer classes mean fewer hours in independent work.

At schools and TAFE colleges (see page 77), your attendance at class is monitored. At universities, it is not. But a condition of the student visa is that you attend 80 per cent of classes. If you miss class for more than five days, you should tell your course coordinator and provide evidence, such as a doctor's certificate, to explain your absence.

At university, there are four types of classes: lectures, tutorials (tutes), laboratory sessions (labs) and practical sessions (pracs). Field trips are a kind of prac. The types of classes are designed to do different things so they have different structures.

LECTURES

Lectures explain the broad themes and ideas of the subject. They are usually held once each week and are 50 to 55 minutes long. Some lectures are partly interactive; most are one-way communication from lecturer to students.

Lecture theatres in popular courses can be crowded. It is a good idea to arrive early to get a good seat.

Lectures need good note-taking. Taking notes in a second language is hard. But some lecturers provide lecture notes at the start of the

Australian students spend a lot of time studying independently. *Courtesy: La Trobe University*

course or on the university web site. Others hand out copies of any transparency or diagram used in the lecture. If there are no notes, ask the lecturers if they can give you some. You can ask on behalf of other international students in your class. Remember, lecture notes do not include everything you need to know. They are the skeleton to which you add material from your own independent study and other classes.

If taking good notes is difficult for you, get help from the study skills advisers in student services.

TUTORIALS AND SEMINARS

Tutorials and seminars are small discussion groups. A tutor encourages students to look critically at a particular topic. Often, students present a short tutorial paper to start the discussion. The tutorial paper is usually handed in for assessment at the end of the tute or in the following week.

Tutorials are about 50 minutes long. Seminars, which are for honours and postgraduate students, normally take two hours.

You are expected to participate actively in tutes. Be prepared by reading about the topic before class. Your tutor will give you a reading list. Sometimes you can buy a pack of reading extracts at the start of the semester.

If you do not understand something in a

Debate and discussion are important in tutorials. *National Library of Australia*

tutorial or lecture, ask your tutor in class. Other students are probably confused too. They will be grateful that you asked the question.

LABORATORY AND PRACTICAL CLASSES

Labs and pracs occur mostly in science and vocational courses. They let students practise doing an experiment or procedure that relates to a lecture.

In labs and pracs, students often work in small teams. These classes usually last for two to three hours.

Students have to write a lab report and hand it in at the end of the session or in the following week.

Australian National University ecology students on a field trip in the Snowy Mountains. *Nich Farrelly*

FIELD TRIPS

Students in some science and vocational subjects go on field trips. Field trips can last for half a day, a full day or sometimes more. The work done on field trips varies a lot from subject to subject. But the aim is to allow students to practise aspects of the subject in real life. For example, on a geology field trip, students get experience at observing rock formations, identifying rocks and recording data. Students usually have to write up a field trip report.

Assessment

The way your work is assessed varies a lot between courses. Some subjects are assessed by many small pieces of work during the semester. This is known as 'continuous assessment'. Others

TABLE 1 *Assessment grades.*

	Pass	Third class honours (H3)	Second class honours (H2B)	Second class honours (H2A)	First class honours (H1)
Pass (P)	50–64				
Credit (Cr)	65–74	65–69	70–74		
Distinction (D)	75–84			75–79	
High Distinction (HD)	85+				80+

Note: *This table is a guide to the grade names and the percentage marks used in Australian assessment. The range of marks may be a little different from the ones given above.*

rely on two or three bigger assignments and/or exams.

Many international students are upset by their first assessments in Australia. They are good students and they are used to getting much better marks. One student from the United States said: 'I was shocked by the marks for my first essay. I was a straight-A student at home and here I got a pass'. Lack of fluent English can cause poorer results. But the Australian system of marking is mostly to blame. It is tough. Few subjects give final grades above the eighties. Scores between 75 and 85 are considered very good. Most results are in the mid- to high 60s. Any result above 50 per cent is a pass. (See table 1.)

As an international student, it is important that you and your family at home understand the Australian system so you know what to expect.

CHEATING

Cheating is a serious offence and is punished severely. Students can fail an assignment or subject if found cheating. Sometimes they can be excluded from their course. Cheating includes taking unauthorised things into an exam and plagiarism.

What is plagiarism? It is using someone's ideas, theories and ways of expressing them as your own work. This means, as the University of Indiana in the United States says, you must 'give credit by a reference to:
• someone else's idea, opinion or theory
• any facts, statistics, graphs or drawings that are not common knowledge
• direct quotations of someone's written or spoken words, or
• your paraphrase of another's idea.'*

Plagiarism can be a small piece of material within an assignment. It can be an entire assignment which is borrowed or bought from another student.

International students can find they are accused of accidental cheating because of different attitudes to education. They don't realise that using a lecturer's ideas or words without referencing is plagiarism. Some don't understand that a paraphrase should be their own words. It shouldn't contain the words, phrases or structure of the original material.

Another tricky area is collaborating with other students on projects that are meant to be done individually. According to a survey of Australian students, this is the most common form of cheating. It is useful to sort out your ideas by talking to other students and tutors, but make sure that your assignment is your own work.

Universities and colleges in Australia now use computer programs to help detect student plagiarism.

*University of Indiana at <http://www.indiana.edu/≈wts.wts.plagiarism.html>

EXAMS

Exams are usually held at the end of each semester. They are between two and three hours long. There are several different types of exam: multiple choice, short answer, problem-solving, short essay and long essay. Some exams are a combination of types.

Most exams test your understanding of the themes or theories of your subject. They don't test your ability to remember detailed facts. Multiple choice exams – in which students should try to answer a question a minute – seem like memory tests. But they really test your understanding of the subject.

Some exams are 'closed book' exams where you can only take pens and calculators into the exam room. In 'open book' exams, you can take approved texts. 'Take home' exams mean you do the exam in your own time and off campus.

Make sure to attend the last lecture before an exam. The lecturer will remind you of the exam format so you know what to expect. And check the details of the date, time and place of the exam yourself. Don't rely on another student to tell you.

If you were sick before the exam or had some other problem, you can ask the examiners to take that into account. This is called 'special consideration'. To apply for special consideration, you must have a doctor's certificate, a letter from a counsellor or other document to prove your claim. If you become ill during the exam, ask the exam supervisor for a letter.

Students who fail an exam may be allowed to sit a 'supplementary', or second, exam if their marks are not too low. Supplementary exams are usually held in December or January.

ESSAYS

Some international students find writing essays is very tough. Academics in Australia want you to show that you have researched the topic's main ideas, thought about them and developed your own argument.

An essay that just describes the main ideas will not get a good mark. In some cultures it is respectful to agree with the teacher. But an essay that repeats the teacher's ideas will not get a good mark in Australia.

The essay is a type of work in which plagiarism (see page 50) easily occurs. To avoid plagiarism, you must always give a reference any time you quote the words of another person. Just as important, you must also reference other people's ideas.

Different disciplines use different ways of referencing. Ask your tutor what is the preferred method in the particular subject and use it. Never mix two different styles of referencing.

In some countries, students get a second chance with their essays. They submit a draft for the teacher's comment and then hand in a revised final version. Or they can resubmit an essay if they fail. This is rarely done in Australia.

Each essay has a word limit. A few words more or less are okay, but you will lose marks if you ignore the limit.

DEADLINES

Every assignment – whether it is an essay, lab report or tutorial paper – has a deadline, which is the latest time by which it must be finished. If there is a good reason why you cannot finish by the deadline, you can ask for an 'extension' of time. Your tutor may ask for a doctor's certificate or similar proof before giving an extension.

Do not ask for an extension on the day an assignment is due. You are unlikely to get it. Go to your tutor as soon as you think you cannot finish the work because of health or personal problems. If academic staff know your situation, they are more likely to give an extension.

ASSESSMENT APPEALS

Students have the right to know their marks for an assignment or exam and how the marks were allotted. Talk to your marker first if you are unhappy with your results. But a talk about your mark is not a chance to bargain. In general, Australians don't like to bargain. They think that bargaining over serious matters such as marks is wrong.

You can ask for the work to be re-marked but the department does not have to do so. If the work has been failed, it will usually have been marked by two people already, unless it is only a small part of the overall assessment.

The real reason for talking to your tutor is so that you can do better next time. Ask your tutor to go over the work with you so you can learn where you went wrong.

If you still think the marks are unfair, you can make a formal appeal. Your university handbook contains the appeal procedure. You can get informal advice on appeals from the student union or formal advice from your department's administrative staff.

Student services

Life as a student is not always easy. Both local students and international students find the move from school to higher education hard. They feel lonely. They feel pressured by their families to do well. They worry about money. Many have to cope with looking after themselves for the first time: finding a place to live, managing a household budget, cooking and cleaning. They get tired from too many late nights, either working or partying.

> **party** – to enjoy oneself at a party, disco, club or other event

Living away from parents can lead to wild behaviour, which can result in pregnancy, drug abuse, excessive drinking and other problems.

Universities provide free support services to help all students. There are two types of official student services: academic and personal. The academic services include general computer rooms, libraries, and help with language or study problems. The personal services include help finding accommodation and counselling about personal or financial problems. The services also include facilities for worship in many faiths, and chaplains or other spiritual advisers. Particularly important for international students is the student health clinic.

In addition, universities and colleges have special international student centres to help with health insurance, visas and banking. They organise cheap tours and trips and social functions. If you have problems that don't relate to

your course, ask the international student centre. If centre staff cannot help directly, they refer you to the right place.

STUDY SKILLS

The change from school to higher study means all students must learn new skills. The demands are even greater on students who have come from a different school system.

All universities help students to improve their study at study skills centres. In some universities, the centres are called learning skills or learning development units.

The centres run short courses throughout the year. The subjects can include essay-writing, note-taking, report-writing, presentation skills, time management, exam techniques, and critical thinking. The courses are free and are usually held at lunchtimes or in the evening.

Lecturers may refer a student to a skills centre for individual help. Centres may sometimes charge a fee for individual sessions.

LIBRARIES AND COMPUTER ROOMS

The quality of libraries and computer rooms varies from institution to institution. But these resources are essential for successful independent learning.

You will spend a lot of time in the library looking for information to use in your assignments. The more you understand about the things the library can provide, the easier your study will be.

A senior university librarian said the most useful thing in a library is the staff. 'Use the library staff. Ask them for help. That's why they are there,' she said. At the start of the year, all libraries run information sessions about the library's services. Go to as many of them as you can.

Most large universities have several libraries: the main library and smaller discipline-based libraries. Your student card lets you study in all the libraries and borrow books. Sometimes a book in the main library is out on loan but there are copies available on the shelf in the smaller libraries. So when you look in the computer catalogue, don't forget to check for books in all the campus libraries.

Librarians are always happy to help students. *Courtesy: La Trobe University*

Even the best libraries have limited money to buy books and journals. But if there is a particular book that you need for a subject, make a book request. The librarians will try to buy it.

Never delay your library research. Start working on an assignment as soon as possible. If you don't, you may find the books you need are on loan to other students.

Always return books on time. If you don't, you can be fined. And some institutions will not give you your final results if you haven't paid your library fines.

Australian universities and colleges continue to increase their use of computer technology. Assignments and administrative work are sometimes done online. Many universities give each student an email account and send important course information by email. If this happens at your university or college, check your email account regularly.

More and more Australian students have their own computers but many still use the communal computer rooms at their university or college. These rooms can become very crowded before assignments are due. So, again, do your work early.

LANGUAGE HELP

Most higher education institutions have specialist English language learning centres on campus.

Even if you are not enrolled in an English language course, you can get help with your English at these centres.

PERSONAL AND FINANCIAL COUNSELLING

Nearly everyone finds it hard to ask for help on personal matters such as a broken romance, loneliness, financial worries or the death of a family member or friend. For international students, it is even more difficult. For students from Asian countries, seeking help from a professional counsellor seems odd. As one campus chaplain said: 'Counselling is culture bound. In Asia, for example, counselling happens within the family'.

But as an international student, you are away from your normal support. You have to use available services. And campus counsellors understand the particular problems that international students have. There is no shame in seeking their help. The service is free.

> ### SURVIVAL TIP
> *If you feel lonely, depressed or unwell for more than a day or two, visit the student health centre, where professional help is available.*

All counselling is private. Nobody except the student and the counsellor know what is said. If needed – to get special consideration for an assignment or exam – a counsellor might tell a tutor that a student has a problem but will not say what the problem is.

Money problems can make international students very worried. Students from poorer countries find the cost of living in Australia is high. Some students know that their families have given up a lot so they can study abroad. Others who are funded by their governments feel their responsibilities very strongly. Special financial counsellors on campus can help these students to manage their budget better.

Gambling is a big problem for some international students. In the casino, they can forget the stress of being away from home. They find gambling exciting and entertaining – until their money has gone. Don't be tempted to think gambling will end your troubles. If you do have gambling problems, see a student counsellor immediately.

STUDENT RIGHTS

In Australia, all students have rights to fair treatment from staff and other students. The educational system tries to protect students from discrimination, harassment, bullying and exploit-ation. International students' rights against exploitation by education providers are protected by federal law.

> **exploitation** – to use people or things unfairly for one's own purposes

In recent years, all Australian governments have passed laws against discrimination. Universities and colleges employ special anti-discrimination officers to make sure the institution treats staff and students properly. The student unions also help students who feel they have suffered discrimination.

What is discrimination? Direct discrimination means a person is treated less favourably because of some characteristic. It could be their religious or political beliefs. It could be a physical disability. It could be their sex, their age or marital status. It could be their race or country of origin.

If you feel you have suffered discrimination, talk to international student services or the student union anti-discrimination officers. They will advise you about the best way to stop the discrimination.

Harassment happens when a person repeat-edly says or does something to you that makes you upset or fearful. It doesn't matter whether the person is a teacher or student, male or female.

On campus, harassment is often sexual harassment. Any unwanted sexual action or remark that makes you frightened or upset could be harassment. Sometimes, of course, it could be a misunderstanding. Advice from a students' rights officer will help you decide what to do.

Willing sexual relationships between academic staff and students are not forbidden. But the staff member can damage his or her career by having a sexual relationship with a student. Any forced sexual intercourse is a crime.

Better marks should never be exchanged for sexual favours. A teacher who suggests such an exchange will be severely punished. So, too, will any student who offers sex for better marks.

Repeated racial insults from teachers or fellow students are also harassment. It may be wise to ignore an insult the first time, but if the insults continue, see your students' rights officer. Other forms of physical or emotional bullying should also be reported.

Unfortunately, there have been cases of exploitation of postgraduate students in Aust-ralian universities. If you think a supervisor or research superior is making you do an unreason-able amount of work, talk to your institution's postgraduate association or international student centre.

Student health

You have to have health insurance as a condition of your student visa (see page 74 for details). But where do you go if you get sick? Your campus student health centre is a good place because the staff know about the special health problems of international students.

People suffering from culture shock – and all international students suffer to some degree – often sleep badly. Tiredness can increase depression and make the body less able to fight disease. Culture shock can also lead to loss of appetite.

Nurses in campus clinics say that diet and skin problems, chest infections, allergies and depression are common.

On-campus student health centres provide medical help and education about health matters.

DIET

International students today are much luckier than earlier generations of students because Australian eating habits have changed. The familiar foods of Asia, the Pacific and Europe are now available in capital cities and larger towns. But many international students still eat badly.

Clinic nurses say students should avoid eating too much Western junk food or instant noodles which can lead to weight gain and deficiency diseases. Students frequently complain of feeling weak or sick in the stomach. This is often because they have not eaten breakfast. You should eat a good breakfast so you can stay alert in class. Also make sure you eat lots of fresh fruit and vegetables.

Few people avoid getting stomach upsets when travelling. Your body takes time to adjust to local water and foods. Expect some stomach upsets when you first arrive. If they continue for more than a day or two, go to the student health centre for advice.

SKIN PROBLEMS

Poor diet causes some skin problems but the Australian climate is the main cause. International students, especially those living in the southern states of Australia, complain of dry, itchy skin. Students from tropical climates are used to more humid air which keeps their skins moist. In cool Australian winters, students from hot countries sometimes sit too close to heaters and overheat their skin.

Two out of three Australians will get a skin cancer at some time in their lives. Although the sun in Australia doesn't seem hot to students from warmer climates, it is dangerous. Australia receives very high ultraviolet (UV) radiation which can cause sunburn in a short time. UV levels are particularly high from September to March and in the middle of the day. To avoid danger, wear a wide-brimmed hat, long-sleeved shirts and sunglasses. Use a sunscreen with a protection rating of 30+ on all exposed skin.

ALLERGIES

Australia has one of the highest rates of asthma in the world. Many asthma attacks are caused by dust, pollen and other things in the air. Hay fever, which causes sneezing, running and itchy eyes, and an itchy throat, is also common. International students often suffer hay fever for the first time in their lives when they arrive in Australia.

Mild allergies can be treated easily but get advice from your student health centre before taking any medicine.

DEPRESSION

Everyone feels sad occasionally. However, depression and suicidal thoughts are common among many Australian students. Unfortunately, international students suffer more depression than local students. This is not surprising. They are living in a strange place. Their usual network of friends and family is far away. Everything is different. Life is very stressful.

Student services are good at helping students with depression. There is no shame in seeking help from them. Talking over your problems privately with an understanding person can be a relief. So, if you feel sad or depressed for more than a day or two, go to your student health centre. If your friends are depressed, encourage them to get help.

But if you need to talk to someone urgently because you are thinking of suicide and it is out of hours, ring the national 24-hour telephone

First year at university or college can be a lonely time.

counselling service, Lifeline. Its number is 13114, everywhere in Australia.

VACCINATIONS

One way to protect your health is to be vaccinated against common diseases. The childhood diseases of measles, mumps and rubella can be dangerous for adults. It is also wise to be vaccinated against polio, diphtheria and tetanus.

If you have not been vaccinated, you can ask the student health staff to vaccinate you. This service is free.

LEGAL AND ILLEGAL DRUGS

Like many countries, Australia has a drug problem. Problems arise with the overuse of legal drugs such as alcohol and tobacco, misuse of prescription drugs, and use of illegal drugs such as heroin, cocaine and cannabis.

Australians have a reputation as heavy drinkers. Australian students are no different. Going to the pub is a popular pastime. But not everyone drinks too much. Even at the pub or parties, it is okay to drink soft drinks.

> **prescription drug** – *a medicine that can only be bought if a doctor has written out a prescription, or direction, for the patient to get the drug*

Remember that too much alcohol is dangerous in many ways. Drunken drivers can kill or injure themselves and other people. Drunken pedestrians can be run over. Alcohol makes people relax their control, so sexual intercourse – and possible pregnancy or disease – is more likely. However, drinking alcohol is legal in Australia and it is up to students to decide for themselves what and how much to drink.

Smoking, although legal, is discouraged. These days less than a quarter of Australians smoke. State laws vary, but smoking bans are becoming more widespread. Smoking is not allowed in public buildings, restaurants, cinemas or public transport.

Some international students are surprised by the open way that drugs are talked about on campus. One student from Malaysia said she was shocked to see needle disposal bins and condom vending machines in public toilets. 'It seemed to encourage casual sex and injecting drugs,' she said. These measures are designed to stop the spread of HIV and hepatitis infection. They do not mean risky behaviour is acceptable.

Using illegal drugs is very unsafe. The quality of such drugs varies and you cannot be sure what you are getting or the effect it will have. Disco drugs – which include ecstasy, speed and the prescription drugs rohypnol and Ritalin – are illegal. You risk losing your student visa if you are caught using them.

PREGNANCY

A serious problem for young women studying away from home is an unwanted pregnancy.

Being away from your parents and the rules of behaviour at home may tempt you to experiment with sex. Australian sexual conduct is freer than that of many countries. But don't be fooled into thinking that all Australians have many sexual partners before marriage. Some do, many don't. Don't be pressured into any behaviour that makes you unhappy. And don't start a sexual relationship just because you are lonely.

If you do have sex, take every precaution. Insist your partner wears a condom, even if you are using other contraception. This protects you against sexually transmitted diseases as well as pregnancy. The student health centre can advise you about contraception.

An unwanted pregnancy can be very damaging. Your religious or cultural beliefs may not allow you to end the pregnancy. But having the baby might ruin your future study and career. You and the baby may not be accepted at home when you return. Your health insurance doesn't cover pregnancy so you will have big costs to pay.

A missed period can be the first sign of pregnancy. Or it can be a result of the stress of living in a foreign country. Many international students have irregular periods or stop having periods completely. If you have missed a period and think you could be pregnant, go to your health centre immediately. If you know you cannot be pregnant, go to the centre anyway for a general health check.

The student union

Australian universities and colleges allow students a voice in how the institutions are run. Students elect representatives each year who sit on university and college policy-making bodies. In this way, student needs are heard at the highest levels. But most students are more interested in how well their representatives run the student union buildings and facilities.

The term *student union* is often used for both the student-run buildings and the group of students who control them. But in some places, the student group is called the Students' Representative Council (SRC) or student guild.

The social hub of the campus is the student union building. It contains shops, cafes, bars and meeting rooms for the many student clubs and activities on campus. It provides printing and copying services, telephones and extra computer rooms. It also houses the student union staff officers, the student publication and, sometimes, the student radio station.

Many student unions run workshops. Topics can include using computers, car maintenance, cooking, Internet web design or résumé writing. Some workshops are free. Others charge a fee.

CLUBS

Every university has a few student clubs; some have more than 100. There are clubs for people interested in everything from drama or politics to chess or martial arts.

International students often say student clubs are the best way to meet local students. The clubs are relaxed and friendly and you share a common interest with the locals. Some clubs are specially designed to allow international and Australian students to meet.

And there is always an international students club. Campuses with big numbers of international students also have national clubs where you can meet students from your home country.

Clubs are a good way to meet fellow students. *Nich Farrelly*

STUDENT ASSISTANCE

Although the universities have good official support services, some students prefer to get help from fellow students. The student unions employ officers who can explain your student rights. They also offer personal and financial counselling and accommodation help. Some give free legal advice.

For international students, the best place to get help is the international student centre. But it is good to remember that you can also get independent help from the student union.

Choosing where to live

Your choice of accommodation has a big effect on your experience of Australia. It is important to think about what you want to achieve in your time away from home. Then you can choose the type of housing that is most likely to support your goals.

You can live with an Australian family under the 'homestay' scheme. You can live in a student hostel or in a hall of residence on campus. Or you can rent a house or flat with friends.

You do not have to stay in one sort of accommodation for your entire course. Many local students live at home or in halls of residence for the first year of university. This makes the move from school to tertiary study easier. They don't have to worry about adjusting to independent living until they have adjusted to university or college life. In later years they move into shared housing with fellow students.

CAMPUS TALK

Here are some special words related to your university or college study that you hear on campus.

Alumni: The alumni are all the former students or staff members of an educational institution. Most universities have alumni associations so you can keep in contact after you leave.

Census date: The census date is the last day for any change of subject enrolment. It usually occurs a few weeks after the start of a semester.

Course outline or study guide: At the start of semester, students receive a course outline which lists the aims of the subject, a lecture and tutorial schedule, and a reading list.

Credit point: Each subject you pass is worth a set number of credit points. You must achieve your course's required total number of credit points in order to graduate.

Discipline: A discipline is an area of study, such as engineering, history, chemistry, art, accounting, or information and communications technology.

ENTER: This stands for Equivalent National Tertiary Entry Ranking. The Australian states have different names for their final year school exams but every student is given a national ENTER score based on their exam results. Most courses use the ENTER to select students.

Exemption: Study at another university or particular work experience that is similar to a subject in your course may be counted towards your degree. If your course coordinator agrees, you can be granted an exemption from a particular subject.

Handbook: The university handbook contains all the official information about university rules and course requirements. Most universities have their handbooks on their web sites. Handbooks for individual faculties contain detailed subject information.

HECS: This stands for Higher Education Contribution Scheme. Students at Australian public universities pay part of their education costs to the federal government. They pay the HECS charge 'up front' at the start of semester or pay it back later through their tax when they begin working.

NUS: The National Union of Students represents about 80 per cent of Australia's university students through each member university's SRC. Some SRCs do not belong. It is the main student voice trying to influence government policy on education and student welfare.

Prerequisite: Some subjects have prerequisites, which are other less-advanced subjects. You must successfully complete the prerequisite subjects before enrolment.

SRC: This is stands for the Students' Representative Council. The SRC is elected by students each year and runs the student union activities. An alternative name is the student guild.

Student diaries: These are given to all students at the start of the year. The diary has important semester dates clearly marked, campus maps and information on students' rights and university regulations.

Transcript: Your transcript is the official document that lists your subject results.

International students don't have that choice. But you can choose accommodation that eases the stress of living in Australia. If you live with people from your home country at first, you are less likely to feel homesick and lonely.

You can arrange accommodation before you arrive in the country. The international student centre at every university and college can help. Most students take temporary accommodation in hotels and hostels before deciding where to live permanently. Help to get housing is also available at the student union.

HOMESTAY

Homestay gives you the greatest contact with Australians of different ages and interests. One student from Hong Kong said he learned a lot from his homestay. 'My firsts in Australia were because of that: my first housewarming party, my first 50th wedding anniversary.'

One big advantage of homestay is that you get a chance to practise Australian English in less stressful surroundings than a classroom. You don't have to be so worried about making mistakes because your homestay hosts are your local family. Another advantage is that most meals are prepared for you. Most of all, you learn about Australia and Australians very quickly.

A disadvantage is that the food is different. You have to live by the rules of the house, which may take some patience and adjustment. Hardest of all, you have to speak English all the time. You can't relax at home by speaking your native language or being with someone who understands your culture.

However, for students who want a deep understanding of Australia, homestay is an excellent choice.

HOSTELS AND UNIVERSITY ACCOMMODATION

On-campus accommodation is not common in Australia. Most students live off campus. However, most universities and some colleges provide some student accommodation in student villages or halls of residence (sometimes called residential colleges). Special places are set aside for postgraduate students who have different needs from undergraduates. The standard of accommodation varies but there are no dormitories like those found in other countries. All students have their own rooms.

Student villages usually comprise furnished self-contained flats where students do their own cooking and cleaning. Most are not on campus but within walking distance.

Halls of residence can vary a lot but usually provide full board. Students have a separate bedroom and dine in common rooms. The halls sometimes provide extra tuition in some university subjects.

> **full board** - *system where accommodation and all meals are provided*
> **half board** - *accommodation and some meals, usually breakfast and lunch, are provided*

Student hostels are normally run by private owners or organisations. They are often much smaller than halls of residence. They offer full board or half board. Because they are small, they can be more like a family home. Students, however, say some hostels have very strict rules.

The advantage of any of these types of accommodation is that they do not provide completely independent living. You can get to know other local and international students in an informal way. A hostel or hall of residence is a good place to practise your English.

A disadvantage is that you live with other students and don't meet Australians of different ages and interests. Another disadvantage is that on-campus living can distract you from study when your fellow students want to party. Halls of residence, in particular, can be expensive.

A room for each student is usual for on-campus accommodation.
Courtesy: Menzies College, La Trobe University

RENTED FLATS AND HOUSES

Many local students rent a private house or flat with other students or friends. Increasingly, international students choose this type of accommodation. Especially in capital cities, such as Sydney, Melbourne and Brisbane, high-rise apartment blocks in the central area often have student tenants. But if your university or college is in the suburbs, a house or flat in a low-rise block is more likely.

Sharing rent can make flats or houses a cheap choice. But rental accommodation is often more expensive than you think. In the centres of the capital cities, rents are high. You have to pay for furniture and household goods, like cooking equipment, sheets and towels. You have to pay a bond of several weeks' rent, which might not be returned to you when you leave. If the house or flat is a long way from your university or college, you have higher transport costs.

Rental accommodation certainly allows you much more freedom in the way you live.

However, there are some disadvantages. You and your flatmates have to cook and clean. The fair division of this work can sometimes cause arguments. You might have problems with your landlord. Unless one of your flatmates is an Australian, you don't get much chance to speak English, or at least Australian English.

If you choose private rental housing, it is essential that you know your rights and respons-

ibilities as a tenant. It is unwise to sign any rental agreement without having it checked first. Your student union and international student services centre are good places to find out. The student housing officer can also help if you have a dispute with your landlord.

> ### SURVIVAL TIP
> *Don't get lost! All formal university and college communication with students is done by mail. Make sure your international student centre and your department have your correct address. You must also tell the Department of Immigration and Multicultural and Indigenous Affairs in writing at least two working days before you move into a different home.*

part five:
the systems

Courtesy: Australian Electoral Commission/Arthur Mostead

'In Australia, students can sit in class and criticise the government a lot. I found that hard to understand at first.'

– a Singaporean student, Flinders University, South Australia

Some systems in Australia, such as education and health, touch the lives of all students. Others, such as the electoral system or the welfare system, don't affect international students. However, it is important to understand how all the systems work. If you know the basics, you can understand newspapers and news broadcasts better. You can follow Australian public debate.

The political system

In the late 19th century, Australia was made up of six British colonies. Each colony had a parliament and made its own laws. But a governor appointed by the British monarch had the final power. Britain could reject any laws it did not like. The passing of the *Australian Constitution Act* in the British Parliament changed that and Australia became a Federation in 1901.

> **federation** – *a political unity which is formed when several separate states unite under a central government. The states keep control of their own internal affairs.*

Today, Australia comprises the six original states – New South Wales, Victoria, Queensland, South Australia, Western Australia and Tasmania – and two territories – the Northern Territory and the Australian Capital Territory.

In the 1840s, some people saw the need to

cooperate about things like quarantine, railways and postal services. But competition between the colonies meant little was done at that time.

A HISTORY OF THE FEDERAL CONSTITUTION

In 1891, the first conference to draft a federal constitution was held. A lot of argument and bargaining occurred at later conferences. The draft was agreed finally and sent to England for approval.

The writers of the Constitution got ideas from Britain, the United States and Switzerland. The basis of the Constitution is a parliamentary system similar to Britain's 'Westminster' system. Such a system relies on a 'separation' of the powers, or functions, of government. The parliament makes the laws. The government administers the laws. The courts interpret the laws if there is a dispute.

Like Britain, Australia is a constitutional monarchy. The Queen of Great Britain and Northern Ireland is also the Queen of Australia. She is represented in Australia by a governor-general, the state governors and the territory administrators.

The way that power was divided between the states and the federal government came from the United States. The United States also provided the model for the Senate, whose members represent the various states and territories.

Switzerland's way of changing the Constitution through a referendum (a vote by the people) was adopted. The Constitution only changes if a majority of voters in the country and in the majority of states vote 'yes' to the proposed change. Change is very hard to achieve. In 100 years, only eight out of 45 referendum questions have succeeded.

The Constitution does two things. It lays out the operating rules of the federal government, or the Commonwealth of Australia. And it regulates the relationship between the states.

The federal government has the power to control commerce, communications, national industrial disputes, defence, external affairs, immigration, and marriage and divorce. The states and territories make laws in other areas. If a state law differs from a federal law, the federal law wins out. Over the years, judgements by the High Court (see page 71) have extended federal powers to areas such as health, education, Indigenous affairs and the environment.

Unlike constitutions in some countries, the Australian Constitution sets out very few individual or human rights. It says the government must allow freedom of religion; but, in general, Australia relies on common law to protect the rights of individuals.

Constitutions set out how the parliaments work. Because each state has a separate consti-

---

CONSTITUTIONAL CRISIS

In 1975, Australia experienced a constitutional crisis which remains significant more than 25 years later.

The Labor government that was elected in 1972 was a controversial government. Under its leader, Gough Whitlam, it introduced many reforms, including no-fault divorce laws and a universal health scheme.

In October 1975, the Senate – where the conservative coalition parties had a majority – delayed passing the legislation needed for the government to pay its accounts, including the salaries of public servants. The delay went against the custom that the Senate cannot vote against a government's money, or supply, bills.

Gough Whitlam advised the governor-general, Sir John Kerr, to call an election of half the Senate. But on 11 November 1975, Kerr dismissed Gough Whitlam. He appointed the leader of the Liberal Party, Malcolm Fraser, as prime minister until a full election was held.

Labor lost the election. Many Labor supporters believed that Kerr was wrong. They argued that the Constitution did not allow the Queen's representative to act against the advice of the prime minister.

The dismissal was one of the most dramatic political events in Australia's history as a nation. It raised issues about the role of the Senate and the governor-general that have not been clarified today.

tution, there are slight differences between them. But all Australian parliaments operate under the type of government known as 'responsible government'.

In this system, only members of parliament are elected. Judges and other high officials are not elected. Parliament provides all the members of government. Outsiders, such as army officers or academics, cannot be part of the government.

The government is formed by the party that wins the most seats in the lower house of parliament. Sometimes two or more parties combine to form a 'coalition' government.

The government is responsible to parliament for its actions. The government must hold an election or resign if it loses its majority in the House of Representatives which is known as 'losing the confidence of the House'. Government ministers are also responsible to parliament for the actions taken by the public servants working in the minister's area of responsibility, or portfolio.

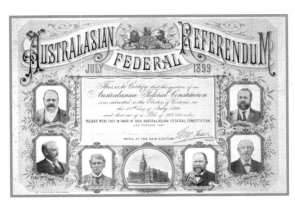

A certificate like this was given to people who voted on 17 July 1899 in the referendum that led to the Federation of Australia. *National Library of Australia*

FEDERAL PARLIAMENT

The Federal Parliament has two chambers: the House of Representatives and the Senate. The House of Representatives is also known as the lower house or people's house. It is the more

important chamber. The leader of the party with the most seats in the House of Representatives becomes prime minister and forms government. The number of seats the party wins in the Senate doesn't count.

A Member of the House of Representatives (MHR) represents one of around 150 electorates throughout the country. The electorates are named after historical figures or places. The number of electorates and their boundaries change as their populations change. The idea is to make sure, as far as possible, that everybody's vote has equal value.

The length of time between elections for the House of Representatives is not fixed. But federal governments must serve a minimum of three years unless they lose the confidence of the House.

The Senate, or upper house, is sometimes called the states' house because its members represent a whole state or territory, not a smaller electorate. Each state has 12 senators and the territories have two. Senators are elected for six years; but half of the Senate retires every three years. They are elected on a quota system, called 'proportional representation'. This means a successful candidate has to receive a certain percentage, or quota, of all the votes cast in an election.

Draft laws, or bills, are introduced into either house by the government or individual members. After debate and amendment, the bill goes to the other house for debate and approval. If it is approved by both houses, the governor-general gives it 'assent' and it becomes law.

Very often, a federal government does not control the Senate. Members of a 'hostile Senate' can delay legislation or try to force changes that the government doesn't want.

Because of the way that senators are elected, smaller parties and independent candidates have a better chance of being elected to the Senate. They can sometimes hold 'the balance of power' because they can vote with the Opposition parties to defeat a bill.

If the Senate rejects a bill from the House of Representatives twice, the government can call a 'double-dissolution' election. If there is a double dissolution, all Senate seats are contested, instead of only half of them. This means there is a good chance that the new Senate will be less hostile. If the government gets back into power, its legislation is more likely to pass. A similar situation applies in the states.

STATE AND TERRITORY PARLIAMENTS

All Australian states, except Queensland, have two-chamber parliaments. In New South Wales, Victoria and Western Australia, the lower house is called the Legislative Assembly. Queensland also calls its single house the Legislative Assembly. In Tasmania and South Australia, the lower house is the House of Assembly. The head of government in each state is a premier.

The two territories, the Australian Capital Territory and the Northern Territory, have one-chamber legislative assemblies. They have chief ministers, not premiers. They have administrators, not governors.

LOCAL GOVERNMENT

Known as the third tier of government, local government has no constitutional status. The

The Victorian State Parliament House was home to the federal government until the Federal Parliament moved to the new national capital, Canberra, in 1927.

local authorities are responsible to the minister of local government in their state. But they provide important services for people. They look after local roads, parking, rubbish collection and building regulations. They provide swimming pools, sports grounds, parks and libraries. They run child care and aged care programs and community health services.

In city areas, the local authorities are called town or city councils; in rural areas, they are called shire councils. Residents and property owners in each council area elect representatives to manage local affairs. Local government gets its money from the land rates paid by property owners, fines and fees collected for things like building permits and pet registrations.

ELECTIONS

Voting in federal and state elections and referendums is compulsory for all Australians over 18. It is also compulsory for residents in local government elections in New South Wales, Victoria and Queensland.

There are various systems of counting the votes. The most important one is the preferential voting system, which applies in the House of Representatives and most state lower houses. It is complicated and means that the result is sometimes not known for many days after voting has taken place.

In this system, voters mark the ballot paper with a number 1 beside the candidate they like best. Then they mark their second preference with a 2, and so on. All first preferences are counted. If a candidate doesn't get a majority, the second preferences of the candidate with the lowest number of first preference votes are counted. This process continues until one candidate receives 50 per cent of the vote plus one.

The political parties produce voting 'tickets', showing which way they want people to vote. At election time, parties often bargain with each other about which party will get second preference on the ticket. This gives smaller parties a chance to influence the actions of the bigger parties.

Australia is dominated by two main political

parties: the Australian Labor Party and the Liberal Party. This has been the case since just after Federation in 1901. It is important to understand that the range of mainstream political opinion in Australia is narrow. Because Australians don't like extremes, the main political parties are neither very radical nor very conservative.

Smaller parties exist. At various times in Australian history, they have been important because they can allocate preferences at elections. They can also hold the balance of power in the upper houses.

Australian voters are cautious. In lower house elections, they vote for the party they want to form government. But they often vote for other parties in the upper house as a way to make sure the government doesn't make too many changes.

THE AUSTRALIAN LABOR PARTY

The Australian Labor Party (ALP) is the country's oldest party. It developed from the trade union movement in the 1890s. Originally a socialist party, it has now dropped the socialist idea of government ownership of part of the economy from its policies and adopted a more free market approach.

The party was elected to office just before World War 1, but a deep split occurred when the prime minister, W. M. 'Billy' Hughes, supported conscription. Hughes was expelled from the party but managed to remain as prime minister. The party declined until Australians elected a Labor government, led by John Curtin, in 1941.

conscription – compulsory enrolment in the armed forces. Compulsory military service no longer exists but it was a topic of hot debate in Australia, especially during World War 1 and the Vietnam War.

John Curtin died in office and was followed by Ben Chifley, who introduced many reforms. But when he tried to nationalise the banks and the airline industry, the voters turned against the party. It was defeated in 1949.

Anti-communist attitudes during the 1950s led to a split in the party. Many of the ALP's anti-communist, Catholic members left to join a new party, the Democratic Labor Party (DLP). The DLP won several Senate seats and, by supporting the conservative government, kept the ALP out of office until 1972.

The Whitlam Labor government lasted only three years (see page 62) but made important changes, including setting up a universal health scheme and abolishing university fees.

During the 1980s and 1990s, the Labor governments of Bob Hawke and Paul Keating adopted stronger free market economics and moved social policies more to the centre. They floated the Australian dollar, deregulated the banks, began dropping tariffs and sold some government assets to private companies. Many of Labor's traditional supporters among workers were unhappy with these moves.

Controversial former prime minister W. M. Hughes (left) with wartime Labor prime minister John Curtin and the Governor-General of Australia (the Duke of Gloucester) in 1945. *National Library of Australia*

THE LIBERAL PARTY

The main conservative party is the Liberal Party, set up under the leadership of Robert Menzies in 1945. The party is committed to free enterprise, although it supported tariff protection for industry and farmers in its early years. Traditionally, it has appealed to middle-class voters.

The first Liberal Party was formed in 1909 when two anti-labour groups – the Protectionists and the Free Traders – united under Alfred Deakin, who became prime minister in 1909. The party was re-formed and renamed several times over the next 30 years. It very often had to

Australia's longest serving prime minister, Robert Gordon Menzies.
National Library of Australia

rely on the support of another conservative party, the Country Party, to win government.

Menzies' Liberal Party, too, formed a coalition government, with the Country Party as the junior partner. By tradition, the leader of the junior coalition partner becomes the deputy prime minister.

First elected in 1949, the Liberals held office for 23 years. Menzies was prime minister for 16 years before he retired in 1966. The Menzies era is seen as the golden years of the party because during that time the country had rapid economic growth and low unemployment. Although conservative, the Menzies government took a generous approach to welfare.

After three years in opposition, the Liberal Party with Malcolm Fraser as leader was elected in 1975. The Fraser government remained in power for eight years, partly because the Labor Opposition was weak. But the popular leadership of Bob Hawke brought Labor back into government. Hawke and, later, Keating led Labor governments for a total of 13 years.

Then John Howard led the Liberal Party to victory in 1996. The Howard government took a more conservative stand than the Fraser government. In foreign policy, it put more emphasis on traditional ties with the United States and Britain. At home, it adopted a strong free market stance and firm anti-labour policies. It also tightened immigration policy.

THE NATIONAL PARTY

The conservative National Party was originally called the Country Party. It was formed to represent farmers and other rural people who felt the city-based parties did not look after their interests.

In recent years, the National Party has tried to broaden its appeal to non-rural voters but its support has steadily dropped, especially in state politics.

MINOR PARTIES

Australians are becoming more critical of the major parties. In the 2001 election, nearly one-quarter of the votes went to candidates for smaller parties and independents.

The Australian Democrats party was formed in 1977 by a former Liberal minister, Don Chipp, as a breakaway party. Originally, it was a centrist party with a policy of making the major parties more accountable. It is now more radical in many policies than the ALP. Despite its small size, it can be powerful when it holds the balance of power in the Senate.

The Greens party grew out of several environmental campaigns in the 1980s. It is particularly strong in Tasmania and Western Australia. It also has one member in the House of Representatives and two senators. Originally an environmental party, it takes a left-of-centre stand on social and international issues.

The One Nation party rose to prominence briefly in the late 1990s. Founded by an independent Queensland MHR, Pauline Hanson, in 1996, One Nation appealed to the rural poor and farmers. These people were upset by the effects of changes in the world economy and policies towards Aboriginals which they thought gave Indigenous Australians unfair advantages over white Australians. With a strong anti-immigration policy and other extreme views, One Nation won 11 seats in the Queensland state election in 1998. But, by the national 2001 election, it got only 4.35 per cent of the primary vote. The result showed, once again, that Australian voters are wary of extremists.

Members of other small single-interest parties and independents also seek election at federal, state and local government elections.

THE MONARCHY

Australians have a complex relationship with the British monarchy. The British Queen is also Queen of Australia. The Australian Constitution gives the monarch powers that are usually given to a head of state. In practice, the monarch passes these powers to the governor-general and the state governors. The Queen appoints and can dismiss a governor-general but only on the advice of the Australian prime minister of the time.

There is a lot of argument about whether the Queen or the governor-general is Australia's head of state. The answer doesn't matter much, except when people discuss whether Australia should be a republic. Republicans argue it is silly for Australia to have a British head of state.

There has always been a strand of republican feeling in Australia, mainly among Australians of Irish background. For them, the British monarch is a symbol of oppression.

At the end of the 20th century, republican sentiment grew. In 1999 a referendum was held on a model of a republic in which a president, elected by the Federal Parliament, became head of state. The president would have the same ceremonial and formal duties as a governor-general.

Opinion polls showed strong support for a republic. But the referendum was defeated because many people wanted to elect the president directly.

The move towards a republic has weakened a little but is likely to return in the future.

POLITICAL PROTEST

The mark of a healthy democracy is the right of people to disagree openly with the government. Although freedom of speech is not mentioned in the Constitution, the High Court ruled that it contains an implied right to free speech in political matters.

Australians use various ways to make their voices heard between elections. The letters pages of newspapers are popular forums. So, too, are talkback radio programs where citizens can speak directly to politicians, including ministers.

Occasionally, people are angry enough to march in the streets. Big demonstrations, known as the moratorium marches, were held in the 1970s to protest against conscription and Australia's involvement in the Vietnam War. In early 2003, even bigger marches were held to protest against war in Iraq.

In general, Australian political demonstrations are peaceful. Violence is very rare.

A demonstration in Canberra against the 2003 Gulf War shows the peaceful nature of most Australian protests. The federal Parliament House is in the background. *Nich Farrelly*

The media

The mass media play an important role in Australian life. They entertain people. They reflect Australian culture in locally made programs. For this reason, many people want to make sure that the media have a large amount of Australian content.

The media also inform. In a democracy, it is vital that people can find out the facts and hear different opinions. Then they can make an informed decision when they vote. Critics say that Australian media can't perform this information task properly because the media are owned by just a few corporations, which means there are not enough different opinions. As well, state laws on defamation restrict debate on matters of public interest.

> **defamation** – *an unreasonable published attack on the reputation of a person, usually someone well known to the public*

GOVERNMENT REGULATION

The Australian government does not control the actual content of any media, except the information on its own web sites. But the federal government does regulate the broadcast media through rules about who can own a broadcast licence and rules on Australian content. The amount and type of media that any one company can own is limited. Foreign ownership is restricted.

The states can affect media content with their laws on obscenity and defamation.

CONCENTRATION OF MEDIA OWNERSHIP

One hundred years ago, Australia's 17 big city daily newspapers were owned by 17 different people. Today, two companies – News Limited and Fairfax – own 10 out of the 12 big city papers. News Limited publishes about 67 per cent of daily newspapers, about 75 per cent of Sunday papers, and nearly half of all suburban newspapers.

Many media companies began as private family-owned companies. Most companies are now listed on the stock exchange but family members are still shareholders or run the companies.

The international media owner Rupert Murdoch and his family are big shareholders in News Limited. The Packer family own a lot of shares in companies that run the Nine TV network and many magazines. When discussing the media, Australians often use the names Murdoch and Packer instead of the proper company names.

Despite the restrictions on foreign ownership, there is a lot of indirect foreign control. The Australian-born Murdoch is a US citizen. Tony O'Reilly is Irish but his family has a big shareholding in APN News and Media which runs a third of Australia's country newspapers.

In general, conservative governments do not like regulating ownership of businesses because they support free enterprise. Labor governments usually advocate controls. But the media are so important that there is some regulation whichever party is in power.

'Cross-media ownership' rules stop media companies from owning all the media in one place, although the rules don't apply to new media such as pay television or datacasting. Attempts to abolish all ownership restrictions cause very heated debate.

COMMERCIAL BROADCASTING

Regular radio broadcasting began in 1921. Television began in 1956, just in time to televise the Olympic Games in Melbourne.

There are just over 200 commercial radio stations in Australia. Half of them are AM stations, half of them are FM. Most play popular music. But several stations, particularly in the capital cities, rely on news and talkback. Talkback stations allow listeners to phone in with their opinions on the news of the day. The talkback stations are very powerful in the political process because they tell politicians what some of the voters think.

A few foreign language commercial radio stations have started in recent years.

There are two types of commercial television: free-to-air and pay TV. In Brisbane, Sydney, Melbourne and Adelaide, there are three free-to-air networks: Nine, Seven and Ten. The networks are made up of stations in each capital. Most programs are broadcast nationally. But each state station produces local news, sports and current affairs programs.

The networks buy programs from the United States and Britain, as well as broadcasting locally produced programs.

Television personality Eddie McGuire hosts the Australian version of the popular TV program *Who Wants To Be A Millionaire. Courtesy: The Nine Network*

Regional TV networks operate in other places in Australia. These are usually linked to the city networks and show many of the same programs.

Pay TV was introduced in the 1990s. Although Australians have a reputation for quickly accepting new communication technologies, they didn't rush to pay a monthly charge to watch TV. By 2002, only 20 per cent of Australian households had pay TV and the two subscription TV companies, Foxtel and Optus, were losing money.

The future of pay TV and digital TV is uncertain.

PUBLIC BROADCASTING

Public broadcasting comprises the national broadcasters – the Australian Broadcasting Corporation (ABC) and the Special Broadcasting Service (SBS) – and community broadcasters.

The Federal Parliament passed a law in 1932 to set up the ABC as an independent non-commercial broadcaster. Its job is to provide quality programs that inform and entertain and add to Australia's sense of identity. It runs 400 television channels and hundreds of radio stations which broadcast local and national programs.

The ABC runs a national youth radio service, Triple J. Many tertiary students think Triple J broadcasts the best mix of local and international music, as well as covering popular culture, social and youth topics properly.

The ABC also has an international service, Radio Australia, which broadcasts in English, Mandarin, Bahasa Indonesia, Vietnamese, Khmer and Tok Pisin throughout the Asia-Pacific region. More recently, it developed a wide-ranging Internet service, ABC Online.

By law, the ABC is independent from government interference in the programs it produces or broadcasts. But the government appoints the directors of the ABC board and the chief executive. Most of the ABC's funds come from a government grant, although it also gets money from various business enterprises. So the government has ways of indirectly influencing the ABC's programs and operation.

Radio presenter Jon Faine takes listeners' phone calls in a 'talkback' segment. *Courtesy: 774 ABC Melbourne*

Many Australians fiercely defend the traditional independence of the ABC from both government pressure and the influence of advertisers. They protest loudly whenever any action threatens that independence.

The SBS is similar to the ABC in structure. Its role is to reflect the multicultural nature of Australia. SBS Radio broadcasts in English and 67 other languages, more than any other broadcaster in the world. Half its television programs are in English; the other half are in about 60 other languages with English subtitles.

Community stations are small and often staffed mainly by volunteers. There are many more community radio stations than television stations.

Community broadcasting appeals to audiences with special interests. For example, there is a network of stations for people with poor eyesight who can't read newspapers and magazines. These stations broadcast readings of articles from the daily press. The student radio stations, run on many campuses, are community broadcasters.

There are a number of foreign language community broadcasting stations.

NEWSPAPERS

The standard of newspapers in Australia is average by world standards. Australia does not have the high quality serious newspapers that are found in Europe or the United States. But it doesn't usually have the sensational popular papers of Britain or the US either. This middle-of-the-road approach is another example of Australians' dislike of extremes.

Australian newspaper circulations, or the number of copies sold, are getting smaller. The number of papers published has also dropped in the past 10 years. There are now no afternoon papers.

There are two national papers: *The Australian* and the business paper, *The Australian Financial Review*. Morning papers, called 'metropolitan' papers, are published in the capital cities, but only Sydney and Melbourne have more than one metropolitan paper. People in capital cities can also read suburban papers, which report local events. The suburban newspapers are free.

Many larger towns have their own daily papers. These are called regional dailies. Other rural areas have newspapers that are usually published once or twice each week.

The foreign language press in Australia began in the 19th century. Most foreign language papers are weekly or monthly but some are dailies. Although most foreign language papers are published in Sydney or Melbourne, they are distributed nationally.

MAGAZINES

Australia has a big magazine industry, even though it has a small population. More than 700 magazines are published regularly. Australian readers also buy many specialist magazines that are published overseas.

A century ago, Australian magazines – such as *The Bulletin* and *The Australian Journal* – were important in promoting Australian literature and

Specialist magazines cover a variety of hobbies and other interests.

ideas. But, these days, the influence of literary and serious news magazines is small.

The most popular types of magazines are women's magazines, sports magazines, 'lifestyle' magazines and 'do-it-yourself' magazines. Lifestyle magazines specialise in one aspect of life, such as food, wine or holidays. The do-it-yourself magazines give advice on activities such as gardening, home decorating and handicrafts.

Then there are hundreds of small magazines for readers interested in a range of specialist topics ranging from surfing to computers to art.

THE INTERNET

Australians welcomed the Internet as eagerly as they accepted other communications technologies. By 2002, half of all Australian homes had access to the Internet. Four years before, only one home in eight had Internet access.

However, the Internet has widened some gaps in society. Richer people are more likely to own computers and use the Internet. City people are bigger Internet users than country people.

Governments throughout Australia have policies to give more people access to the Internet so that everyone gets a fair go. Most local libraries provide free Internet access and the number of schools using the Internet is increasing every year.

But as access increases, more Australians worry about children finding pornography sites on the Internet.

The legal system

The law in Australia is a mixture of statute law, or laws made in the parliaments, and common law. There is also 'designated legislation', which occurs when a parliament hands over the power to make laws to another organisation. The most common example in Australia is local councils, which can make laws, or 'ordinances', about local matters.

The law is divided into criminal law and civil law. Criminal law deals with those cases where the accused, if found guilty, will be punished.

Australia upholds principles of criminal law which are based on the British tradition. These principles say a person is innocent until proved guilty of a crime. An accused person doesn't need to prove innocence. The prosecution, often called the Crown, must prove the accused is almost certainly guilty; that is, that the case is 'proved beyond reasonable doubt'. People can only be tried on the facts of the case being heard by the court. The court can't be told about the accused person's past behaviour.

Another important part of the Australian system, which also came from Britain, is the jury system. In criminal law, a jury of citizens (usually 12 people) decides whether an accused person is guilty of all crimes, except minor ones.

Civil law deals with cases where people want compensation, usually money damages, for something wrong that they think another person or organisation has done to them. They 'sue', or take to court, the person who they think has harmed them. Sometimes civil cases are decided by small juries.

When any court, except the High Court, makes a decision, the people involved can seek permission to appeal to a higher court to change the decision.

THE COURTS

Because Australia is a federation, it has two legal systems: the federal system and the state or territory system. Sometimes these systems overlap. The top court in the country is the High Court. It hears appeals from lower state courts and other federal courts. It also makes decisions if a part of the Constitution is challenged.

The High Court has seven judges, who are appointed by the federal government. Only three or five judges hear most cases. But all the judges hear very important cases. When all seven judges hear a case, it is called a Full Bench of the High Court. All cases are decided by a majority of judges.

The Family Court, which hears divorce cases and decides what will happen to the children of a marriage and the property of the husband and wife, is a federal court. So, too, is the Federal Court which deals with laws that apply nationally. These include some industrial laws and bankruptcy laws. It hears appeals from state courts on federal matters such as taxation.

The Victorian Supreme Court hears a case. *Courtesy: Supreme Court of Victoria/John French*

The state courts have three tiers. The lower courts, where all criminal cases and most civil cases begin, are the Magistrates' Courts. In some states they are called local courts or courts of petty sessions.

The Magistrates' Courts hear minor civil and family law cases. They hear criminal cases. In serious criminal cases, such as murder, the magistrate decides if there is enough evidence to send a person for trial in a higher court. This process is called a 'committal hearing'.

The Children's Courts and Coroner's Courts are lower courts, too. Coroner's Courts hear evidence when people die unexpectedly or violently. Sometimes, the coroner commits a person for trial on a charge of murder. Children's Courts deal with most cases where the accused is a child.

The second tier comprises the District or County Courts. These are known as intermediate courts. They deal with appeals in civil cases from the Magistrates' Courts. They hear trials for more serious crimes such as armed robbery.

The third tier is the state Supreme Courts. They hear appeals from the intermediate and lower courts. They also hold trials for serious crimes, such as rape and murder.

ROYAL COMMISSIONS AND JUDICIAL INQUIRIES

Royal commissions, which are set up by governments, inquire into various issues of public importance. They don't investigate a single event, which is what happens in a normal court.

The head of the commission, the royal commissioner, is usually a retired judge. The commissioner has the powers of a court to call witnesses and question them.

After hearing the evidence, the commissioner writes a report and makes recommendations to the government about action that should be taken. For example, the commissioner may recommend changes in the law or that someone should be charged with an offence.

Over the last 20 years, royal commissions have investigated many matters. Aboriginal deaths in police custody, organised crime, the collapse of Australia's biggest insurance company HIH, and the operation of the building industry are some of the topics. Because royal commissions usually deal with political issues, they often cause a lot of public debate.

Judicial inquiries are like royal commissions, except their powers are not as wide.

THE POLICE

Every state and territory has its own police force. The Australian Federal Police system operates at the national level. By world standards, the level of corruption in Australian police forces is reasonably low. It is not common practice and it is illegal to pay police to stop their inquiries or to ignore wrongdoing.

When police are corrupt or they treat suspects brutally, there is usually a public outcry. Most states have anti-corruption commissions to deal with police corruption or corruption in government.

Police in Victoria question a driver. *Courtesy: Victoria Police*

A PERSON'S RIGHTS

The rights of individuals are protected under Australian law. People have rights when they are questioned by police or charged with most crimes. However, the law gives less protection to suspected terrorists.

Police can question someone if they believe the person has committed a crime or if they think the person has information that could help them solve a crime. In all states, if police question you about a motoring offence, you must give them your name and address. But you do not have to answer any other questions. In most states, you have to give your name and address if questioned about other matters.

> **arrest** – an arrest happens when a police officer tells someone that he or she must go to the police station with the officer for questioning about a crime.
>
> **charge** – the formal statement of the crime of which a person is accused

Even if people are arrested, they do not have

to answer questions. However, anything they say can be written down and used as evidence. If arrested, people are wise not to say anything until they have advice from a lawyer.

There is no automatic right to make a phone call or to have a lawyer present during questioning. But the police usually contact someone on behalf of an arrested person.

Police don't have a general right to search a suspect unless the person is arrested. Police have a right to search the premises where they arrest someone. But they can't search other private property without a search warrant.

The welfare system

Australians are in two minds about government welfare payments. On the one hand, they think governments should help improve things for Australians. On the other hand, they don't like people to get too much help. The right levels of welfare payments and who should get them is debated all the time.

> **means test** – a system that counts someone's wealth to see if that person needs financial help. Under a means test, the amount of welfare money a person gets is decided by the amount of income and property the person already has.

But the country has a long tradition of government assistance. During the 19th century, charities and voluntary organisations provided help for poor people. The colonies of Victoria and New South Wales introduced a means-tested old age pension in 1900, long before Britain and the United States.

The federal government began paying means-tested pensions to older Australians and invalid pensions to people unable to work through illness in 1908. It also introduced an allowance for mothers in 1912.

However, it was not until Labor came to power during World War 2, that the welfare system grew. Labor introduced national child endowment (a regular payment for each child after the first one), pensions for widows and payments for unemployed people. Extra types of payments – such as disability pensions for disabled people – were introduced in the 1970s.

In the late 1990s, it became harder to get welfare payments. For example, people who receive unemployment payments must now prove they are looking for work. This system of giving people certain things to do before they can receive welfare is called 'mutual obligation'.

The federal welfare system is run by a central agency called Centrelink. Centrelink pays all of the 30 different kinds of welfare payment that are currently available.

State and territory governments provide some help, often in the form of low-cost housing. Private employers are also part of the welfare system. By law, they must have insurance to pay for workers who are injured at work. Usually, they also pay a sick worker's wage for some time.

The health system

In colonial and early 20th-century Australia, the main cause of death was infectious disease. By the mid-20th century, better housing, clean water supplies, sewerage and cleaner handling of food had helped stop the spread of infectious diseases. The introduction of drugs, such as penicillin and other antibiotics, also helped cure them.

Over the past 50 years, the situation changed. Heart attacks and strokes, cancers and injuries became the biggest killers. Health authorities began to stress preventing illness as well as curing it. Campaigns now urge Australians to avoid 'lifestyle diseases' that are caused by poor diet, smoking, too much drinking and too little exercise.

The standard of health care in Australia is high. Capital city hospitals, in particular, have advanced equipment. They are staffed by well-qualified doctors, nurses and other health professionals. Many of them carry out medical research of international quality.

All care is provided by hospital staff. Family and friends are not expected to help care for patients as they are in some countries.

The health system is a mixture of services provided by government and private enterprise.

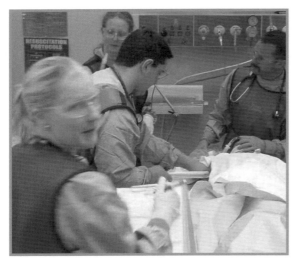

Australian hospitals offer a high quality of medical care. *Courtesy: The Alfred Hospital, Melbourne*

PAYING FOR HEALTH SERVICES

Supplying good health care is expensive. Australians pay for it with a mixture of government funding, health insurance and patient payments.

Since 1975, the country has had a national health scheme. It is called Medicare. The money to run Medicare comes partly from a special taxation levy and partly from general taxation.

Medicare guarantees basic health care for all residents, whether they can afford to pay or not. It pays for treatment by a hospital-appointed doctor in a public hospital. It provides free, or subsidised, treatment by general practitioners, specialists and optometrists.

The federal government sets a 'schedule fee' for all medical services. Medicare pays a high percentage of this fee. This is supposed to cover costs and give doctors a fair profit. But most doctors say this is impossible, so many of them charge more than the schedule fee. The patient pays the difference, unless they have private insurance that covers what is called 'the gap'.

Many doctors 'bulk bill', especially for patients on welfare payments. 'Bulk billing' means the

> **general practitioner** – *a doctor who does not specialise in any one branch of medicine but looks after the general health of patients. Also called GPs or family doctors*

doctors send the bills straight to Medicare and the patient doesn't have to pay the gap.

The public hospitals are run by state or territory governments. There are also private hospitals which are run as commercial businesses. Patients in these hospitals either pay the bills themselves or have their insurance companies pay.

THE PHARMACEUTICAL BENEFITS SCHEME (PBS)

The PBS aims to make essential medicines available to Australians at low cost. Nearly 1500 drugs are on the PBS list. Some of these are very expensive but most patients pay only around $25 for any listed medicine. People on welfare benefits, such as aged pensioners and the unemployed, pay much less. People pay full price for any medicines not covered by the scheme.

When new drugs are introduced, there is often a lot of public argument about whether they should be included in the scheme. The huge cost of the PBS is also a matter of debate.

PRIVATE HEALTH INSURANCE

The rising cost of public health care has led the government to encourage more Australians to pay for themselves through private health insurance.

The largest private health insurer is Medibank Private but there are a number of others. The companies are competitive and offer many different types of insurance. Many schemes pay part of patients' costs for alternative therapies such as acupuncture and naturopathy, as well as standard Western medical treatment.

However, poorer Australians cannot afford private health insurance. They have to rely on public hospitals, which are overcrowded. Sometimes patients have to wait months for treatment or surgery for conditions that are not life-threatening.

Critics argue that the present system doesn't treat patients equally. The cost and efficiency of the health system is a constant topic of discussion.

OVERSEAS STUDENT HEALTH COVER

International students – except some Norwegian and Swedish students – must pay for Overseas

Student Health Cover (OSHC) as a condition of their visas. At present, students can choose between three insurers who provide OSHC.

The OSHC provides the same sort of basic cover as Medicare and the PBS. It also pays for an emergency ambulance. Various restrictions apply. For example, OSHC does not pay for the contraceptive pill. Find out the restrictions from the international student centre at your university or college.

International students can go to any GP but have to pay the difference between the doctor's fee and the OSHC refund. The university student health services bulk bill so students don't have to pay.

In an emergency, especially out of office hours, it is best to go to the emergency department of the local public hospital for free treatment.

The financial system

Australia is a free market economy, although until recently some industries – such as tele-communications, electricity and gas supply, and transport – were mainly state-owned. One example of the move to privatisation is the Commonwealth Bank of Australia.

> **privatisation** – the process by which land and industries are changed from government ownership to private ownership

The Commonwealth Bank was set up by the Australian government in 1911 as a trading and savings bank to compete with the many private banks. Gradually it took over the role of a central bank, or the bank that runs a government's monetary policy by setting official interest rates.

At the beginning of the 1960s, the government set up the Reserve Bank of Australia as the central bank. The Commonwealth Bank went back to being a trading and savings bank. At the same time, the government placed strict controls on all banks. This led to an increase in other types of financial institutions – such as credit unions, finance companies and building societies – because they weren't regulated.

Federal government policy prevents any merger of the top four Australian banks. *S.A. White, Westpac image Courtesy: Westpac*

In the 1980s, most government controls on the banks were lifted. One remaining regulation sets limits on the rate of loans for housing. This recognises the importance of home-ownership to Australians.

Foreign banks were allowed into Australia. New local banks were established. Then, in 1991, the government started to sell its share in the Commonwealth Bank. The bank was later fully privatised and is now one of the 'big four' private banks, which also include the National, Westpac and ANZ.

These days, most financial institutions offer online banking.

BANK FEES

The Australian banks are very profitable but unpopular with the public. In recent years, they have closed many branches, especially in rural areas. Customers are also cross about big increases in the fees that the banks charge for everyday transactions, such as deposits and withdrawals. Most state governments also impose taxes on bank transactions.

It is sensible to check what fees the various banks charge, before you open an account.

OPENING A BANK ACCOUNT

Everyone in Australia has to show proof of identity before they can open a bank account. As an international student, if you have been in the country for fewer than six weeks, all you need is your passport. If you have been in Australia longer, you will need your student card too.

Because banks are so competitive, it is worth finding out which banks offer student accounts. The bank fees on these are cheaper. Your international student centre can advise you.

CREDIT CARDS

Australians have a high level of debt. This is partly because many have big home loans and partly because they use credit cards a lot. Credit card charges are high but they vary from bank to bank. Check the interest and other charges you will have to pay for using your credit card.

Some educational institutions pass on credit card charges to students who pay their fees by credit card. Check your institution's policy on this before paying your fees.

THE GST

In 2000, the federal government introduced a 10 per cent goods and services tax (the GST) on everything except fresh food, health services, education and childcare expenses. But some things at university – such as food and accommodation on field trips and non-essential books – do include the GST.

The GST is already included in the price of all items. But you will see the GST part stated on receipts.

The education system

Like many institutions in Australia, the education system was originally based on English models. There is a mix of state or public schools and private schools, which are often religious schools.

SCHOOLS

School education is the responsibility of state and territory governments. The governments run the public schools. But they also affect private schools because they set the basic curriculums and run the examination systems. Moves to make the systems and standards uniform across the country are planned.

Australian children start school at about six years old. *St John's College, Preston/Darren James*

Education is compulsory for all children until they reach 15 or 16, depending on state rules. Some children go to pre-school part time for a year or two before starting primary school at the age of five or six. They spend six or seven years in primary school.

At age 11 or 12, they go to secondary school. The final year of school is Year 12. Nearly 80 per cent of students stay at school until they finish Year 12.

In the past, there were basically two kinds of state secondary school: high schools which taught academic subjects and technical schools which taught mostly practical subjects and prepared students for skilled jobs. These days, schools teach both academic and vocational education and training (VET) subjects.

> *vocational education* – education that trains people in the skills needed for a trade or occupation

The public school system is under stress. More Australian parents are choosing a private education for their children because they think the standards of teaching and student behaviour are better in private schools. But nearly 70 per cent of students are still educated in public schools.

EDUCATION FUNDING

The federal government has an influence on the school system because it gives money to state governments and to the private schools.

Government grants to private schools have been an issue in Australian politics for many years. The colonial governments in the 19th century subsidised church schools. The subsidies stopped when free, compulsory and secular schooling was introduced in the 1870s. This created a system of free public schools and fee-paying private schools.

In 1974, the federal government began a new system of grants to independent private schools and church schools. The most needy schools, many of which were run by the Catholic Church, got more money for each student than the wealthier schools. The grant system still exists. In the past, critics protested because they said government money shouldn't be used to support religious schools. These days, critics say wealthy schools get money at the expense of poorer schools, whether they are private religious schools or state schools.

TERTIARY EDUCATION

Tertiary education is not much more than 100 years old in Australia. It began as a dual system of universities and colleges. The colleges were teachers' colleges or colleges of advanced edu-cation which taught vocational subjects. Tertiary education was not free, but scholarships allowed some poorer students to go to university or teachers' college. State and federal governments subsidised the running of the tertiary educational institutions but fees were still high.

In the mid-1970s, all tertiary education became free. But in 1988, the federal government introduced a higher education contribution scheme (HECS). Students paid about 20 per cent of the cost of their courses.

At the same time, higher education was reorganised. Most of the colleges were merged with the universities. The vocational Technical and Further Education (TAFE) system remained separate.

More recently, governments have encouraged the institutions to pay more of their costs. Fee-paying courses for international students and some local students were introduced. The institutions set up commercial sections to make money by selling staff expertise and research.

The introduction of commercial matters into education was unpopular with many staff members and students. Some people worry that the HECS debt means poorer students can't afford a tertiary education. Others say that commercial demands mean that the standards of teaching and research will decline. However, free market competition in the tertiary sector is likely to increase in future.

part six:
shaping the land

Osmar White

'I expected to see kangaroos everywhere and native people. But I only saw big flat fields with sheep in them. And the mountains were so small, compared to home.'

– a Swiss student, Australian National University, Canberra

Aboriginal Australians are part of the land. White Australians, too, depend more on the land than many of them realise. The land has shaped Australian history. At the same time, Australians have shaped and changed the land.

The birth of the land

Australia was once part of the giant continent, Gondwana, which included Africa, South America and India. About 150 million years ago, Australia and Antarctica split from Gondwana. About a million years later, Australia broke away from Antarctica and began moving north.

About 20,000 years ago, rising seas cut Tasmania off from the mainland. Some 8000 years later, the sea rose between Australia and Papua New Guinea, creating the Torres Strait.

Australia is the world's flattest continent. Its average height is only 274 metres above sea level. It has always been flatter than many other countries. It was in the middle of Gondwana so it didn't fold at the edges to make high mountains like the Himalayas. For the same reason, it doesn't have much volcanic activity. Volcanoes, mountains and rivers all help to produce rich soils. Australia's soils are shallow and poor, and lack the nutrients, or foods, needed for strong plant growth.

THE GREAT DIVIDING RANGE

The country's most significant mountains are in the Great Dividing Range. The Great Divide runs down the east coast from northern Queensland to Victoria and then turns to the west. But it isn't a single range. It is made up of several loosely connected mountain groups. None of the range is very high. The highest peak is Mount Kosciuszko, which is only 2228 metres high.

Many of Australia's mountains and hills are rounded and weathered because the country is so old.

DESERTS AND WATER

Lack of water has affected Australia's history. Except for Antarctica, Australia is the driest continent in the world. It has low average rainfalls, which are often unreliable. About 70 per cent of the country is arid or semi-arid and cannot support agriculture. Half of the country receives less than 300 mm of rain a year. Much of the rain soaks into the ground and does not run off to form rivers and lakes. High temperatures also mean that a lot of moisture evaporates or is used by thirsty plants.

Many of eastern Australia's rivers don't flow directly to the coast. They flow inland to join together in the country's biggest river system, the Murray–Darling system. The rivers drain more than a million square kilometres of land in New South Wales, Victoria, South Australia and Queensland. The water finally reaches the Murray River.

The land drained by the system is known as the Murray–Darling Basin. This area grows more than 40 per cent of Australia's agricultural produce.

Lack of reliable water supplies has helped restrict white settlement to the outer edges of the continent. But some desert areas can be used to graze cattle or establish mining because of stores of underground, or artesian, water. A hole, or bore, is drilled into the water store and pressure forces the water to the surface.

The biggest of these is the Great Artesian Basin, which lies under about 1.57 million square kilometres of Central Australia. Over the years, the store of underground water has been used and many bores are now dry.

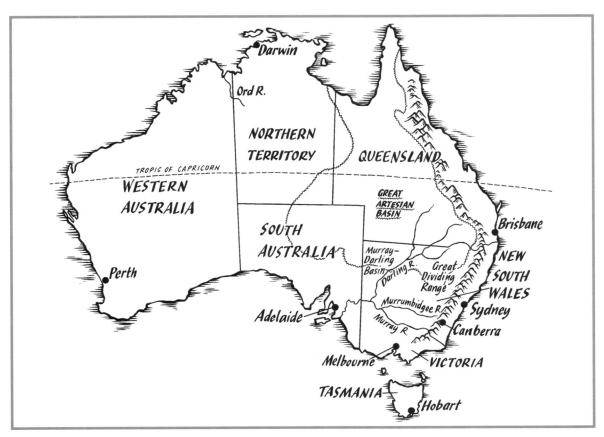

A geographical map shows how most Australian capital cities and rivers are in the south-east.

THE CLIMATES

Because of its size, Australia has many climates. The Tropic of Capricorn cuts across the northern part of Australia so about 40 per cent of the country lies in the tropics. In the south, the island state of Tasmania lies in the cool roaring forties.

> **roaring forties** – *the area of ocean between 40°S and 50°S in which strong winds blow from the west*

In the north, the climate is tropical. Monsoon winds bring moist air from the north-west during summer. This time of high rainfall, between December and March, is known as 'the wet'. The north also has cyclones during the wet.

In the southern two-thirds of the country, the climate ranges from warm temperate to cool temperate. There are four distinct seasons. Winter temperatures can be low, but rarely freezing, in the southern states.

A famous poem about Australia talks of a land of 'droughts and flooding rains'. Drought is caused by the El Niño Southern Oscillation, a weather pattern which happens when the southern Pacific Ocean heats up. This causes the wind direction to reverse. Instead of bringing moist air towards eastern Australia, the rain-bearing clouds are blown away.

An El Niño occurs about every four or five years, causing drought and bushfires. Droughts are often followed by floods.

Native animals

When a platypus specimen first reached Europe, some people were sure that this strange animal from Australia was a fake, sewn together from bits of other animals. But the platypus and the echidna are the world's only monotremes, or egg-laying mammals. The platypus is a living reminder of ancient, extinct creatures.

> **mammal** – *a class of animals in which the young feed on their mother's milk*

The platypus is the strangest of Australia's animals, but the best known is the kangaroo. There are about 50 species of kangaroo, ranging in size from the big red kangaroo of the outback to wallabies and smaller rat-kangaroos. Kangaroos are marsupials, mammals that give birth to very tiny babies. The babies then develop inside a pouch where they suck their mother's milk.

Australia is home to most of the world's marsupial species. About half of Australia's 230 mammal species are marsupials. As well as kangaroos, there are koalas, wombats, bandicoots, possums, the meat-eating Tasmanian devil and many others. The large meat-eating marsupial, the Tasmanian tiger, is probably extinct, although some people are still looking for it.

Koalas are marsupials, not bears, and should not be called 'koala bears'.

Kangaroos, wallabies and echidnas are sometimes seen during the day but most Australian native animals are hard to see because they move around at night. Many of the country's 750 species of birds are easy to see, especially the brightly coloured and noisy parrots. Some birds – such as the emu and the lyrebird – are modern relatives of Gondwana birds.

There are nearly 500 species of lizard, including the giant goanna and the frill-necked lizard.

Two types of crocodile, the saltwater and the freshwater crocodile, are found in the north.

Ancient Australia had many giant relatives of today's creatures. Fossils of these creatures, known as the megafauna, are still being discovered.

The dingo, or native dog, is not really an Australian native. It was brought from Asia around 4000 years ago. The dingo is an efficient hunter. To save their sheep from dingo attacks, farmers built many fences to keep the dingos out. These fences didn't work so, in 1946, the government built a single fence which stretched 5400 kilometres from the Great Australian Bight in South Australia to near the Queensland coast. This single fence worked better.

Native plants

Australian vegetation comes in a variety of types, including wet tropical forests in the north, temperate rainforests in the south, dry woodland, coastal heathland and the desert plants of the inland.

Nearly all Australian trees and shrubs do not lose their leaves in winter but grow throughout the year, dropping leaves, branches and bark all the time. This habit builds up a lot of dry material on the ground that helps bushfires to burn.

Many Australian plants have adapted to frequent bushfires; they actually need fire to reproduce. Others have adapted to dry conditions and poor soils.

The biggest family of native plants are the myrtles. They include more than 500 species of eucalypts, or gum trees. Only one species, the big river red gum, is seen nearly everywhere. These large spreading trees are found beside rivers and dry riverbeds, even in arid country.

Gum tree leaves are full of volatile oils, which evaporate easily. The blue-green colour of Australian forests and woodlands is caused by light reflecting off these oils as they evaporate.

Some gums are valuable timber species and have been cut down for many years. In the past 20 years, conservationists have fought to make the timber industry leave the native forests, especially the 'old growth' areas which have not been disturbed by settlement or timber-getting.

The river red gum is found throughout Australia.

Another big family of native plants are the acacias, known as wattles. There are about 900 wattle species. They are the dominant species in arid and semi-arid areas but are also found in high rainfall areas. The golden wattle is Australia's official flower. Its bright gold flowers and green leaves inspired the colours worn by many Australian sporting teams.

Wattle seeds provided food for Indigenous Australians. Other edible foods include the bunya nut, warrigal greens, quandongs, bush tomatoes and candlenuts. Some of these 'bush foods' are now being grown commercially.

Aboriginal Australia before 1788

When Aboriginals first arrived in Australia, the climate was wetter than it is today. Megafauna still roamed the country. But there were few large animals that were a danger to humans. Gradually, the people spread out across the country.

The various Aboriginal groups adapted to the different environments they found. In the south, they wore thick possum-skin cloaks; in warmer areas, they wore few clothes. They learned the behaviour of the animals and the plant seasons in their territory.

EARLY INDIGENOUS LIFESTYLES

Most Indigenous Australians were hunter-gatherers. In some places, such as the Torres Strait islands, they planted gardens of yams and coconuts and became farmers. Archaeologists have also found eel farm ponds in New South Wales.

Most Aboriginal groups were partly nomadic. They moved around within their territory, depending on the availability of food. Occasionally, they moved hundreds of kilometres across other clans' territories for ceremonial gatherings or to trade goods such as ochre, greenstone and bunya nut.

Although they were not farmers, Aboriginals developed a complex system of land management, which in some places included 'firestick farming'. Firestick farming uses fire to clear the undergrowth. This encourages new vegetation that attracts animals to feed. It also makes it easier to see the animals and kill them. Firestick farming is thought to be responsible for the creation of open woodland in Australia, the rise of fire-dependent plant species and loss of soil nutrients.

Aboriginal people banned hunting or food gathering in certain areas from time to time. This allowed animal and plant populations time to recover.

Mostly, Aboriginal groups had no permanent

Small controlled fires, like this one in the Northern Territory, are part of Aboriginal 'firestick farming' methods. *Ben Glezer*

dwellings. They built simple shelters from bark and branches. These were left behind when the group moved on to a new food source. But there is evidence that some Tasmanian Aboriginals lived permanently in caves. Ancient stone buildings in Victoria were probably semi-permanent dwellings, used in the months when there were lots of eels to trap in nearby rivers.

The early Aboriginals were efficient hunter-gatherers so they had plenty of time to pass on their culture to their children in songs, stories, dances and paintings. Some rock paintings are as old as 18,000 years; others may be much older. Certain rock paintings in the north-west depict human figures that do not look like Aboriginals. Some people believe these show the first encounters that the Indigenous Australians had with Europeans.

Search for the great south land

No one is sure who were the first non-Aboriginals to visit Australia. The Chinese navigator Cheng Ho probably reached Australia when he sailed into the Indian Ocean in the early 15th century. Later that century, the Dutch and the Portuguese established trade routes to the East Indies and heard rumours of a great south land, rich in gold and spices.

EUROPEAN EXPLORERS

Various Portuguese and Spanish explorers may have landed, but no lasting evidence of this has been found. Certainly, the Spaniard Luis Vaez de Torres saw the coast of the Cape York Peninsula when he sailed past in 1606.

The same year, the first confirmed landing by Europeans occurred when a Dutchman, Willem Jansz, landed on Cape York. Ten years later, another Dutchman, Dirk Hartog, landed on an island off the coast of Western Australia. Although Jansz said the natives were 'wild and cruel', the Dutch were still interested in the great south land. Several ships landed on the west coast, which is why there are several Dutch place names in Western Australia. But the country was not attractive to traders.

However, in 1642, Abel Tasman was sent from Batavia (Djakarta) to find the south land. His two ships sailed into the Indian Ocean and then turned south-east. In November, the explorers saw land, which Tasman called Van Diemen's Land (later renamed Tasmania). In December, the Dutchmen landed and took possession of the land for Holland. Then they left, without having seen any Aboriginals.

In 1773, a French captain, Marion du Fresne, made the first contact with the Tasmanian Aboriginals. It was a fatal encounter, for the French killed several Aboriginals after a misunderstanding caused the local people to attack. The French continued exploring. In 1792, Admiral d'Entrecasteaux and his companions spent nearly three months exploring Tasmania's southern coast. Then the French explorers left, having mapped and named many features of the coast. Like the Dutch, they thought the island was part of the Australian mainland.

ENGLISH EXPLORATION

The first English sailor to see Australia was John Brooke who saw the west coast in 1622. His ship was wrecked. But Brooke and some of his men survived and rowed to Java (in Indonesia) in small boats. Another Englishman, William Dampier, landed on the north-west coast in 1688. He didn't like the country.

In 1768, Captain James Cook left England on the *Endeavour*. Also on board were two botanists, Joseph Banks and Daniel Solander, because the voyage was mainly a scientific expedition. Cook mapped the coast of New Zealand before turning west. On 20 April 1770, a crew member saw land: the east coast of Australia.

The *Endeavour* travelled north along the coast, stopping at Botany Bay and several other places to collect scientific specimens. In June, the ship hit a coral reef and almost sank. The party spent six weeks repairing it at the site of present-day Cooktown in Queensland.

Cook then carefully sailed up the coast until he reached the Torres Strait. On 22 August, he formally took possession of all the east coast of Australia for England. He called the land New South Wales.

Captain Cook lands at Botany Bay in 1770. *La Trobe Picture Collection, State Library of Victoria*

The convict years

Britain used to send her convicts to America. But the American War of Independence (1775–83) stopped transportation. Joseph Banks said Botany Bay was a good place for a new penal colony. Although Australia was so far away, the British government agreed.

> **transportation** – *the English policy of sending convicts to overseas prison settlements*

In 1787, Captain Arthur Phillip – in charge of the First Fleet of 11 ships – set sail for Botany Bay, with 759 convicts and 294 soldiers and sailors.

The Fleet arrived on 18 January 1788 but found there was no fresh water. Phillip decided to move to Sydney Cove on Port Jackson. He landed there on 26 January and raised the British flag. He was the colony's first governor.

The early years of settlement were very hard. Fresh food was scarce, partly because few of the convicts or soldiers knew how to farm. The food brought from England began to run out. When the Second Fleet arrived in mid-1790, the colony was almost starving. Convicts who stole food got 1000 lashes of the whip as punishment.

Life for convicts could be very harsh. But for some, transportation to Australia was the beginning of a new and better life.

Some people stress the brutality of the convict

system. In the special penal colonies, which were set up at Port Arthur in Tasmania, Moreton Bay (Brisbane) in Queensland and on Norfolk Island (off the New South Wales coast), conditions were cruel. The convicts – usually those who had committed more crimes in the colonies – worked in chains, were often flogged and sometimes hanged.

For other convicts, life was better. The convicts' skills – as bricklayers, carpenters, shepherds and so on – were used to build the colony. Many were 'assigned' to work for free settlers. Sometimes, their masters were cruel; sometimes they were not. Female convicts were encouraged to marry. When they did, they were no longer regarded as convicts.

At the end of their sentences, ex-convicts were given land and assigned other convicts to help them. Many were successful and became accepted members of colonial society.

By the time transportation completely ended in 1852, Britain had sent more than 150,000 convicts to Australia. Some historians say transportation was a kind of forced migration which allowed the new colonies to develop and become part of the growing economy of the British Empire.

Australians' attitudes towards the convict past have changed. Until about 50 years ago, people were ashamed to admit they had convict ancestors. Today, people are proud to have a convict ancestor.

> **anti-authoritarianism** – the idea that individual freedom is more important than obedience to an authority

Some people say the convict past is central to Australians' sense of national identity. They say the convict system created the anti-authoritarianism that is still part of the Australian character. Also, the fact that many former convicts were success-ful showed that the British class system could be overcome. Perhaps the convict past explains the tendency of Australians to make heroes out of outlaws like Ned Kelly or anyone who shows little respect for rules and the authorities.

Exploring the land

Land exploration in Australia was driven by necessity, curiosity and a sense of adventure.

For the first 25 years, the Europeans stayed close to the coast, exploring a short distance north and south of Sydney. Sea exploration continued and George Bass and Matthew Flinders proved that Van Diemen's Land was an island. Flinders sailed all the way round Australia, mapping the coastline.

As Sydney grew, there was pressure for the colony to expand. Land was needed to grow food and graze animals so the colony could be independent.

The barrier to expansion to the west was the Blue Mountains. In 1813, a way was found across the mountains, opening up good grazing land. The movement west then stopped when the rivers were found to disappear in marshes.

People wanted to know what sort of land lay further west but the explorers turned their

An old engraving shows convicts in chains, ready to go to colonies like Australia. *Dixson Library, State Library of New South Wales*

attention to the south and north. They travelled to the fertile Darling Downs in Queensland and south beyond the Murray River.

> **pastoralist** – *a person who owns land for raising sheep and cattle*

By 1828, much of the south-east corner of the country had been explored. But a big question remained. Did the west-flowing rivers end in a huge inland sea? Charles Sturt tried to answer that question. He followed several rivers and found they joined the Murray River. His exploration opened up the rich Murray–Darling Basin. Then, in 1835, Tasmanian pastoralists crossed Bass Strait and settled in the Port Phillip District (later renamed Victoria).

In the 1840s, the desire to find out what lay in the heart of Australia replaced the need for good land as the reason for exploration. Edward Eyre crossed the Nullarbor and Ludwig Leichhardt travelled from the Darling Downs in Queensland to Port Essington, near present-day Darwin.

Later expeditions tried to cross the country from south to north. The Burke and Wills ex-pedition in 1860 reached the Gulf of Carpentaria in the far north, but most of the group died on the return journey.

The last expedition to discover significant areas of land was Alexander Forrest's expedition in 1879. He found the Ord River and the vast areas of grazing land in the Kimberley region of Western Australia.

By the time of Federation in 1901, the age of exploration had passed. Most of Australia was known, although not always in much detail.

Taming the land

When the British arrived in Australia, they found a strange, untamed land. It had no crops or herds of grazing animals. It was covered with strange trees. It was dry and brown. It didn't look like home. The new arrivals began the long and difficult task of changing Australia so that it could support a population used to a European lifestyle.

The history of taming Australia is a story of hard work, achievement, inventiveness and courage. It is also a history of some dreadful mistakes.

INTRODUCED SPECIES

The British first introduced animal and plant species to Australia to provide food. Other species were introduced later, partly to re-create the environment and traditional activities of Britain.

In the 19th century, people wanted to introduce animals that were hunted in Britain, such as deer, foxes and rabbits. They wanted to hear the songs of familiar birds such as sparrows, thrushes and blackbirds. Many of these animals are now classed as pests and do great damage to native plants and animals.

A rabbit plague in South Australia. *APL/John & Lorraine Carnemolle*

Other introduced animals were useful on farms. But some went wild and had a serious impact on the Australian environment. They included pigs, buffalo, donkeys, cats and goats. The cane toad, introduced to keep sugar cane fields free of insect pests, became a threat to native fauna in tropical Australia.

Introduced plants – such as blackberries, bracken fern, prickly pear and water hyacinth – became weeds in their new Australian environment.

PROTECTING AUSTRALIA

Because Australia is an island continent, it doesn't have many of the animal and plant diseases that are found elsewhere. To protect its farming industries and its native animal and plant species, Australia has very strict quarantine laws.

THE PASTORAL INDUSTRY

For much of white Australia's history, the wool industry was central to economic prosperity. In 1797, John Macarthur imported some merino sheep from Spain. He and his wife Elizabeth developed the country's first fine wool sheep flocks at Camden Park, near Sydney.

By the 1830s, wool was Australia's most important export and in the 1850s Australia was supplying half of Britain's needs. People said Australia 'rode on the sheep's back'. The wool industry sustained the long economic boom which started with the gold rushes of the 1850s and lasted until the depression of the 1890s when many sheep farmers went out of business.

Cattle were also important in the early years. As more people came to Australia, the home market for meat grew. But beef exports didn't start until the second half of the 20th century when canned meat and, later, frozen meat were sent to the distant markets of Europe. Today, about 60 per cent of Australian beef exports go to Japan, Korea, Taiwan and South-East Asia.

The 19th-century pastoralists had to find more land for their sheep and cattle. In New South Wales and Victoria, many of them grazed their animals illegally on land the colonial governments had not given them. These people were called squatters. Many became very rich.

The great pastoral families saw themselves as a kind of Australian aristocracy. They became leaders in society and conservative politics.

But it is the pastoral workers who live on in songs and literature and Australian mythology. The shearers, boundary riders, drovers and swagmen matched the idea of the typical Australian.

Australia is known for its high quality wool. *La Trobe Picture Collection, State Library of Victoria/Roy Dunstan*

They were self-reliant, direct and hard working. Where they went, their sure-footed stock horses and trusty working dogs – the kelpie and the Australian cattle dog – went too. Even today, Australian advertisers use images of such men to sell trucks and beer.

The pastoral industry has contributed a great deal to Australia. But there has been a cost. The fragile soils and vegetation of Australia suffer under the hard hoofs of sheep and cattle. The provision of permanent water supplies for stock reduces ground water. It has also caused big increases in kangaroo numbers in the outback. Many kangaroos are shot, which makes animal rights campaigners at home and abroad angry.

AGRICULTURE

Australia's farmers are efficient. They export large quantities of wheat, sugar, dairy products, barley, rice, cotton, fruit and wine. But the part that agriculture plays in the economy declined a lot after World War 2.

Today's farmers face big problems: salinity, where salt in the soil makes the land barren, declining water quality, increasing costs and unreliable world markets.

The nature of the country's soils and weather make the land more suitable for grazing than intensive crop growing. The first white settlers discovered this when they arrived at Sydney Cove. It took New South Wales more than a century to become self-sufficient in food.

As settlers moved into new areas to grow crops and graze animals, they began to clear the land. It was hard work but they did it effectively.

For example, in 1870, most of Victoria, except the western plains and the goldfields, was forest. A hundred years later, only a third was forest.

Land clearing in Western Australia. *National Library of Australia/Frank Hurley*

Extensive clearing led to erosion because the soil was not protected from wind and floods. Much land became so eroded it was no longer productive. Removing trees also raised the watertable, or the upper limit of underground water. This brought the salt in the deep soil to the surface, causing dry land salinity.

Land clearing continues today and is a topic of debate, because it also contributes to 'greenhouse gases' and destroys native habitats. About 90 per cent of all clearing occurs in Queensland, where about 425,000 hectares are cleared every year.

Low rainfall and frequent drought are another problem. After a severe drought in the late 1870s, farmers began to irrigate their land. Irrigation schemes were started on the Murray River in the 1880s. Within 100 years, there were irrigation schemes in all states, supplying the Murray–Darling Basin region (throughout Queensland, New South Wales, Victoria and South Australia), the Ord region in Western Australia and other agricultural areas.

At first, irrigation was successful. It allowed the growing of crops, such as rice and cotton. It enabled small farmers to grow fruit, vines, vegetables and tobacco. It encouraged people to move away from the coast.

But, today, Australians realise that irrigation has a bad side because it cuts river flows, which affects animal and plant life. Less water in the rivers makes the water salty and dirtier. For instance, the water of the Murray River – on which Adelaide depends for its water supply – is now almost undrinkable.

Australians are resourceful and practical people. Their ability to solve problems is shown in many advances in agriculture. Two examples are the 19th-century inventions of the stripper harvester, which enabled a single man to harvest a crop, and the stump jump plough, which let farmers plough semi-cleared land. Farmers and scientists bred plants and animals to suit Australia's special conditions. One early example was William Farrar's Federation wheat which resisted the disease called rust.

Many rural observers hope today's Australians will be equally resourceful in solving the big problems that European-style agriculture has caused.

Mineral wealth

Australia's poor surface soils made agriculture hard work. But great wealth lay under the surface. Minerals have been very important in the country's development. In 2000, the mining industry supplied nearly a third of all Australian exports. Australia is the world's biggest exporter of coal and also exports large amounts of iron ore, gold, petroleum, nickel and other minerals.

Mining was a major reason for the creation of many inland towns, the arrival of thousands of immigrants and the development of essential infrastructure. It provided the basic needs for the growth of industry, such as fuel and raw materials.

Within 12 years of white settlement, the colony of New South Wales was exporting coal from small deposits found at Newcastle. In the 1840s, silver, lead and copper were being mined in South Australia. But gold was the metal that changed Australia from a pastoral and agricultural economy to an industrial one.

GOLD

Early discoveries of gold were kept secret. The authorities thought gold would upset the order of the colony, which was just starting to get rid of its convict settlement image.

When gold was found on the US west coast, however, many people left for California. When Edward Hargraves returned from California and dug up six kilograms of gold near Bathurst, the New South Wales government announced the find in May 1851. The gold discovery could stop the colony's population decline.

The Victorian economy suffered a lot as people rushed to New South Wales. So the government offered a reward for the first person

Artist Nicholas Chevalier engraved this image of miners prospecting for gold in 1864. *La Trobe Picture Collection, State Library of Victoria*

to find gold within 320 kilometres of Melbourne. Gold deposits at Clunes, near Ballarat in central Victoria, were announced in July 1851. More gold was found soon after at nearby Buninyong and at Bendigo. The rush was on. Within five months, about 7776 kilograms of gold had been found in the region.

Gold did upset the order of society. So many people went to the goldfields that labour became scarce and expensive. But gold also created demand for goods and services. Farms and businesses started near the fields to serve the thousands of new arrivals. Victoria's population grew from 76,000 to more than half a million. Many of the newcomers were young men with skills needed in the colony.

In the early years, the miners argued with the Victorian authorities about unfair treatment and having to pay for miner's licences. The disputes led to the Eureka rebellion at Ballarat, which some people say marked the birth of Australian democracy.

The first Australian finds were alluvial gold which meant individual miners could dig it out easily with simple tools. These miners mostly worked alone or with one or two mates and in secret.

When the alluvial gold ran out, many individual miners left for new fields in New

> **alluvial gold** – bits of gold that have been washed away from the main body of gold and dropped in the earth and sand left behind by floods

South Wales, Queensland and Western Australia. Others formed companies which were able to afford the equipment needed to dig deep mines and find the rich reefs of gold. The mining industry was born. Gold finds at Coolgardie and Kalgoorlie in Western Australia in the 1890s depended on deep mine technology.

Gold led to a burst of economic growth in Australia and exploration for the precious metal led to the discovery of other important minerals.

OTHER MINERALS

In 1883 a rich deposit of silver, lead and zinc was found at Broken Hill in New South Wales. The find gave birth to Broken Hill Proprietary Limited, or BHP (now BHP Billiton), which was Australia's biggest company for many years.

In the 1870s and 1880s, tin and coal were found in several states and by the early 20th century, mining, with its associated smelters and refineries, was well established and technically advanced. But big drops in metal prices after

THE EUREKA REBELLION

Trouble began at Ballarat when a miner was killed and his suspected killer set free. A government inquiry found evidence of corruption among goldfields officials, who often harassed miners several times a day, demanding to see their mining licences.

A miners' organisation, the Ballarat Reform League, called for the vote, an end to the licence tax and the opening up of land to small settlers.

On 29 November 1854, the rebel miners unfurled the Southern Cross flag and burned their licences. Then they armed themselves behind a stockade (a wooden fort), at Eureka. At daybreak on 3 December, government troops attacked, killing about 30 miners. Five soldiers were killed.

The rebels were tried early the next year, but juries refused to find them guilty.

A replica of the flag flown by miners during the Eureka Rebellion. It shows the Southern Cross. *National Library of Australia*

For many people, the Eureka Stockade is one of the first examples of Australian courage, mateship and resistance to authority. It was Australia's bloodiest civil disturbance, yet the death toll was less than 50.

World War 1 and the Depression of the 1930s meant that the industry didn't grow much.

A series of discoveries of base metals which began in the late 1940s and ran until the late 1960s changed the fortunes of mining. Oil and natural gas reserves were found around the same time.

> **base metals** – *non-precious metals such as iron, copper, nickel, bauxite and uranium*

New exploration and mining techniques were developed. Mining towns grew up in the Northern Territory, Western Australia and Queensland. Australia became a major mineral exporting country. The growing economies of Japan and Korea were major customers.

By the late 1970s, the industry's growth had slowed. Two things played a part in this: public concern about the effect of mining on the environment and the granting of land rights to Aboriginals, which meant companies had to get permission from traditional owners before they could explore or mine.

However, the industry expanded again in the 1990s. Many Australian companies began operating overseas. Some merged with overseas companies to become world mining giants.

Industry, science and technology

Australia's economy relies heavily on the primary industries of mining and farming. However, manufacturing and the use of science and technology are also important.

MANUFACTURING

Early Australian manufacturing industries – such as flour milling, brewing and ship building – were based on the colonies' agricultural, pastoral and mineral products. The gold rushes of the 1850s created more demand. Railways were built; houses and public buildings were constructed; agricultural and mining machinery was made.

Australia's first steel plant opened in 1915. By the 1920s, local industries included engineering, motor car assembly, chemical and rubber industries, and textiles. However, many of the industries were supported by high tariffs which protected them from international competition because the tariffs made goods from overseas more expensive.

World War 2 encouraged the development of aviation, optical and armaments industries. However, it was the years between 1945 and 1970 that saw the manufacturing sector grow most strongly. Australia's first locally designed and made car, the Holden, began production in 1948. The motor vehicle, electrical goods, heavy engineering, metal fabrication and chemical industries all boomed.

Nine different models of Australia's own car, the Holden. *National Library of Australia/Holden Ltd*

But the Australian economy is not large and there is a limited amount of money for investment. By 1970, the expanding mining sector was attracting most of the available investment capital. Investment in manufacturing declined. Competition from Japanese goods – despite tariff barriers – was becoming stronger.

Government tariff policy changed. Import duties would be reduced gradually over several years so that Australian industries could compete on equal terms with other countries. The ending of protection had a big effect on both primary and secondary industries. Industries had to cut costs. Jobs – particularly in industries like textiles, clothing and footwear – were cut as manufacturers moved their factories to countries where wages were lower. Australian companies whose products were household names – like Arnott's Biscuits, Bushells Tea and Taubmans paints – became takeover targets for foreign companies.

The effects of these changes are still felt

today. Job losses and foreign takeovers arouse much public debate and anger.

SCIENCE AND TECHNOLOGY

Most Australians are more likely to be able to name the country's Olympic gold medal winners than its Nobel Prize winners. Yet Australia has a fine reputation in science and technology.

The list of Australian inventions is long: the Xerox copying process, the black box flight recorder to track an aircraft's movements, the electric drill, latex gloves, the bionic ear to restore hearing to the deaf, polymer banknotes, the gene shears technique used in genetic engineering, and many more.

Each year, Australian scientists publish nearly 2 per cent of the world's scientific papers. This proportion is very large for a country with such a small population.

Australians have always been particularly good at medical sciences. Four of Australia's six Nobel Prizes were given for physiology or medicine. But the country also has a reputation in fields as diverse as astronomy, marine biology, remote sensing and wool technology.

Most of the country's research is done in the public laboratories of universities or the Commonwealth Scientific and Industrial Research Organisation (CSIRO). Funding for research by private companies is small, although governments have tried to encourage private sector research and development.

In recent years, the government has said public laboratories must earn more money from working with business. Some scientists say this will have a bad effect on basic research; but it is likely that the proportion of government money going to scientific research will continue to decline.

Race relations

Australia is proud of its present multicultural character. However, it has a history of race conflict, and tensions continue today. The main targets of racist policies in the past were Indigenous people and Asians, particularly the Chinese.

INDIGENOUS AUSTRALIANS

The coming of white settlers was a disaster for Indigenous Australians. Their land was taken. They were killed by settlers or by imported diseases, such as typhoid and influenza. Public debate about how many Aboriginals were deliberately killed is very heated. Some say that focusing on massacres by whites is 'black armband history', which doesn't respect the role of settlers in building the nation. Others say the killings are a stain on Australia's history.

Today, Indigenous Australians are still disadvantaged. They have poorer health, lower life expectancy, more poverty and more unemployment. Imprisoned at a much higher rate than other Australians, they often die in prison.

LAND RIGHTS

Indigenous people have fought for recognition of their rights to land for more than 30 years. Until recently, Australian law accepted the idea that land could be colonised if it was not inhabited. This idea was called *terra nullius*, or unoccupied land. Indigenous people had lived in Australia for thousands of years but the British colonial government said the land was *terra nullius*.

In 1982, five Torres Strait Islanders – including Eddie Mabo – went to the High Court to get title to their land. Ten years later, the High Court decided the Mabo case. It said that native title had existed and, in some cases, could continue after colonisation. In 1993, the *Native Title Act* set up a system for deciding claims to native title.

Another case – the Wik case in 1996 – was also important because the High Court said that native title could co-exist with pastoral leases. Many native title claims are still not decided because each one is judged separately.

THE STOLEN GENERATIONS

By 1901, all the Australian colonies had passed laws that restricted Aboriginals' rights to own property and find work. In most states after Federation, a government official was the legal guardian of all Aboriginal children.

Children of mixed blood were taken away from their Aboriginal families, often by force. The policy, which continued until the early

1970s, aimed to absorb mixed race children into white Australian society.

In 1997, a report called these children 'the stolen generations'. The report was the first full investigation of the results of a policy that left deep emotional scars on many Indigenous Australians.

Moves towards reconciliation include a national 'Sorry Day' on 26 May each year.

RECONCILIATION

The stolen generations report shocked many non-Indigenous Australians who wanted to say sorry to Indigenous Australians for the wrongs done to them. Throughout the country, Indigenous and non-Indigenous Australians now work together in many ways to put right past injustice. But the reconciliation process is slow and still opposed by some Australians.

> **reconciliation** – the act of settling a dispute or bringing two opponents together in harmony

IMMIGRATION RESTRICTIONS

The first Chinese people came to Australia in the 1840s as bonded labourers. Later, many single men came to find gold. But other miners disliked them because they were hardworking and came from a different culture. There were race riots on the Victorian goldfields in the 1850s. In 1861, about 250 Chinese were injured in an attack at Lambing Flat in New South Wales. The New South Wales government immediately passed a law to restrict Chinese immigration, similar to existing laws in South Australia and Victoria.

Small populations of Indians, Afghans, Sri Lankans, Japanese and Malays in Central and northern Australia were less visible.

In 1901, the new federal government passed the *Commonwealth Immigration Restriction Act*, more often called the White Australia Policy because it prevented non-white immigrants from entering the country. Pacific Islanders were banned from working in the Queensland cane fields and forced to go home. Non-European Australians were denied welfare payments.

The government said the policy would maintain living standards by preventing cheap labour and would avoid racial conflict.

After World War 1, quotas were put on southern European and Jewish migration. But soon after World War 2, a few non-Europeans – such as supporters of the Chinese Nationalists and Japanese war brides – were allowed into Australia.

Gradually, the White Australia Policy was dismantled; all remaining immigration restrictions based on race disappeared in 1973.

RACISM TODAY

Despite government laws banning racial discrimination, some Australians are racist – but probably no more than any other people.

Public expressions of racism are a response to world events, such as the destruction of the World Trade Centre in New York in 2001 and the nightclub bombings in Bali in 2002. After these events, Arabic and Muslim communities reported more racist incidents.

However, it is important to remember that Australians are generally tolerant. People sometimes say they do not like a particular ethnic group; but, at the same time, they are good friends with a person from that group. As they do so often, Australians respond to the individual, not the group.

Australians at war

The Australian experience of war is unusual. Indigenous Australians say Europeans invaded their country, but modern Australia has never been invaded. European Australians have never shed each others' blood in civil wars. Yet the Australian sense of identity is closely linked to the qualities of its fighting forces. In little more than a century, Australians have fought in 10 wars and provided troops to 14 international peacekeeping missions.

Australiaa's history of involvement in conflict shows how it supported more powerful allies that it hoped would help if Australia was threatened: first, Britain and, later, the United States.

Even before Australia became a nation, Australians were fighting overseas with Britain in South Africa in the Boer War (1899–1902) and in China's Boxer Rebellion (1900). They got a reputation as good fighters, but lacking discipline. Australians won six Victoria Crosses (VCs) in the Boer War.

> **Victoria Cross** - the highest award given by the British for bravery in the presence of the enemy

WORLD WAR 1 (1914–1918)

World War 1 had a huge impact on Australia, even though it was fought on the other side of the world. It gave rise to the Anzac legend (see page xxx54). More than 58,000 men died, which was about one in 10 Australian men aged between 18 and 45. War memorials – in the shape of obelisks, stone soldiers or community halls, and bearing the names of the soldiers who died or fought – were built in the cities and almost every country town.

When war between Britain and Germany seemed certain, the Australian prime minister

Australian troops set up a wireless station at Anzac Cove on the Gallipoli Peninsula, Turkey, in April 1915. *Australian War Memorial A03787*

offered help. The volunteer troops of the Australian Imperial Forces (AIF) marched away to war. They landed in Gallipoli in Turkey as part of the campaign to defeat the Ottoman Empire, but suffered huge casualties.

After the retreat from Gallipoli, the AIF was split. The Light Horsemen, who had learned how to handle horses back home on Australian farms, went to the Sinai Desert. They took part in the Battle of Beersheba and helped the British conquer the Ottoman forces.

The rest of the troops fought in the trenches of Belgium and northern France. Nearly 120,000 Australians died or were wounded in France at the Battle of the Somme in 1916, at Ypres in 1917 and other battles on the Western Front. The men, who called themselves 'diggers', were stuck in the trenches.

Then, under the command of General John Monash, the AIF joined the British and other Allied troops in the final assault which ended in the armistice on 11 November 1918.

WORLD WAR 2 (1939–1945)

When Britain declared war on Germany in 1939, Prime Minister Robert Menzies automatically committed troops to Europe to help Britain. At the same time, the government was worried about the growing power of Japan in the Asia-Pacific region.

The first troops – who called themselves the Second AIF – joined the British in the Middle East and the Mediterranean. Again they showed themselves to be brave fighters, winning several Victoria Crosses at Tobruk and El Alamein.

Thousands of Australian airmen served with the British Air Force and Australian Navy ships served beside those of Britain.

The entry of Japan into the war in 1941 changed Australia's view. The Japanese captured Malaya, Burma and the Dutch East Indies (Indonesia). In February 1942, 15,000 Australian troops were captured during the invasion of Singapore. In the same month, the Japanese bombed Darwin, killing nearly 300 people.

The British were unable to help defend Australia. So the Australian government looked to the United States for support. The US general, Douglas MacArthur, became commander of the Allied forces in the south-west Pacific.

In July 1942, the Japanese tried to reach Australia through Papua New Guinea. Inexperienced Australian troops had to retreat along the mountainous Kokoda Track, but a few months later they pushed the Japanese back and recaptured Kokoda.

In September 1945, these former prisoners of war were waiting to return home to Australia at 'Bicycle Camp' on the Indonesian island of Java. *Australian War Memorial 123669*

When the war ended in 1945, Australia had lost about 35,000 men and women. In the Asia-Pacific region, half of the dead were prisoners of war (POWs). Just as the Anzacs became heroes at Gallipoli, the POWs who suffered and died on the Thai-Burma Railway or in prison camps such as Changi (Singapore) and Sandakan (Malaysia) became the heroes of World War 2.

WARS IN ASIA

Robert Menzies committed Australian troops to four more conflicts in Asia. Like many people, he believed in the 'domino theory' which said that after the communist victory in China, all Asia might become communist.

In 1950 he committed troops to the Korean War. The same year, more troops left for British-controlled Malaya to help fight communist insurgents. During the confrontation between Malaysia and Indonesia between 1963 and 1966, Australian troops again served in Malaysia.

> *insurgent* – someone who engages in armed resistance to a government

In 1962, the government announced that a few army instructors would go to Vietnam to help the South Vietnamese Army. Regular forces were sent three years later. By 1968, 8000 Australians were serving in Vietnam, mainly in Phuoc Tuy province.

There was opposition to Australia's involvement in the undeclared war in Vietnam. Much of it focused on the conscription of 18-year-olds. However, it was not until 1969 that the anti-war movement gained majority support. In 1970, troops began returning home. In December 1972, the new Labor government ordered the last 179 men back.

The Vietnam veterans didn't receive a hero's welcome. The war was too unpopular. For many years, they felt rejected by the Australian people.

WARS IN THE MIDDLE EAST

The Labor government of Bob Hawke sent Australians to the 1991 Gulf War. The shortness of the war meant it had little impact on Australians at home.

But when Prime Minister John Howard sent

troops to the Middle East in February 2003 before the Second Gulf War started, Australians were divided. Many did not want Australia to be involved in a war that the United Nations had not agreed to.

Although they were divided, the Australian people agreed on one thing. They would not blame the troops as they had after the Vietnam War.

Australia's place in the world

Australia's place in the world is full of contradictions. Australia is basically a European culture, thousands of kilometres from Europe. It is a country whose political system was established more than a century ago, surrounded by the newly independent nations of Asia and the Pacific. It is a developed nation with developing neighbours. It has a tiny population living on the edge of a huge landmass. It began as a British colony, but became a colonial power itself in Papua New Guinea.

For the first 100 years and more, Australia's place was easy to describe. It was a faraway part of the British Empire. Australians saw themselves as British. Britain was their mother country. Australia had no independent foreign service. It relied on British diplomats to represent it abroad. But British interests did not always agree with Australian ones. So in the late 1930s,

Labor politician Dr Herbert Evatt was a strong supporter of international cooperation. He was president of the United Nations General Assembly in 1948–49. *Courtesy: Evatt Collection, Flinders University Library*

Australia set up its first independent diplomatic missions.

The nation's view of its place in the world began to change. The events of World War 2 showed that Australia could no longer rely on automatic British help. The wartime Labor government developed a more independent policy, which emphasised regional and international cooperation. After the war, the Australian foreign minister, Dr H. V. Evatt, was active in the newly-formed United Nations.

Soon, Australia's neighbours were in turmoil as they fought for independence from colonial

---

AUSTRALIA AS A COLONIAL POWER

The Queensland colonial government wanted to protect the shipping route through the Torres Strait. But when it urged Britain to take possession of east New Guinea, Britain said 'no'. By the time the British finally raised the flag in 1884, the Germans had already claimed the north-east part of New Guinea.

The new Australian government accepted British New Guinea (Papua) as a territory in 1901. During World War 1, Australian troops occupied the German sector. After the war, the League of Nations allowed Australia to administer the north-east area.

Papua New Guinea (PNG) became Australia's green armour against the Japanese during World War 2. The Japanese never took the capital, Port Moresby.

Australia continued as a colonial power until PNG's independence in 1975. Today, a big proportion of Australia's development aid goes to its closest neighbour.

powers. The British economy was in crisis. The Cold War – between communist and non-communist countries – had begun. And Australia voted the Liberal-Country Party coalition into power in 1949.

Although Liberal prime minister Robert Menzies was an old-style British monarchist, his government recognised that the world was different. In 1951, Australia signed the ANZUS Treaty, which was a defence alliance with the US and New Zealand. It began taking more notice of its Asian neighbours. It joined the South-East Asia Treaty Organisation (SEATO) in 1954. It set up the Colombo Plan, which aimed to discourage communism by giving development aid to Asian nations.

The shift towards Asia intensified in the 1970s and 1980s. By this time, Australia's trading future was based firmly in the local region. In the past, its trade had been with Britain and Europe, but Britain was becoming part of Europe. Australia's new trading partners were Japan, Korea and, after 1972, China.

By Australia's centenary in 2001, the country's foreign policy was moving away from the strong regional focus of the previous 20 years, although it was closely involved in East Timor's transition to independence.

The next 100 years are likely to see Australia adapting and changing its policy and allegiances as it continues to try to find its appropriate role on the world stage.

part seven:
the essentials

The more you know and understand a country, the more you will enjoy living in it. As an international student, you will have a rewarding – and sometimes uncomfortable – experience. You can learn a lot about Australia and its people through reading, talking to Australians, watching their behaviour, asking questions and analysing your observations.

Here are seven statements to remember on your Australian journey of discovery.

1 Australia is a place of contradictions

Australia is an old country and a new one. It is one of the oldest continents on earth. Its soils, its mountains, its plants and animals are all ancient. Its Aboriginal peoples represent the world's oldest continuous culture. But modern Australia

is a society of newcomers, who are building a nation from many different cultures.

Australia has a very peaceful history. It has not experienced large-scale war or civil disturbance. Yet its most enduring myths are those born on the battlefields of Europe, the Middle East and the Pacific.

Australia is a conservative country with a radical streak. Since Federation, Australians have elected conservative governments more often than leftist ones. But the country has a strong trade union tradition. It was one of the first countries to give women the vote and to introduce government social welfare schemes.

Australia is a comfortable, urban society but its stories, myths and dreams are often based on the ideals of living in the harsh environment of the bush. Australians love leisure but their folk heroes are hardworking battlers.

Australians are open and direct but they value their privacy. These qualities affect much of their social behaviour and customs.

Most Australians are friendly and helpful to strangers, but it takes hard work to develop deep friendships with them. Although they seem confident and loud, they are often cautious and uncommunicative about their real feelings.

2 Australia is one of the world's most successful multiracial societies

The conflict between Australia's Indigenous peoples and the thousands of immigrants who arrived after 1788 has been long and painful. But modern Australia is making real efforts to overcome the bitterness of the past and to reconcile the differences between black and white.

The waves of immigrants from the 18th century to the present day have sometimes been met with suspicion and ignorance. Occasional racist outbursts reflect world events. But Australia does not suffer bloody or constant racial or religious conflict.

3 Australians are still in the process of change

For the first 150 years of modern Australian history, the country was definitely British. The settlers tried to remake the strange landscape into a copy of the country they had left behind, at big environmental cost. They adopted the political, legal and educational systems of England. They went to war for Britain. They imported some of the old ill feelings between the English and the Irish, the Protestants and the Catholics.

Australia became less British and more independent in outlook after World War 2. The ethnic mix of its population became more varied. It looked to Asia and the United States to replace Britain as its major trading partners. Young Australians began to travel first to Asia, not England, and to use American, not British, words and phrases.

Australians no longer suffer from 'cultural cringe', where everything Australian was not as good as everything from Britain or America. But they are still not fully confident about their place in the world.

4 Australians believe they are egalitarian, irreverent and anti-authority

Australia is not an equal society. There are divisions between rich and poor, white and black, privileged and underprivileged. But Australians are sincere when they say they are egalitarian. They believe that people should have a fair go, or equality of opportunity. After that, it is up to individuals what they make of their lives.

Australians don't respect people just because of their role in society or their birth. For example, teachers don't have a right to respect because they are teachers. They earn respect because they are good teachers.

Australians tend to treat people with high status the same as they do those with lesser status. They dislike people who seem arrogant.

Australians are basically law-abiding, but they like people who bend the rules or who don't respect authority.

5 Australians put more value on the individual than the group

Australians are part of the Western tradition of individualism. They value their communities, their families and their friends. But they also think that individuals should be able to choose how they live their lives. This means they judge people on their individual qualities rather than as a member of a group. They approve of self-reliance and independence. They don't like being told what to do.

6 The key to successful study in Australia is to ask questions

Your university and college teachers expect all students to be responsible for their own learning. They expect you to organise your own work schedule, do independent research, and meet deadlines. Most of all, they expect you to question everything and think for yourself, instead of just accepting someone else's ideas.

Teachers are always willing to help students. But you have to ask. There is no shame in asking for help about academic or personal problems.

All professional staff at universities and colleges will respect your privacy.

7 Australians have a casual approach to life

Australians are relaxed and informal about most aspects of daily living. There are some rules about polite behaviour but Australians aren't too upset if the rules are broken. As long as someone's behaviour doesn't interfere with another person's activities or beliefs, Australians are tolerant and easygoing.

Reading List

Aboriginal Australia and the Torres Strait Islands: Guide to Indigenous Australia, Sarina Singh, David Andrew, Bryan Andy, Monique Choy, Hugh Finlay, Paul Greenway, Kath Kenny, Philip Morrissey, Dennis O'Byrne, Belinda Scott, Lonely Planet, Footscray, Vic., 2001.
Although basically a travel guide, this book contains general essays about Aboriginal and Torres Strait cultures and the modern challenges they face. Much of it gives information from the Aboriginal viewpoint.

English: One Language, Different Cultures, ed. Eddie Ronowicz and Colin Yallop, Cassell, London, 1999.
This useful book looks at English in various countries, including Australia. It contains exercises for international students to help you understand how language and culture are closely linked.

Help: The Leaving Home Guide, Jane Norris and Kym Ortenburg, Pluto Press, Sydney, 2000.
Written for young Australians, this small book is useful for anyone leaving home for the first time. It contains basic advice about Australian laws on tenancy, insurance, buying a car, health and sex. For international students who want to share a house with local students, it is an invaluable guide to the etiquette of house-sharing in Australia.

Leaving Home: The Ultimate Guide, Samantha Koch, Allen & Unwin, St Leonards, NSW, 2003.
This book concentrates on how to prepare for independent living. It has some useful checklists for basic home equipment, and things to do before you move and when you leave a rented home in Australia.

Studying in Australia: A Guide for International Students, Teresa De Fazio, Allen & Unwin, St Leonards, NSW, 1999.
This handy guide to tertiary study in Australia has details of the Australian tertiary education system and university or college life. Practical sections cover study skills – such as note-taking, writing, report-writing, referencing, giving presentations – the library and time management. It includes checklists and step-by-step guidelines to preparing assignments and developing critical thinking.

Studying in Australia: The STUDY ABROAD Student's Guide to Success, Aveline Pérez, Learning Skills Unit, University of Melbourne, Melbourne, 2002.
This is another guide for short-term international students that has reliable information on the way Australian universities operate, as well as lots of study hints.

Pocket History of Australia: From Aboriginal Arrival to the Present Day, Murray David Publishing, Cameron House Publishing, Wingfield, SA, 2002.
This little book is designed for school students and contains sections on each state's history and a timeline of important events.

The Penguin Book of Australian Slang: A Dinkum Guide to Oz English, Lenie Johansen, Penguin, Ringwood, Vic., 1996.
This book contains a full listing of Australian words and colloquial phrases. It is easy to find idioms because they are listed alphabetically under the first word of the phrase rather than the keyword. There are also useful word lists grouped by subject such as clothes, cars and sex.

Glossary

A good Australian dictionary gives the Australian meaning of many words and phrases, as well as the standard British or American meaning. The dictionary is always the best place to start looking. Remember to look up the main word, wherever it occurs in the phrase. For example *no sweat* (an expression of assurance as in 'I'll do that for you, no sweat') is in the dictionary under *sweat*, not *no*.

Here are some meanings of Australian phrases which are not in standard dictionaries. Where necessary, sample sentences show how they are used. Phrases marked with a star may be impolite, vulgar or insulting.

a bit much – excessive, rude behaviour (When Jack started eating before everyone sat down, I thought it was a bit much.)

About time! – Finally! At last! (I've decided to give up smoking. – About time!)

above (oneself) – conceited (Since she won the prize, Jill has been above herself.)

all the same to (one) – not important (Whether I have rice or potatoes, it's all the same to me.)

Are you with me? – 'Do you understand' or 'Will you support me?' (I am going to ask the lecturer to hand out lecture notes in future. Are you with me?)

awesome – excellent, exciting (The band's latest album is awesome.)

BA – short for 'bloody awful' (My exam results were BA.)

backflip – an unexpected change, especially in political or social policy (The Treasurer has done a backflip. Last week she announced tax cuts. Today she said there were none.)

Beats me! – an exclamation meaning 'I don't know'

*been around – experienced; also, sexually promiscuous

Be your age! – Behave sensibly! Used when someone is behaving in an irritating way.

bingle – a minor car crash

booze-up – a drinking party

brush-off – rude rejection of something (Jill gave Jack the brush-off when he asked her out for a date.)

cactus – wrecked, ruined, spoiled (I lost my wallet so the whole weekend was cactus.)

cask wine – cheap wine in an airtight bag with a pouring tap inside a cardboard box. An Australian invention.

chardonnay socialist – a well-off person who claims to care about the welfare of the poor

checkout chick – female operator of a supermarket cash register

con artist – a swindler or someone who persuades people to do what he or she wants (Jack borrowed Jill's car for the weekend. He's a real con artist.)

cover band – a band that plays the music of other musicians

crowd surf – to be picked up and passed over the heads of a crowd at a concert

cut to the chase – to say what you mean or get to the main point

drover's dog – a nobody, a person with no special qualities (That essay's so bad. A drover's dog could have written it.)

dunny paper – toilet paper

Ekka – Brisbane's Agricultural Exhibition

FJ Holden – the most popular model of the Australian designed car. Made between 1953 and 1956, it is now a collector's item.

*four-eyes – a person who wears spectacles

Fremantle doctor – a refreshing breeze in Perth, Western Australia

the Gabba – the Queensland Cricket Association ground at Woolloongabba in Brisbane

gents – a public toilet for men (Can you tell me where the gents is?)

give (something) a go – to try (Do you want to come rock-climbing? – Yes. I'll give it a go.)

*go apeshit – react with unrestrained emotion of any kind – happiness, anger, joy etc. (Jill went apeshit when her dad bought her a car.)

go bananas – to become very cross; to become crazy or insane (Jack went bananas when someone stole his laptop.)

gone – in serious trouble (The tutor found that Jill had cheated. She's gone.)

good guy – a hero. Often used with 'bad guy' meaning villain. (In old Western movies, the good guys wear white hats. The bad guys wear black hats.)

happy hour – time at a pub or club when cheap drinks are served

hen's party – party for women only

hip pocket nerve – desire for money (The government's tax cuts will appeal to voters' hip pocket nerve.)

hoon – a person who drives fast, loud cars; also, the act of fast, dangerous driving

Hoover™ – to use a vacuum cleaner (It's your turn to Hoover the lounge room.)

if you ask me – in my opinion (If you ask me, that lecture was a waste of time.)

iffy – dubious or odd; not sure (Don't eat that fish. It smells iffy. / We're still iffy about whether to go surfing this weekend.)

itchy feet – a strong desire to travel (Since he went to Thailand last year, Jack's got itchy feet.)

item – to be involved romantically (Are Jack and Jill an item?)

join the queue! – exclamation to another person indicating you both want, or are waiting for, the same thing. (Haven't you got your results yet? Join the queue!)

keep your hair/shirt on – don't lose your temper

kick on – continue to enjoy oneself after most people have stopped (After the concert, we kicked on at a club until 4 a.m.)

klick – kilometre

L-plates – compulsory signs on the front and back of cars to show they are being driven by a learner driver

label – assign to a category, sometimes without reason (Jim was labelled a drunk because he sometimes went to the pub.)

land up in – find oneself in (Don't do that or you'll land up in trouble.)

lap (something) up – enjoy (The band lapped up the audience's applause.)

lash out – spend without worrying about the expense; criticise (Jill lashed out and bought eight new dresses. / Jack lashed out at her because she didn't need eight dresses.)

latest – news, most recent information (What's the latest?)

leftie – one who supports left-wing policies (He's been a leftie since he was a schoolboy.)

let it all hang out – be uninhibited, show emotion

the MCG – the Melbourne Cricket Ground

mean business – be serious about doing something (He wants to be a millionaire and he means business.)

mob – in Aboriginal English, a person's nation (*see below*)

monty – a certainty (His team is a monty to win.)

morning after pill – a prescription pill taken within 72 hours of unprotected sex to prevent implantation of the fertilised egg

nation – preferred term for an Aboriginal tribe

nerd – a socially inept person; a person who is more interested in computers than people

nibblies – snacks (She asked me to take some nibblies to the party.)

nip – go somewhere for a short time (I'll nip out to the shop to buy some milk.)

not cricket – unacceptable behaviour (Seducing your friend's girlfriend is not cricket.)

not so hot – unwell; disappointing

no standing anytime – a parking sign warning drivers not to stop in the designated area

not with (someone) – to fail to understand (Explain that again please. I'm not with you.)

pc – short for politically correct; that is, language, ideas or actions that avoid offending minority groups (Jill doesn't use the phrase 'deaf and dumb' because it's not pc.)

performance – display of bad temper or emotion (He put on a performance when he lost the game.)

P-plates – compulsory signs on the back and front of a car, showing the driver has a probationary licence

rabbit food – lettuce or other salad greens

redneck – a prejudiced and uneducated person

rip into (someone) – abuse or berate

roadworthy – legally fit to be on the roads; a certificate testifying this is needed when selling a car (Is your old car roadworthy? Yes, I've got a roadworthy certificate to prove it.)

sanger – a sandwich

*****shat off** – very angry (I'm shat off with Jack.)

shock jock – a radio announcer with strongly conservative views and prejudices

*****slimeball** – repulsive person

slip, slop, slap – an advertising slogan used to encourage Australians to be careful in the sun. It stands for slip on protective clothing, slop on sunscreen and slap on a hat

Speedos™ – tight, revealing swimming costumes, first designed in Australia in 1927

spit the dummy – be angry (Jill spat the dummy when her boyfriend arrived to collect her two hours late.)

spot fine – a fine for a traffic or other minor offence, such as littering, that must be paid immediately

STD – Subscriber Trunk Dialling, the capacity to phone long distance. (Does the hotel have STD phones in every room?)

STIs – Sexually Transmitted Infections. Sometimes also known as STDs, which stands for sexually transmitted diseases

stuffed – exhausted

suit – a term for a business man, implying greed and conformity

ticker – strength of character and determination (He hasn't got the ticker to finish his course.)

time out – a short break, often to allow people time to consider their position (This argument is getting heated. Let's take some time out.)

Toorak tractor – a large four-wheel drive vehicle

too right! – an emphatic yes (Are you coming to the party? Too right!)

totalled – wrecked, destroyed (He drove into a truck and his car was totalled.)

tragic – a devoted fan, usually of a sport (Jack is a cricket tragic. He never misses a match.)

unAustralian – a term of abuse used about people who do things the speaker disagrees with (Drinking warm beer is unAustralian.)

under the counter – illegally or secretly (That shopkeeper sells cigarettes to children under the counter.)

very funny! – an exclamation expressing displeasure or indicating that what has occurred is not funny (You've split coffee on my new blouse. Very funny!)

the WACA – the West Australian Cricket Association ground in Perth

youse – a plural form of 'you' that is acceptable in Aboriginal English but thought to be a sign of poor education in other people (Are youse going to the footy?)

zines – small independent magazines published for special interest groups

zit – a pimple, especially on the face